Styles of Radical Will

by Susan Sontag

Styles of Radical

Will

SUSAN SONTAG

FARRAR, STRAUS AND GIROUX   NEW YORK

Acknowledgment is made to the editors of *Aspen, Partisan Review, Sight and Sound,* and *Tulane Drama Review,* in whose pages some of these essays first appeared, and to the Quadrangle Press (Chicago) for the use of the essay on E. M. Cioran. *A Trip to Hanoi* was first published in *Esquire Magazine.*

FOR JOSEPH CHAIKIN

Contents

I

The Aesthetics of Silence

1

Every era has to reinvent the project of "spirituality" for itself.
(Spirituality = plans, terminologies, ideas of deportment
aimed at resolving the painful structural contradictions inherent in the human situation, at the completion of human
consciousness, at transcendence.)

In the modern era, one of the most active metaphors for the
spiritual project is "art." The activities of the painter, the
musician, the poet, the dancer, once they were grouped
together under that generic name (a relatively recent move),
have proved a particularly adaptable site on which to stage the
formal dramas besetting consciousness, each individual work
of art being a more or less astute paradigm for regulating or

reconciling these contradictions. Of course, the site needs continual refurbishing. Whatever goal is set for art eventually proves restrictive, matched against the widest goals of consciousness. Art, itself a form of mystification, endures a succession of crises of demystification; older artistic goals are assailed and, ostensibly, replaced; outworn maps of consciousness are redrawn. But what supplies all these crises with their energy—an energy held in common, so to speak—is the very unification of numerous, quite disparate activities into a single genus. At the moment when "art" comes into being, the modern period of art begins. From then on, any of the activities therein subsumed becomes a profoundly *problematic* activity, all of whose procedures and, ultimately, whose very right to exist can be called into question.

From the promotion of the arts into "art" comes the leading myth about art, that of the absoluteness of the artist's activity. In its first, more unreflective version, the myth treated art as an *expression* of human consciousness, consciousness seeking to know itself. (The evaluative standards generated by this version of the myth were fairly easily arrived at: some expressions were more complete, more ennobling, more informative, richer than others.) The later version of the myth posits a more complex, tragic relation of art to consciousness. Denying that art is mere expression, the later myth rather relates art to the mind's need or capacity for self-estrangement. Art is no longer understood as consciousness expressing and therefore, implicitly, affirming itself. Art is not consciousness per se, but rather its antidote—evolved from within consciousness itself. (The evaluative standards generated by this version of the myth proved much harder to get at.)

The newer myth, derived from a post-psychological conception of consciousness, installs within the activity of art many of the paradoxes involved in attaining an absolute state of being described by the great religious mystics. As the activity of the mystic must end in a *via negativa*, a theology of

God's absence, a craving for the cloud of unknowing beyond knowledge and for the silence beyond speech, so art must tend toward anti-art, the elimination of the "subject" (the "object," the "image"), the substitution of chance for intention, and the pursuit of silence.

In the early, linear version of art's relation to consciousness, a struggle was discerned between the "spiritual" integrity of the creative impulses and the distracting "materiality" of ordinary life, which throws up so many obstacles in the path of authentic sublimation. But the newer version, in which art is part of a dialectical transaction with consciousness, poses a deeper, more frustrating conflict. The "spirit" seeking embodiment in art clashes with the "material" character of art itself. Art is unmasked as gratuitous, and the very concreteness of the artist's tools (and, particularly in the case of language, their historicity) appears as a trap. Practiced in a world furnished with second-hand perceptions, and specifically confounded by the treachery of words, the artist's activity is cursed with mediacy. Art becomes the enemy of the artist, for it denies him the realization—the transcendence—he desires.

Therefore, art comes to be considered something to be overthrown. A new element enters the individual artwork and becomes constitutive of it: the appeal (tacit or overt) for its own abolition—and, ultimately, for the abolition of art itself.

2

The scene changes to an empty room.

Rimbaud has gone to Abyssinia to make his fortune in the slave trade. Wittgenstein, after a period as a village schoolteacher, has chosen menial work as a hospital orderly. Duchamp has turned to chess. Accompanying these exemplary renunciations of a vocation, each man has declared that he regards his previous achievements in poetry, philosophy, or art as trifling, of no importance.

But the choice of permanent silence doesn't negate their work. On the contrary, it imparts retroactively an added power and authority to what was broken off—disavowal of the work becoming a new source of its validity, a certificate of unchallengeable seriousness. That seriousness consists in not regarding art (or philosophy practiced as an art form: Wittgenstein) as something whose seriousness lasts forever, an "end," a permanent vehicle for spiritual ambition. The truly serious attitude is one that regards art as a "means" to something that can perhaps be achieved only by abandoning art; judged more impatiently, art is a false way or (the word of the Dada artist Jacques Vaché) a stupidity.

Though no longer a confession, art is more than ever a deliverance, an exercise in asceticism. Through it, the artist becomes purified—of himself and, eventually, of his art. The artist (if not art itself) is still engaged in a progress toward "the good." But whereas formerly the artist's good was mastery of and fulfillment in his art, now the highest good for the artist is to reach the point where those goals of excellence become insignificant to him, emotionally and ethically, and he is more satisfied by being silent than by finding a voice in art. Silence in this sense, as termination, proposes a mood of ultimacy antithetical to the mood informing the self-conscious artist's traditional serious use of silence (beautifully described by Valéry and Rilke): as a zone of meditation, preparation for spiritual ripening, an ordeal that ends in gaining the right to speak.

So far as he is serious, the artist is continually tempted to sever the dialogue he has with an audience. Silence is the furthest extension of that reluctance to communicate, that ambivalence about making contact with the audience which is a leading motif of modern art, with its tireless commitment to the "new" and/or the "esoteric." Silence is the artist's ultimate other-worldly gesture: by silence, he frees himself from servile bondage to the world, which appears as patron, client, consumer, antagonist, arbiter, and distorter of his work.

Still, one cannot fail to perceive in this renunciation of "society" a highly social gesture. The cues for the artist's eventual liberation from the need to practice his vocation come from observing his fellow artists and measuring himself against them. An exemplary decision of this sort can be made only after the artist has demonstrated that he possesses genius and exercised that genius authoritatively. Once he has surpassed his peers by the standards which he acknowledges, his pride has only one place left to go. For, to be a victim of the craving for silence is to be, in still a further sense, superior to everyone else. It suggests that the artist has had the wit to ask more questions than other people, and that he possesses stronger nerves and higher standards of excellence. (That the artist *can* persevere in the interrogation of his art until he or it is exhausted scarcely needs proving. As René Char has written, "No bird has the heart to sing in a thicket of questions.")

3

The exemplary modern artist's choice of silence is rarely carried to this point of final simplification, so that he becomes literally silent. More typically, he continues speaking, but in a manner that his audience can't hear. Most valuable art in our time has been experienced by audiences as a move into silence (or unintelligibility or invisibility or inaudibility); a dismantling of the artist's competence, his responsible sense of vocation—and therefore as an aggression against them.

Modern art's chronic habit of displeasing, provoking, or frustrating its audience can be regarded as a limited, vicarious participation in the ideal of silence which has been elevated as a major standard of "seriousness" in contemporary aesthetics.

But it is also a contradictory form of participation in the ideal of silence. It is contradictory not only because the artist continues making works of art, but also because the isolation of the work from its audience never lasts. With the passage of time and the intervention of newer, more difficult works, the artist's transgression becomes ingratiating, eventually legitimate. Goethe accused Kleist of having written his plays for an "invisible theatre." But eventually the invisible theatre becomes "visible." The ugly and discordant and senseless become "beautiful." The history of art is a sequence of successful transgressions.

The characteristic aim of modern art, to be *unacceptable* to its audience, inversely states the unacceptability to the artist of the very presence of an audience—audience in the modern sense, an assembly of voyeuristic spectators. At least since Nietzsche observed in *The Birth of Tragedy* that an audience of spectators as we know it, those present whom the actors ignore, was unknown to the Greeks, a good deal of contemporary art seems moved by the desire to eliminate the audience from art, an enterprise that often presents itself as an attempt to eliminate "art" altogether. (In favor of "life"?)

Committed to the idea that the power of art is located in its power to *negate*, the ultimate weapon in the artist's inconsistent war with his audience is to verge closer and closer to silence. The sensory or conceptual gap between the artist and his audience, the space of the missing or ruptured dialogue, can also constitute the grounds for an ascetic affirmation. Beckett speaks of "my dream of an art unresentful of its insuperable indigence and too proud for the farce of giving and receiving." But there is no abolishing a minimal transaction, a minimal exchange of gifts—just as there is no talented and rigorous asceticism that, whatever its intention, doesn't produce a gain (rather than a loss) in the capacity for pleasure.

And none of the aggressions committed intentionally or inadvertently by modern artists has succeeded in either abolishing the audience or transforming it into something else, a community engaged in a common activity. They cannot. As long as art is understood and valued as an "absolute" activity, it will be a separate, elitist one. Elites presuppose masses. So far as the best art defines itself by essentially "priestly" aims, it presupposes and confirms the existence of a relatively passive, never fully initiated, voyeuristic laity that is regularly convoked to watch, listen, read, or hear—and then sent away.

The most the artist can do is to modify the different terms in this situation vis-à-vis the audience and himself. To discuss the idea of silence in art is to discuss the various alternatives within this essentially unalterable situation.

4

How literally does silence figure in art?

Silence exists as a *decision*—in the exemplary suicide of the artist (Kleist, Lautréamont), who thereby testifies that he has gone "too far"; and in the already cited model renunciations by the artist of his vocation.

Silence also exists as a *punishment*—self-punishment, in the exemplary madness of artists (Hölderlin, Artaud) who demonstrate that sanity itself may be the price of trespassing the accepted frontiers of consciousness; and, of course, in penalties (ranging from censorship and physical destruction of artworks to fines, exile, prison for the artist) meted out by "society" for the artist's spiritual nonconformity or subversion of the group sensibility.

Silence doesn't exist in a literal sense, however, as the *experience* of an audience. It would mean that the spectator was aware of no stimulus or that he was unable to make a response. But this can't happen; nor can it even be induced programmatically. The non-awareness of any stimulus, the inability to make a response, can result only from a defective presence on the part of the spectator, or a misunderstanding of his own reactions (misled by restrictive ideas about what would be a "relevant" response). As long as audiences, by definition, consist of sentient beings in a "situation," it is impossible for them to have no response at all.

Nor can silence, in its literal state, exist as the *property* of an artwork—even of works like Duchamp's readymades or Cage's 4'33", in which the artist has ostentatiously done no more to satisfy any established criteria of art than set the object in a gallery or situate the performance on a concert stage. There is no neutral surface, no neutral discourse, no neutral theme, no neutral form. Something is neutral only with respect to some-thing else—like an intention or an expectation. As a property of the work of art itself, silence can exist only in a cooked or non-literal sense. (Put otherwise: if a work exists at all, its silence is only one element in it.) Instead of raw or achieved silence, one finds various moves in the direction of an ever receding horizon of silence—moves which, by definition, can never be fully consummated. One result is a type of art that many people characterize pejoratively as dumb, depressed, acquies-cent, cold. But these privative qualities exist in a context of the artist's objective intention, which is always discernible. Cultivating the metaphoric silence suggested by conventionally lifeless subjects (as in much of Pop Art) and constructing "minimal" forms that seem to lack emotional resonance are in themselves vigorous, often tonic choices.

And, finally, even without imputing objective intentions to the artwork, there remains the inescapable truth about per-ception: the positivity of all experience at every moment of it. As Cage has insisted, "There is no such thing as silence. Some-thing is always happening that makes a sound." (Cage has described how, even in a soundless chamber, he still heard two things: his heartbeat and the coursing of the blood in his head.) Similarly, there is no such thing as empty space. As long as a human eye is looking, there is always something to see. To look at something which is "empty" is still to be looking, still to be seeing something—if only the ghosts of one's own expectations. In order to perceive fullness, one must retain an acute sense of the emptiness which marks it off; conversely, in order to perceive emptiness, one must apprehend other zones of the world as full. (In *Through the Looking Glass*, Alice comes upon a shop "that seemed to be full of all manner of curious things—but the oddest part of it all was that whenever she looked hard at any shelf, to make out exactly what it had on it, that particular shelf was always quite empty, though the others round it were crowded full as they could hold.")

"Silence" never ceases to imply its opposite and to depend on its presence: just as there can't be "up" without "down" or "left" without "right," so one must acknowledge a surrounding environment of sound or language in order to recognize silence. Not only does silence exist in a world full of speech and other sounds, but any given silence has its identity as a stretch of time being perforated by sound. (Thus, much of the beauty of Harpo Marx's muteness derives from his being surrounded by manic talkers.)

A genuine emptiness, a pure silence is not feasible—either conceptually or in fact. If only because the artwork exists in a world furnished with many other things, the artist who creates silence or emptiness must produce something dialectical: a full void, an enriching emptiness, a resonating or eloquent silence. Silence remains, inescapably, a form of speech (in many instances, of complaint or indictment) and an element in a dialogue.

5

Programs for a radical reduction of means and effects in art—including the ultimate demand for the renunciation of art itself—can't be taken at face value, undialectically. Silence and allied ideas (like emptiness, reduction, the "zero degree") are boundary notions with a very complex set of uses, leading terms of a particular spiritual and cultural rhetoric. To describe silence as a rhetorical term is, of course, not to condemn this rhetoric as fraudulent or in bad faith. In my opinion, the myths of silence and emptiness are about as nourishing and viable as might be devised in an "unwholesome" time—which is, of necessity, a time in which "unwholesome" psychic states furnish the energies for most superior work in the arts. Yet one can't deny the pathos of these myths.

This pathos appears in the fact that the idea of silence allows, essentially, only two types of valuable development. Either it is taken to the point of utter self-negation (as art) or else it is practiced in a form that is heroically, ingeniously inconsistent.

6

The art of our time is noisy with appeals for silence.

A coquettish, even cheerful nihilism. One recognizes the imperative of silence, but goes on speaking anyway. Discovering that one has nothing to say, one seeks a way to say *that*.

Beckett has expressed the wish that art would renounce all further projects for disturbing matters on "the plane of the feasible," that art would retire, "weary of puny exploits, weary of pretending to be able, of being able, of doing a little better the same old thing, of going further along a dreary road." The alternative is an art consisting of "the expression that there is nothing to express, nothing from which to express, no power to express, no desire to express, together with the obligation to express." From where does this obligation derive? The very aesthetics of the death wish seems to make of that wish something incorrigibly lively.

Apollinaire says, "J'ai fait des gestes blancs parmi les solitudes." But he *is* making gestures.

Since the artist can't embrace silence literally and remain an artist, what the rhetoric of silence indicates is a determination to pursue his activity more deviously than before. One way is indicated by Breton's notion of the "full margin." The artist is enjoined to devote himself to filling up the periphery of the art space, leaving the central area of usage blank. Art becomes privative, anemic—as suggested by the title of Duchamp's only effort at film-making, "Anemic Cinema," a work from 1924–26. Beckett projects the idea of an "impoverished painting," painting which is "authentically fruitless, incapable of any image whatsoever." Jerzy Grotowski's manifesto for his Theatre Laboratory in Poland is called "Plea for a Poor Theatre." These programs for art's impoverishment must not be understood simply as terroristic admonitions to audiences, but rather as strategies for improving the audience's experience.

The notions of silence, emptiness, and reduction sketch out new prescriptions for looking, hearing, etc.—which either promote a more immediate, sensuous experience of art or confront the artwork in a more conscious, conceptual way.

7

Consider the connection between the mandate for a reduction of means and effects in art, whose horizon is silence, and the faculty of attention. In one of its aspects, art is a technique for focusing attention, for teaching skills of attention. (While the whole of the human environment might be so described—as a pedagogic instrument—this description particularly applies to works of art.) The history of the arts is tantamount to the discovery and formulation of a repertory of objects on which to lavish attention. One could trace exactly and in order how the eye of art has panned over our environment, "naming," making its limited selection of things which people then become aware of as significant, pleasurable, complex entities. (Oscar Wilde pointed out that people didn't see fogs before certain nineteenth-century poets and painters taught them how to; and surely, no one saw as much of the variety and subtlety of the human face before the era of the movies.)

Once the artist's task seemed to be simply that of opening up new areas and objects of attention. That task is still acknowledged, but it has become problematic. The very faculty of attention has come into question, and been subjected to more rigorous standards. As Jasper Johns says: "Already it's a great deal to see anything *clearly*, for we don't see *anything* clearly."

Perhaps the quality of the attention one brings to bear on something will be better (less contaminated, less distracted), the less one is offered. Furnished with impoverished art, purged by silence, one might then be able to begin to transcend the frustrating selectivity of attention, with its inevitable distortions of experience. Ideally, one should be able to pay attention to everything.

/ 14

The tendency is toward less and less. But never has "less" so ostentatiously advanced itself as "more."

In the light of the current myth, in which art aims to become a "total experience," soliciting total attention, the strategies of impoverishment and reduction indicate the most exalted ambition art could adopt. Underneath what looks like a strenuous modesty, if not actual debility, is to be discerned an energetic secular blasphemy: the wish to attain the unfettered, unselective, total consciousness of "God."

8

Language seems a privileged metaphor for expressing the mediated character of art-making and the artwork. On the one hand, speech is both an immaterial medium (compared with, say, images) and a human activity with an apparently essential stake in the project of transcendence, of moving beyond the singular and contingent (all words being abstractions, only roughly based on or making reference to concrete particulars). On the other hand, language is the most impure, the most contaminated, the most exhausted of all the materials out of which art is made.

This dual character of language—its abstractness, and its "fallenness" in history—serves as a microcosm of the unhappy character of the arts today. Art is so far along the labyrinthine pathways of the project of transcendence that one can hardly conceive of it turning back, short of the most drastic and punitive "cultural revolution." Yet at the same time, art is foundering in the debilitating tide of what once seemed the crowning achievement of European thought: secular historical consciousness. In little more than two centuries, the consciousness of history has transformed itself from a liberation, an opening of doors, blessed enlightenment, into an almost insupportable burden of self-consciousness. It's scarcely possible for the artist to write a word (or render an image or make a gesture) that doesn't remind him of something already achieved.

As Nietzsche says: "Our pre-eminence: we live in the age of comparison, we can verify as has never been verified before." Therefore "we enjoy differently, we suffer differently: our instinctive activity is to compare an unheard number of things."

Up to a point, the community and historicity of the artist's means are implicit in the very fact of intersubjectivity: each person is a being-in-a-world. But today, particularly in the arts using language, this normal state of affairs is felt as an extraordinary, wearying problem.

Language is experienced not merely as something shared but as something corrupted, weighed down by historical accumulation. Thus, for each conscious artist, the creation of a work means dealing with two potentially antagonistic domains of meaning and their relationships. One is his own meaning (or lack of it); the other is the set of second-order meanings that both extend his own language and encumber, compromise, and adulterate it. The artist ends by choosing between two inherently limiting alternatives, forced to take a position that is either servile or insolent. Either he flatters or appeases his audience, giving them what they already know, or he commits an aggression against his audience, giving them what they don't want.

Modern art thus transmits in full the alienation produced by historical consciousness. Whatever the artist does is in (usually conscious) alignment with something else already done, producing a compulsion to be continually checking his situation, his own stance against those of his predecessors and contemporaries. To compensate for this ignominious enslavement to history, the artist exalts himself with the dream of a wholly ahistorical, and therefore unalienated, art.

9

Art that is "silent" constitutes one approach to this visionary, ahistorical condition.

Consider the difference between *looking* and *staring*. A look is voluntary; it is also mobile, rising and falling in intensity as its foci of interest are taken up and then exhausted. A stare has, essentially, the character of a compulsion; it is steady, unmodulated, "fixed."

Traditional art invites a look. Art that is silent engenders a stare. Silent art allows—at least in principle—no release from attention, because there has never, in principle, been any soliciting of it. A stare is perhaps as far from history, as close to eternity, as contemporary art can get.

10

Silence is a metaphor for a cleansed, non-interfering vision, appropriate to artworks that are unresponsive before being seen, unviolable in their essential integrity by human scrutiny. The spectator would approach art as he does a landscape. A landscape doesn't demand from the spectator his "understanding," his imputations of significance, his anxieties and sympathies; it demands, rather, his absence, it asks that he not add anything to *it*. Contemplation, strictly speaking, entails self-forgetfulness on the part of the spectator: an object worthy of contemplation is one which, in effect, annihilates the perceiving subject.

Toward such an ideal plenitude to which the audience can add nothing, analogous to the aesthetic relation to nature, a great deal of contemporary art aspires—through various strategies of blandness, of reduction, of deindividuation, of alogicality. In principle, the audience may not even add its thought. All objects, rightly perceived, are already full. This is what Cage must mean when, after explaining that there is no such thing as silence because something is always happening that makes a sound, he adds, "No one can have an idea once he starts really listening."

Plenitude—experiencing all the space as filled, so that ideas cannot enter—means impenetrability. A person who becomes silent becomes opaque for the other; somebody's silence opens up an array of possibilities for interpreting that silence, for imputing speech to it.

GRAND HAIR DESIGNS

3167 S. GRAND • 771 8820

GOOD FOR ONE <u>FREE</u> HAIRCUT

FROM **TERRY** or **DERRIC**

FIRST TIME ONLY PLEASE

GRAND HAIR DESIGNS

The way in which this opaqueness induces spiritual vertigo is the theme of Bergman's *Persona*. The actress's deliberate silence has two aspects: Considered as a decision apparently relating to herself, the refusal to speak is apparently the form she has given to the wish for ethical purity; but it is also, as behavior, a means of power, a species of sadism, a virtually inviolable position of strength from which she manipulates and confounds her nurse-companion, who is charged with the burden of talking.

But the opaqueness of silence can be conceived more positively, as free from anxiety. For Keats, the silence of the Grecian urn is a locus of spiritual nourishment: "unheard" melodies endure, whereas those that pipe to "the sensual ear" decay. Silence is equated with arresting time ("slow time"). One can stare endlessly at the Grecian urn. Eternity, in the argument of Keats' poem, is the only interesting stimulus to thought and also the sole occasion for coming to the end of mental activity, which means interminable, unanswered questions ("Thou, silent form, dost tease us out of thought/ As doth eternity"), in order to arrive at a final equation of ideas ("Beauty is truth, truth beauty") which is both absolutely vacuous and completely full. Keats' poem quite logically ends in a statement that will seem, if the reader hasn't followed his argument, like empty wisdom, a banality. As time, or history, is the medium of definite, determinate thought, the silence of eternity prepares for a thought beyond thought, which must appear from the perspective of traditional thinking and the familiar uses of the mind as no thought at all—though it may rather be the emblem of new, "difficult" thinking.

11

Behind the appeals for silence lies the wish for a perceptual and cultural clean slate. And, in its most hortatory and ambitious version, the advocacy of silence expresses a mythic project of total liberation. What's envisaged is nothing less than the liberation of the artist from himself, of art from the particular artwork, of art from history, of spirit from matter, of the mind from its perceptual and intellectual limitations.

As some people know now, there are ways of thinking that we don't yet know about. Nothing could be more important or precious than that knowledge, however unborn. The sense of urgency, the spiritual restlessness it engenders, cannot be appeased, and continues to fuel the radical art of this century. Through its advocacy of silence and reduction, art commits an act of violence upon itself, turning art into a species of auto-manipulation, of conjuring—trying to bring these new ways of thinking to birth.

Silence is a strategy for the transvaluation of art, art itself being the herald of an anticipated radical transvaluation of human values. But the success of this strategy must mean its eventual abandonment, or at least its significant modification.

Silence is a prophecy, one which the artist's actions can be understood as attempting both to fulfill and to reverse.

As language points to its own transcendence in silence, silence points to its own transcendence—to a speech beyond silence.

But can the whole enterprise become an act of bad faith if the artist knows *this*, too?

12

A famous quotation: "Everything that can be thought at all can be thought clearly. Everything that can be said at all can be said clearly. But not everything that can be thought can be said."

Notice that Wittgenstein, with his scrupulous avoidance of the psychological issue, doesn't ask why, when, and in what circumstances someone would *want* to put into words "everything that can be thought" (even if he could), or even to utter (whether clearly or not) "everything that could be said."

13

Of everything that's said, one can ask: *why?* (Including: why should I say *that?* And: why should I say anything at all?)

Moreover, strictly speaking, nothing that's *said* is true. (Though a person can *be* the truth, one can't ever say it.)

Still, things that are said can sometimes be helpful—which is what people ordinarily mean when they regard something *said* as being true. Speech can enlighten, relieve, confuse, exalt, infect, antagonize, gratify, grieve, stun, animate. While language is regularly used to inspire to action, some verbal statements, either written or oral, are themselves the performing of an action (as in promising, swearing, bequeathing). Another use of speech, if anything more common than that of provoking actions, is to provoke further speech. But speech can silence, too. This indeed is how it must be: without the polarity of silence, the whole system of language would fail. And beyond its generic function as the dialectical opposite of speech, silence—like speech—also has more specific, less inevitable uses.

One use for silence: certifying the absence or renunciation of thought. Silence is often employed as a magical or mimetic procedure in repressive social relationships, as in the Jesuit regulations about speaking to superiors and in the disciplining of children. (This should not be confused with the practice of certain monastic disciplines, such as the Trappist order, in which silence is both an ascetic act and bears witness to the condition of being perfectly "full.")

Another, apparently opposed, use for silence: certifying the completion of thought. In the words of Karl Jaspers, "He who has the final answers can no longer speak to the other, breaking off genuine communication for the sake of what he believes in."

Still another use for silence: providing time for the continuing or exploring of thought. Notably, speech closes off thought. (An example: the enterprise of criticism, in which there seems no way for a critic not to assert that a given artist is *this*, he's *that*, etc.) But if one decides an issue isn't closed, it's not. This is presumably the rationale behind the voluntary experiments in silence that some contemporary spiritual athletes, like Buckminster Fuller, have undertaken, and the element of wisdom in the otherwise mainly authoritarian, philistine silence of the orthodox Freudian psychoanalyst. Silence keeps things "open."

Still another use for silence: furnishing or aiding speech to attain its maximum integrity or seriousness. Everyone has experienced how, when punctuated by long silences, words weigh more; they become almost palpable. Or how, when one talks less, one begins feeling more fully one's physical presence in a given space. Silence undermines "bad speech," by which I mean dissociated speech—speech dissociated from the body (and, therefore, from feeling), speech not organically informed by the sensuous presence and concrete particularity of the speaker and by the individual occasion for using language. Unmoored from the body, speech deteriorates. It becomes false, inane, ignoble, weightless. Silence can inhibit or counteract this tendency, providing a kind of ballast, monitoring and even correcting language when it becomes inauthentic.

Given these perils to the authenticity of language (which doesn't depend on the character of any isolated statement or even group of statements, but on the relation of speaker, utterance, and situation), the imaginary project of saying clearly "everything that can be said" suggested by Wittgenstein's remarks looks fearfully complicated. (How much time would one have? Would one have to speak quickly?) The philosopher's hypothetical universe of clear speech (which assigns to silence only "that whereof one cannot speak") would seem to be a moralist's, or a psychiatrist's, nightmare— at the least a place no one should lightheartedly enter. Is there anyone who *wants* to say "everything that could be said"? The psychologically plausible answer would seem to be no. But yes is plausible, too—as a rising ideal of modern culture. Isn't that what many people *do* want today—to say everything that can be said? But this aim cannot be maintained without inner conflict. In part inspired by the spread of the ideals of psychotherapy, people are yearning to say "everything" (thereby, among other results, further undermining the crumbling distinction between public and private endeavors, between information and secrets). But in an overpopulated world being connected by global electronic communication and jet travel at a pace too rapid and violent for an organically sound person to assimilate without shock, people are also suffering from a revulsion at any further proliferation of speech and images. Such different factors as the unlimited "technological reproduction" and near universal diffusion of printed language and speech as well as images (from "news" to "art objects"), and the degeneration of public language within the realms of politics and advertising and entertainment, have produced, especially among the better-educated inhabitants of modern mass society, a devaluation of language. (I should argue, contrary to McLuhan, that a devaluation of the power and credibility of images has taken place no less profound than, and essentially similar to, that afflicting language.) And, as the prestige of language falls, that of silence rises.

I am alluding, at this point, to the sociological context of the contemporary ambivalence toward language. The matter, of course, goes much deeper than this. In addition to the specific sociological determinants, one must recognize the operation of something like a perennial discontent with language that has been formulated in each of the major civilizations of the Orient and Occident, whenever thought reaches a certain high, *excruciating* order of complexity and spiritual seriousness.

Traditionally, it has been through the religious vocabulary, with its meta-absolutes of "sacred" and "profane," "human" and "divine," that the disaffection with language itself has been charted. In particular, the antecedents of art's dilemmas and strategies are to be found in the radical wing of the mystical tradition. (Cf., among Christian texts, the *Mystica*

Theologia of Dionysius the Areopagite, the anonymous *Cloud of Unknowing*, the writings of Jakob Boehme and Meister Eckhart; and parallels in Zen, Taoist, and Sufi texts.) The mystical tradition has always recognized, in Norman Brown's phrase, "the neurotic character of language." (According to Boehme, Adam spoke a language different from all known languages. It was "sensual speech," the unmediated expressive instrument of the senses, proper to beings integrally part of sensuous nature—that is, still employed by all the animals except that sick animal, man. This, which Boehme calls the only "natural language," the sole language free from distortion and illusion, is what man will speak again when he recovers paradise.) But in our time, the most striking developments of such ideas have been made by artists (and certain psychotherapists) rather than by the timid legatees of the religious traditions.

Explicitly in revolt against what is deemed the desiccated, categorized life of the ordinary mind, the artist issues his own call for a revision of language. A good deal of contemporary art is moved by this quest for a consciousness purified of contaminated language and, in some versions, of the distortions produced by conceiving the world exclusively in conventional verbal (in their debased sense, "rational" or "logical") terms. Art itself becomes a kind of counterviolence, seeking to loosen the grip upon consciousness of the habits of lifeless, static verbalization, presenting models of "sensual speech."

If anything, the volume of discontent has been turned up since the arts inherited the problem of language from religious discourse. It's not just that words, ultimately, are inadequate to the highest aims of consciousness; or even that they get in the way. Art expresses a double discontent. We lack words, and we have too many of them. It raises two complaints about language. Words are too crude. And words are also too busy—inviting a hyperactivity of consciousness that is not only dysfunctional, in terms of human capacities of feeling and acting, but actively deadens the mind and blunts the senses.

Language is demoted to the status of an event. Something takes place in time, a voice speaking which points to the before and to what comes after an utterance: silence. Silence, then, is both the precondition of speech and the result or aim of properly directed speech. On this model, the artist's activity is the creating or establishing of silence; the efficacious artwork leaves silence in its wake. Silence, administered by the artist, is part of a program of perceptual and cultural therapy, often on the model of shock therapy rather than of persuasion. Even if the artist's medium is words, he can share in this task: language can be employed to check language, to express muteness. Mallarmé thought it was the job of poetry, using words, to clean up our word-clogged reality—by creating silences around things. Art must mount a full-scale attack on language itself, by means of language and its surrogates, on behalf of the standard of silence.

14

In the end, the radical critique of consciousness (first delineated by the mystical tradition, now administered by unorthodox psychotherapy and high modernist art) always lays the blame on language. Consciousness, experienced as a burden, is conceived of as the memory of all the words that have ever been said.

Krishnamurti claims that we must give up psychological, as distinct from factual, memory. Otherwise, we keep filling up the new with the old, closing off experience by hooking each experience onto the last.

We must destroy continuity (which is insured by psychological memory), by going to the *end* of each emotion or thought.

And after the end, what supervenes (for a while) is silence.

15

In his Fourth Duino Elegy, Rilke gives a metaphoric statement of the problem of language and recommends a procedure for approaching as near the horizon of silence as he considers feasible. A prerequisite of "emptying out" is to be able to perceive what one is "full of," what words and mechanical gestures one is stuffed with, like a doll; only then, in polar confrontation with the doll, does the "angel" appear, a figure representing an equally inhuman though "higher" possibility, that of an entirely unmediated, translinguistic apprehension. Neither doll nor angel, human beings remain situated within the kingdom of language. But for nature, then things, then other people, then the textures of ordinary life to be experienced from a stance other than the crippled one of mere spectatorship, language must regain its chastity. As Rilke describes it in the Ninth Elegy, the redemption of language (which is to say, the redemption of the world through its interiorization in consciousness) is a long, infinitely arduous task. Human beings are so "fallen" that they must start with the simplest linguistic act: the naming of things. Perhaps no more than this minimal function can be preserved from the general corruption of discourse. Language may very well have to remain within a permanent state of reduction. Though perhaps, when this spiritual exercise of confining language to naming is perfected, it may be possible to pass on to other, more ambitious uses of language, nothing must be attempted which will allow consciousness to become reestranged from itself.

For Rilke the overcoming of the alienation of consciousness is conceivable; and not, as in the radical myths of the mystics, through transcending language altogether. It suffices to cut back drastically the scope and use of language. A tremendous spiritual preparation (the contrary of "alienation") is required for this deceptively simple act of naming. It is nothing less than the scouring and harmonious sharpening of the senses (the very opposite of such violent projects, with roughly the same end and informed by the same hostility to verbal-rational culture, as "systematically deranging the senses").

Rilke's remedy lies halfway between exploiting the numbness of language as a gross, fully installed cultural institution and yielding to the suicidal vertigo of pure silence. But this middle ground of reducing language to naming can be claimed in quite another way than his. Contrast the benign nominalism proposed by Rilke (and proposed and practiced by Francis Ponge) with the brutal nominalism adopted by many other artists. The more familiar recourse of modern art to the aesthetics of the inventory is not made—as in Rilke—with an eye to "humanizing" things, but rather to confirming their inhumanity, their impersonality, their indifference to and separateness from human concerns. (Examples of the "inhumane" preoccupation with naming: Roussel's *Impressions of Africa;* the silk-screen paintings and early films of Andy Warhol; the early novels of Robbe-Grillet, which attempt to confine the function of language to bare physical description and location.)

Rilke and Ponge assume that there *are* priorities: rich as opposed to vacuous objects, events with a certain allure. (This is the incentive for trying to peel back language, allowing the "things" themselves to speak.) More decisively, they assume that if there are states of false (language-clogged) consciousness, there are also authentic states of consciousness—which it's the function of art to promote. The alternative view denies the traditional hierarchies of interest and meaning, in which some things have more "significance" than others. The distinction between true and false experience, true and false consciousness is also denied: in principle, one should desire to pay attention to everything. It's this view, most elegantly formulated by Cage though its practice is found everywhere, that leads to the art of the inventory, the catalogue, surfaces; also "chance." The function of art isn't to sanction any specific experience, except the state of being open to the multiplicity of experience—which ends in practice by a decided stress on things usually considered trivial or unimportant.

The attachment of contemporary art to the "minimal" narrative principle of the catalogue or inventory seems almost to

parody the capitalist world-view, in which the environment is
atomized into "items" (a category embracing things and persons, works of art and natural organisms), and in which every
item is a commodity—that is, a discrete, portable object. A
general leveling of value is encouraged in the art of inventory,
which is itself only one of the possible approaches to an ideally
uninflected discourse. Traditionally, the effects of an artwork
have been unevenly distributed, to induce in the audience a
certain sequence of experience: first arousing, then manipulating, and eventually fulfilling emotional expectations. What
is proposed now is a discourse without emphases in this traditional sense. (Again, the principle of the stare as opposed to
the look.)

Such art could also be described as establishing great "distance" (between spectator and art object, between the spectator and his emotions). But, psychologically, distance often is
linked with the most intense state of feeling, in which
the coolness or impersonality with which something is
treated measures the insatiable interest that thing has for us.
The distance that a great deal of "anti-humanist" art proposes
is actually equivalent to obsession—an aspect of the involvement in "things" of which the "humanist" nominalism of Rilke
has no intimation.

16

"There is something strange in the acts of writing and speaking," Novalis wrote in 1799. "The ridiculous and amazing
mistake people make is to believe they use words in relation to
things. They are unaware of the nature of language—which is
to be its own and only concern, making it so fertile and
splendid a mystery. When someone talks just for the sake of
talking he is saying the most original and truthful thing he can
say."

Novalis' statement may help explain an apparent paradox: that in the era of the widespread advocacy of art's

silence, an increasing number of works of art babble. Verbosity and repetitiveness are particularly noticeable in the temporal arts of prose fiction, music, film, and dance, many of which cultivate a kind of ontological stammer—facilitated by their refusal of the incentives for a clean, anti-redundant discourse supplied by linear, beginning-middle-and-end construction. But actually, there's no contradiction. For the contemporary appeal for silence has never indicated merely a hostile dismissal of language. It also signifies a very high estimate of language—of its powers, of its past health, and of the current dangers it poses to a free consciousness. From this intense and ambivalent valuation proceeds the impulse for a discourse that appears both irrepressible (and, in principle, interminable) and strangely inarticulate, painfully reduced. Discernible in the fictions of Stein, Burroughs, and Beckett is the subliminal idea that it might be possible to out-talk language, or to talk oneself into silence.

This is not a very promising strategy, considering what results might reasonably be anticipated from it. But perhaps not so odd, when one observes how often the aesthetic of silence appears alongside a barely controlled abhorrence of the void.

Accommodating these two contrary impulses may produce the need to fill up all the spaces with objects of slight emotional weight or with large areas of barely modulated color or evenly detailed objects, or to spin a discourse with as few possible inflections, emotive variations, and risings and fallings of emphasis. These procedures seem analogous to the behavior of an obsessional neurotic warding off a danger. The acts of such a person must be repeated in the identical form, because the danger remains the same; and they must be repeated endlessly, because the danger never seems to go away. But the emotional fires feeding the art-discourse analogous to obsessionalism may be turned down so low one can almost forget they're there. Then all that's left to the ear is a kind of steady hum or drone. What's left to the eye is the neat filling of a space with things, or, more accurately, the patient transcription of the surface detail of things.

In this view, the "silence" of things, images, and words is a prerequisite for their proliferation. Were they endowed with a more potent, individual charge, each of the various elements of the artwork would claim more psychic space and then their total number might have to be reduced.

17

Sometimes the accusation against language is not directed against all of language but only against the written word. Thus Tristan Tzara urged the burning of all books and libraries to bring about a new era of oral legends. And McLuhan, as everyone knows, makes the sharpest distinction between written language (which exists in "visual space") and oral speech (which exists in "auditory space"), praising the psychic and cultural advantages of the latter as the basis for sensibility.

If written language is singled out as the culprit, what will be sought is not so much the reduction as the metamorphosis of language into something looser, more intuitive, less organized and inflected, non-linear (in McLuhan's terminology) and—noticeably—more verbose. But, of course, it is just these qualities that characterize many of the great prose narratives of our time. Joyce, Stein, Gadda, Laura Riding, Beckett, and Burroughs employ a language whose norms and energies come from oral speech, with its circular repetitive movements and essentially first-person voice.

"Speaking for the sake of speaking is the formula of deliverance," Novalis said. (Deliverance from what? From speaking? From art?)

In my opinion, Novalis has succinctly described the proper approach of the writer to language and offered the basic criterion for literature as an art. But to what extent oral speech is the privileged model for the speech of literature as an art is still an open question.

18

A corollary of the growth of this conception of art's language as autonomous and self-sufficient (and, in the end, self-reflective) is a decline in "meaning" as traditionally sought in works of art. "Speaking for the sake of speaking" forces us to relocate the meaning of linguistic or para-linguistic statements. We are led to abandon meaning (in the sense of references to entities outside the artwork) as the criterion for the language of art in favor of "use." (Wittgenstein's famous thesis, "the meaning is the use," can and should be rigorously applied to art.)

"Meaning" partially or totally converted into "use" is the secret behind the widespread strategy of *literalness*, a major development of the aesthetics of silence. A variant on this: hidden literality, exemplified by such different writers as Kafka and Beckett. The narratives of Kafka and Beckett seem puzzling because they appear to invite the reader to ascribe high-powered symbolic and allegorical meanings to them and, at the same time, repel such ascriptions. Yet when the narrative is examined, it discloses no more than what it literally means. The power of their language derives precisely from the fact that the meaning is so bare.

The effect of such bareness is often a kind of anxiety—like the anxiety produced when familiar things aren't in their place or playing their accustomed role. One may be made as anxious by unexpected literalness as by the Surrealists' "disturbing" objects and unexpected scale and condition of objects conjoined in an imaginary landscape. Whatever is wholly mysterious is at once both psychically relieving and anxiety-provoking. (A perfect machine for agitating this pair of contrary emotions: the Bosch drawing in a Dutch museum that shows trees furnished with two ears at the sides of their trunks, as if they were listening to the forest, while the forest floor is strewn with eyes.) Before a fully conscious work of art, one feels something like the mixture of anxiety, detachment, pruriency, and relief that a physically sound person feels when he glimpses an amputee. Beckett speaks favorably of a work of art which would be a "total object, complete with missing parts, instead of partial object. Question of degree."

But exactly what is a totality and what constitutes completeness in art (or anything else)? That problem is, in principle, unresolvable. Whatever way a work of art is, it could have been—could be—different. The necessity of *these* parts in this order is never given; it is conferred.

The refusal to admit this essential contingency (or openness) is what inspires the audience's will to confirm the closedness of a work by interpreting it, and what creates the feeling common among reflective artists and critics that the artwork is always somehow in arrears of or inadequate to its "subject." But unless one is committed to the idea that art "expresses" something, these procedures and attitudes are far from inevitable.

19

This tenacious concept of art as "expression" has given rise to the most common, and dubious, version of the notion of silence—which invokes the idea of "the ineffable." The theory supposes that the province of art is "the beautiful," which implies effects of unspeakableness, indescribability, ineffability. Indeed, the search to express the inexpressible is taken as the very criterion of art; and sometimes becomes the occasion for a strict—and to my mind untenable—distinction between prose literature and poetry. It is from this position that Valéry advanced his famous argument (repeated in a quite different context by Sartre) that the novel is not, strictly speaking, an art form at all. His reason is that since the aim of prose is to communicate, the use of language in prose is perfectly straightforward. Poetry, being an art, should have quite different aims: to express an experience which is essentially ineffable; using language to express muteness. In contrast to prose writers, poets are engaged in subverting their own instrument and seeking to pass beyond it.

This theory, so far as it assumes that art is concerned with beauty, is not very interesting. (Modern aesthetics is crippled by its dependence upon this essentially vacant concept. As if art were "about" beauty, as science is "about" truth!) But even if the theory dispenses with the notion of beauty, there is still a more serious objection. The view that expressing the ineffable is an essential function of poetry (considered as a paradigm of all the arts) is naïvely unhistorical. The ineffable, while surely a perennial category of consciousness, has certainly not always made its home in the arts. Its traditional shelter was in religious discourse and, secondarily (as Plato relates in his 7th Epistle), in philosophy. The fact that contemporary artists are concerned with silence—and, therefore, in one extension, with the ineffable—must be understood historically, as a consequence of the prevailing contemporary myth of the "absoluteness" of art. The value placed on silence doesn't arise by virtue of the *nature* of art, but derives from the contemporary ascription of certain "absolute" qualities to the art object and to the activity of the artist.

The extent to which art *is* involved with the ineffable is more specific, as well as contemporary: art, in the modern conception, is always connected with systematic transgressions of a formal sort. The systematic violation of older formal conventions practiced by modern artists gives their work a certain aura of the unspeakable—for instance, as the audience uneasily senses the negative presence of what else could be, but isn't being, said; and as any "statement" made in an aggressively new or difficult form tends to seem equivocal or merely vacant. But these features of ineffability must not be acknowledged at the expense of one's awareness of the positivity of the work of art. Contemporary art, no matter how much it has defined itself by a taste for negation, can still be analyzed as a set of assertions of a formal kind.

For instance, each work of art gives us a form or paradigm

or model of *knowing* something, an epistemology. But viewed as a spiritual project, a vehicle of aspirations toward an absolute, what any work of art supplies is a specific model for meta-social or meta-ethical *tact*, a standard of decorum. Each artwork indicates the unity of certain preferences about what can and cannot be said (or represented). At the same time that it may make a tacit proposal for upsetting previously consecrated rulings on what can be said (or represented), it issues its own set of limits.

20

Contemporary artists advocate silence in two styles: loud and soft.

The loud style is a function of the unstable antithesis of "plenum" and "void." The sensuous, ecstatic, translinguistic apprehension of the plenum is notoriously fragile: in a terrible, almost instantaneous plunge it can collapse into the void of negative silence. With all its awareness of risk-taking (the hazards of spiritual nausea, even of madness), this advocacy of silence tends to be frenetic and overgeneralizing. It is also frequently apocalyptic and must endure the indignity of all apocalyptic thinking: namely, to prophesy the end, to see the day come, to outlive it, and then to set a new date for the incineration of consciousness and the definitive pollution of language and exhaustion of the possibilities of art-discourse.

The other way of talking about silence is more cautious. Basically, it presents itself as an extension of a main feature of traditional classicism: the concern with modes of propriety, with standards of seemliness. Silence is only "reticence" stepped up to the nth degree. Of course, in the translation of this concern from the matrix of traditional classical art, the tone has changed—from didactic seriousness to ironic open-mindedness. But while the clamorous style of proclaiming the rhetoric of silence may seem more passionate, its more subdued advocates (like Cage, Johns) are saying something equally drastic. They are reacting to the same idea of art's absolute aspirations (by programmatic disavowals of art); they share the same disdain for the "meanings" established by bourgeois-rationalist culture, indeed for culture itself in the familiar sense. What is voiced by the Futurists, some of the Dada artists, and Burroughs as a harsh despair and perverse vision of apocalypse is no less serious for being proclaimed in a polite voice and as a sequence of playful affirmations. Indeed, it could be argued that silence is likely to remain a viable notion for modern art and consciousness only if deployed with a considerable, near systematic irony.

21

It is in the nature of all spiritual projects to tend to consume themselves—exhausting their own sense, the very meaning of the terms in which they are couched. (This is why "spirituality" must be continually reinvented.) All genuinely ultimate projects of consciousness eventually become projects for the unraveling of thought itself.

Art conceived as a spiritual project is no exception. As an abstracted and fragmented replica of the positive nihilism expounded by the radical religious myths, the serious art of our time has moved increasingly toward the most excruciating inflections of consciousness. Conceivably, irony is the only feasible counterweight to this grave use of art as the arena for the ordeal of consciousness. The present prospect is that artists will go on abolishing art, only to resurrect it in a more retracted version. As long as art bears up under the pressure of chronic interrogation, it would seem desirable that some of the questions have a certain playful quality.

But this prospect depends, perhaps, on the viability of irony itself.

From Socrates on, there are countless witnesses to the value of irony for the private individual: as a complex, serious method of seeking and holding one's truth, and as a means of saving one's sanity. But as irony becomes the good taste of what is, after all, an essentially collective activity—the making of art—it may prove less serviceable.

One need not judge as categorically as Nietzsche, who thought the spread of irony throughout a culture signified the floodtide of decadence and the approaching end of that culture's vitality and powers. In the post-political, electronically connected cosmopolis in which all serious modern artists have taken out premature citizenship, certain organic connections between culture and "thinking" (and art is certainly now, mainly, a form of thinking) appear to have been broken, so that Nietzsche's diagnosis may need to be modified. But if irony has more positive resources than Nietzsche acknowledged, there still remains a question as to how far the resources of irony can be stretched. It seems unlikely that the possibilities of continually undermining one's assumptions can go on unfolding indefinitely into the future, without being eventually checked by despair or by a laugh that leaves one without any breath at all.

(1967)

The Pornographic Imagination

No one should undertake a discussion of pornography before
acknowledging the pornograph*ies*—there are at least three—
and before pledging to take them on one at a time. There
is a considerable gain in truth if pornography as an item in
social history is treated quite separately from pornography
as a psychological phenomenon (according to the usual view,
symptomatic of sexual deficiency or deformity in both the
producers and the consumers), and if one further distinguishes
from both of these another pornography: a minor but interesting modality or convention within the arts.

It's the last of the three pornographies that I want to focus
upon. More narrowly, upon the literary genre for which,
lacking a better name, I'm willing to accept (in the privacy of

serious intellectual debate, not in the courts) the dubious label of pornography. By literary genre I mean a body of work belonging to literature considered as an art, and to which inherent standards of artistic excellence pertain. From the standpoint of social and psychological phenomena, all pornographic texts have the same status; they are documents. But from the standpoint of art, some of these texts may well become something else. Not only do Pierre Louys' *Trois Filles de leur Mère,* Georges Bataille's *Histoire de l'Oeil* and *Madame Edwarda,* the pseudonymous *Story of O* and *The Image* belong to literature, but it can be made clear why these books, all five of them, occupy a much higher rank as literature than *Candy* or Oscar Wilde's *Teleny* or the Earl of Rochester's *Sodom* or Apollinaire's *The Debauched Hospodar* or Cleland's *Fanny Hill.* The avalanche of pornographic potboilers marketed for two centuries under and now, increasingly, over the counter no more impugns the status as literature of the first group of pornographic books than the proliferation of books of the caliber of *The Carpetbaggers* and *Valley of the Dolls* throws into question the credentials of *Anna Karenina* and *The Great Gatsby* and *The Man Who Loved Children.* The ratio of authentic literature to trash in pornography may be somewhat lower than the ratio of novels of genuine literary merit to the entire volume of sub-literary fiction produced for mass taste. But it is probably no lower than, for instance, that of another somewhat shady sub-genre with a few first-rate books to its credit, science fiction. (As literary forms, pornography and science fiction resemble each other in several interesting ways.) Anyway, the quantitative measure supplies a trivial standard. Relatively uncommon as they may be, there are writings which it seems reasonable to call pornographic—assuming that the stale label has any use at all—which, at the same time, cannot be refused accreditation as serious literature.

The point would seem to be obvious. Yet, apparently, that's far from being the case. At least in England and America, the reasoned scrutiny and assessment of pornography is held firmly within the limits of the discourse employed by psychologists, sociologists, historians, jurists, professional moralists, and social critics. Pornography is a malady to be diagnosed and an occasion for judgment. It's something one is for or against. And taking sides about pornography is hardly like being for or against aleatoric music or Pop Art, but quite a bit like being for or against legalized abortion or federal aid to parochial schools. In fact, the same fundamental approach to the subject is shared by recent eloquent defenders of society's right and obligation to censor dirty books, like George P. Elliott and George Steiner, and those like Paul Goodman, who foresee pernicious consequences of a policy of censorship far worse than any harm done by the books themselves. Both the libertarians and the would-be censors agree in reducing pornography to pathological symptom and problematic social commodity. A near unanimous consensus exists as to what pornography is—this being identified with notions about the *sources* of the impulse to produce and consume these curious goods. When viewed as a theme for psychological analysis, pornography is rarely seen as anything more interesting than texts which illustrate a deplorable arrest in normal adult sexual development. In this view, all pornography amounts to is the representation of the fantasies of infantile sexual life, these fantasies having been edited by the more skilled, less innocent consciousness of the masturbatory adolescent, for purchase by so-called adults. As a social phenomenon—for instance, the boom in the production of pornography in the societies of Western Europe and America since the eighteenth century—the approach is no less unequivocally clinical. Pornography becomes a group pathology, the disease of a whole culture, about whose cause everyone is pretty well agreed. The mounting output of dirty books is attributed to a festering legacy of Christian sexual repression and to sheer physiological ignorance, these ancient disabilities being now compounded by more proximate historical events, the impact of drastic dislocations in traditional modes of family and political order and unsettling change in the roles of the sexes. (The problem of pornography is one of "the dilemmas of a society in transition," Goodman said in an essay several years ago.) Thus, there is a fairly complete consensus about the *diagnosis* of pornography itself. The disagreements arise only in the estimate of the psychological and social *consequences* of its dissemination, and therefore in the formulating of tactics and policy.

The more enlightened architects of moral policy are undoubtedly prepared to admit that there is something like a "pornographic imagination," although only in the sense that pornographic works are tokens of a radical failure or deformation of the imagination. And they may grant, as Goodman, Wayland Young, and others have suggested, that there also exists a "pornographic society": that, indeed, ours is a flourishing example of one, a society so hypocritically and repressively constructed that it must inevitably produce an effusion of pornography as both its logical expression and its subversive, demotic antidote. But nowhere in the Anglo-American community of letters have I seen it argued that some pornographic books are interesting and important works of art. So long as pornography is treated as only a social and psychological phenomenon and a locus for moral concern, how could such an argument ever be made?

2

There's another reason, apart from this categorizing of pornography as a topic of analysis, why the question whether or not works of pornography can be literature has never been genuinely debated. I mean the view of literature itself maintained by most English and American critics—a view which in excluding pornographic writings *by definition* from the precincts of literature excludes much else besides.

Of course, no one denies that pornography constitutes a branch of literature in the sense that it appears in the form of printed books of fiction. But beyond that trivial connection, no more is allowed. The fashion in which most critics construe the nature of prose literature, no less than their view of the nature of pornography, inevitably puts pornography in an adverse relation to literature. It is an airtight case, for if a pornographic book is defined as one not belonging to literature (and vice versa), there is no need to examine individual books.

Most mutually exclusive definitions of pornography and literature rest on four separate arguments. One is that the utterly singleminded way in which works of pornography address the reader, proposing to arouse him sexually, is antithetical to the complex function of literature. It may then be argued that pornography's aim, inducing sexual excitement, is at odds with the tranquil, detached involvement evoked by genuine art. But this turn of the argument seems particularly unconvincing, considering the respected appeal to the reader's moral feelings intended by "realistic" writing, not to mention the fact that some certified masterpieces (from Chaucer to Lawrence) contain passages that do properly excite readers sexually. It is more plausible just to emphasize that pornography still possesses only one "intention," while any genuinely valuable work of literature has many.

Another argument, made by Adorno among others, is that works of pornography lack the beginning-middle-and-end form characteristic of literature. A piece of pornographic fiction concocts no better than a crude excuse for a beginning; and once having begun, it goes on and on and ends nowhere.

Another argument: pornographic writing can't evidence any care for its means of expression as such (the concern of literature), since the aim of pornography is to inspire a set of nonverbal fantasies in which language plays a debased, merely instrumental role.

Last and most weighty is the argument that the subject of literature is the relation of human beings to each other, their complex feelings and emotions; pornography, in contrast, disdains fully formed persons (psychology and social portraiture), is oblivious to the question of motives and their credibility and reports only the motiveless tireless transactions of depersonalized organs.

Simply extrapolating from the conception of literature maintained by most English and American critics today, it would follow that the literary value of pornography has to be nil. But these paradigms don't stand up to close analysis in themselves, nor do they even fit their subject. Take, for instance, *Story of O.* Though the novel is clearly obscene by the usual standards, and more effective than many in arousing a reader sexually, sexual arousal doesn't appear to be the sole function of the situations portrayed. The narrative does have a definite beginning, middle, and end. The elegance of the writing hardly gives the impression that its author considered language a bothersome necessity. Further, the characters do possess emotions of a very intense kind, although obsessional and indeed wholly asocial ones; characters do have motives, though they are not psychiatrically or socially "normal" motives. The characters in *Story of O* are endowed with a "psychology" of a sort, one derived from the psychology of lust. And while what can be learned of the characters within the situations in which they are placed is severely restricted—to modes of sexual concentration and explicitly rendered sexual behavior—O and her partners are no more reduced or foreshortened than the characters in many nonpornographic works of contemporary fiction.

Only when English and American critics evolve a more sophisticated view of literature will an interesting debate get underway. (In the end, this debate would be not only about pornography but about the whole body of contemporary literature insistently focused on extreme situations and behavior.) The difficulty arises because so many critics continue to identify with prose literature itself the particular literary conventions of "realism" (what might be crudely associated with the major tradition of the nineteenth-century novel). For examples of alternative literary modes, one is not confined only to much of the greatest twentieth-century writing—to *Ulysses*, a book not about characters but about media of transpersonal exchange, about all that lies outside individual psychology and personal need; to French Surrealism and its most recent offspring, the New Novel; to German "expressionist" fiction; to the Russian post-novel represented by Biely's *St. Petersburg* and by Nabokov; or to the nonlinear, tenseless narratives of Stein and Burroughs. A definition of literature that faults a work for being rooted in "fantasy" rather than in the realistic rendering of how lifelike persons in familiar situations live with each other couldn't even handle such venerable conventions as the pastoral, which depicts relations between people that are certainly reductive, vapid, and unconvincing.

An uprooting of some of these tenacious clichés is long overdue: it will promote a sounder reading of the literature of the past as well as put critics and ordinary readers better in touch with contemporary literature, which includes zones of writing that structurally resemble pornography. It is facile, virtually meaningless, to demand that literature stick with the "human." For the matter at stake is not "human" versus "inhuman" (in which choosing the "human" guarantees instant moral self-congratulation for both author and reader) but an infinitely varied register of forms and tonalities for transposing *the human voice* into prose narrative. For the critic, the proper question is not the relationship between the book and "the world" or "reality" (in which each novel is judged as if it were a unique item, and in which the world is regarded as a far less complex place than it is) but the complexities of consciousness itself, as the medium through which a world exists at all and is constituted, and an approach to single books of fiction which doesn't slight the fact that they exist in dialogue with each other. From this point of view, the decision of the old novelists to depict the unfolding of the destinies of sharply individualized "characters" in familiar, socially dense situations within the conventional notation of chronological sequence is only one of many possible decisions, possessing no inherently superior claim to the allegiance of serious readers. There is nothing innately more "human" about these procedures. The presence of realistic characters is not, in itself, something wholesome, a more nourishing staple for the moral sensibility.

The only sure truth about characters in prose fiction is that they are, in Henry James' phrase, "a compositional resource." The presence of human figures in literary art can serve many purposes. Dramatic tension or three-dimensionality in the rendering of personal and social relations is often *not* a writer's aim, in which case it doesn't help to insist on that as a generic standard. Exploring ideas is as authentic an aim of prose fiction, although by the standards of novelistic realism this aim severely limits the presentation of lifelike persons. The constructing or imaging of something inanimate, or of a portion of the world of nature, is also a valid enterprise, and entails an appropriate rescaling of the human figure. (The form of the pastoral involves both these aims: the depiction of ideas and of nature. Persons are used only to the extent that they constitute a certain kind of landscape, which is partly a stylization of "real" nature and partly a neo-Platonic landscape of ideas.) And equally valid as a subject for prose narrative are the extreme states of human feeling and consciousness, those so peremptory that they exclude the mundane flux of feelings and are only contingently linked with concrete persons—which is the case with pornography.

One would never guess from the confident pronouncements on the nature of literature by most American and English critics that a vivid debate on this issue had been proceeding for several generations. "It seems to me," Jacques Rivière wrote in the *Nouvelle Revue Française* in 1924, "that we are witnessing a very serious crisis in the concept of what literature is." One of several responses to "the problem of the possibility and the limits of literature," Rivière noted, is the marked tendency for "art (if even the word can still be kept) to become a completely nonhuman activity, a supersensory function, if I may use that term, a sort of creative astronomy." I cite

Rivière not because his essay, "Questioning the Concept of
Literature," is particularly original or definitive or subtly
argued, but simply to recall an ensemble of radical notions
about literature which were almost critical commonplaces
forty years ago in European literary magazines.

To this day, though, that ferment remains alien, unassimi-
lated, and persistently misunderstood in the English and
American world of letters: suspected as issuing from a collective cultural failure of nerve, frequently dismissed as outright
perversity or obscurantism or creative sterility. The better
English-speaking critics, however, could hardly fail to notice
how much great twentieth-century literature subverts those
ideas received from certain of the great nineteenth-century
novelists on the nature of literature which they continue to
echo in 1967. But the critics' awareness of genuinely new
literature was usually tendered in a spirit much like that of the
rabbis a century before the beginning of the Christian era
who, humbly acknowledging the spiritual inferiority of their
own age to the age of the great prophets, nevertheless firmly
closed the canon of prophetic books and declared—with more
relief, one suspects, than regret—the era of prophecy ended.
So has the age of what in Anglo-American criticism is still
called, astonishingly enough, "experimental" or "avant-garde"
writing been repeatedly declared closed. The ritual celebra-
tion of each contemporary genius's undermining of the older
notions of literature was often accompanied by the nervous
insistence that the writing brought forth was, alas, the last of
its noble, sterile line. Now, the results of this intricate, one-
eyed way of looking at modern literature have been several
decades of unparalleled interest and brilliance in English and
American—particularly American—criticism. But it is an interest and brilliance reared on bankruptcy of taste and something
approaching a fundamental dishonesty of method. The critics'
retrograde awareness of the impressive new claims staked out
by modern literature, linked with their chagrin over what was
usually designated as "the rejection of reality" and "the failure

of the self" endemic in that literature, indicates the precise point at which most talented Anglo-American literary criticism leaves off considering structures of literature and transposes itself into criticism of culture.

I don't wish to repeat here the arguments that I have advanced elsewhere on behalf of a different critical approach. Still, some allusion to that approach needs to be made. To discuss even a single work of the radical nature of *Histoire de l'Oeil* raises the question of literature itself, of prose narrative considered as an art form. And books like those of Bataille could not have been written except for that agonized reappraisal of the nature of literature which has been preoccupying literary Europe for more than half a century; but lacking that context, they must prove almost unassimilable for English and American readers—except as "mere" pornography, inexplicably fancy trash. If it is even necessary to take up the issue of whether or not pornography and literature are antithetical, if it is at all necessary to assert that works of pornography *can* belong to literature, then the assertion must imply an overall view of what art is.

To put it very generally: art (and art-making) is a form of consciousness; the materials of art are the variety of forms of consciousness. By no *aesthetic* principle can this notion of the materials of art be construed as excluding even the extreme forms of consciousness that transcend social personality or psychological individuality.

In daily life, to be sure, we may acknowledge a moral obligation to inhibit such states of consciousness in ourselves. The obligation seems pragmatically sound, not only to maintain social order in the widest sense but to allow the individual to establish and maintain a humane contact with other persons (though that contact can be renounced, for shorter or longer periods). It's well known that when people venture into the far reaches of consciousness, they do so at the peril of their sanity, that is, of their humanity. But the "human scale" or humanistic standard proper to ordinary life and conduct seems misplaced when applied to art. It oversimplifies. If within the last century art conceived as an autonomous activity has come to be invested with an unprecedented stature—the nearest thing to a sacramental human activity acknowledged by secular society—it is because one of the tasks art has assumed is making forays into and taking up positions on the frontiers of consciousness (often very dangerous to the artist as a person) and reporting back what's there. Being a free-lance explorer of spiritual dangers, the artist gains a certain license to behave differently from other people; matching the singularity of his vocation, he may be decked out with a suitably eccentric life style, or he may not. His job is inventing trophies of his experiences—objects and gestures that fascinate and enthrall, not merely (as prescribed by older notions of the artist) edify or entertain. His principal means of fascinating is to advance one step further in the dialectic of outrage. He seeks to make his work repulsive, obscure, inaccessible; in short, to give what is, or seems to be, *not* wanted. But however fierce may be the outrages the artist perpetrates upon his audience, his credentials and spiritual authority ultimately depend on the audience's sense (whether something known or inferred) of the outrages he commits upon himself. The exemplary modern artist is a broker in madness.

The notion of art as the dearly purchased outcome of an immense spiritual risk, one whose cost goes up with the entry and participation of each new player in the game, invites a revised set of critical standards. Art produced under the aegis of this conception certainly is not, cannot be, "realistic." But words like "fantasy" or "surrealism," that only invert the guidelines of realism, clarify little. Fantasy too easily declines into "mere" fantasy; the clincher is the adjective "infantile." Where does fantasy, condemned by psychiatric rather than artistic standards, end and imagination begin?

Since it's hardly likely that contemporary critics seriously mean to bar prose narratives that are unrealistic from the domain of literature, one suspects that a special standard is being applied to sexual themes. This becomes clearer if one thinks of another kind of book, another kind of "fantasy." The ahistorical dreamlike landscape where action is situated, the peculiarly congealed time in which acts are performed—these occur almost as often in science fiction as they do in pornography. There is nothing conclusive in the well-known fact that most men and women fall short of the sexual prowess that people in pornography are represented as enjoying; that the size of organs, number and duration of orgasms, variety and feasibility of sexual powers, and amount of sexual energy all seem grossly exaggerated. Yes, and the spaceships and the teeming planets depicted in science-fiction novels don't exist either. The fact that the site of narrative is an ideal *topos* disqualifies neither pornography nor science fiction from being literature. Such negations of real, concrete, three-dimensional social time, space, and personality—and such "fantastic" enlargements of human energy—are rather the ingredients of another kind of literature, founded on another mode of consciousness.

The materials of the pornographic books that count as literature are, precisely, one of the extreme forms of human consciousness. Undoubtedly, many people would agree that the sexually obsessed consciousness can, in principle, enter into literature as an art form. Literature about lust? Why not? But then they usually add a rider to the agreement which effectually nullifies it. They require that the author have the proper "distance" from his obsessions for their rendering to count as literature. Such a standard is sheer hypocrisy, revealing once again that the values commonly applied to pornography are, in the end, those belonging to psychiatry and social affairs rather than to art. (Since Christianity upped the ante and concentrated on sexual behavior as the root of virtue, everything pertaining to sex has been a "special case" in our culture, evoking peculiarly inconsistent attitudes.) Van Gogh's paintings retain their status as art even if it seems his manner of painting owed less to a conscious choice of representational means than to his being deranged and actually seeing reality the way he painted it. Similarly, *Histoire de l'Oeil* does not become case history rather than art because, as Bataille reveals in the extraordinary autobiographical essay appended to the narrative, the book's obsessions are indeed his own.

What makes a work of pornography part of the history of art rather than of trash is not distance, the superimposition of a consciousness more conformable to that of ordinary reality upon the "deranged consciousness" of the erotically obsessed. Rather, it is the originality, thoroughness, authenticity, and power of that deranged consciousness itself, as incarnated in a work. From the point of view of art, the exclusivity of the consciousness embodied in pornographic books is in itself neither anomalous nor anti-literary.

Nor is the purported aim or effect, whether it is intentional or not, of such books—to excite the reader sexually—a defect. Only a degraded and mechanistic idea of sex could mislead someone into thinking that being sexually stirred by a book like *Madame Edwarda* is a simple matter. The singleness of intention often condemned by critics is, when the work merits treatment as art, compounded of many resonances. The physical sensations involuntarily produced in someone reading the book carry with them something that touches upon the reader's whole experience of his humanity—and his limits as a personality and as a body. Actually, the singleness of pornography's intention is spurious. But the aggressiveness of the intention is not. What seems like an end is as much a means, startlingly and oppressively concrete. The end, however, is less concrete. Pornography is one of the branches of literature— science fiction is another—aiming at disorientation, at psychic dislocation.

In some respects, the use of sexual obsessions as a subject for literature resembles the use of a literary subject whose validity far fewer people would contest: religious obsessions. So compared, the familiar fact of pornography's definite, aggressive impact upon its readers looks somewhat different. Its celebrated intention of sexually stimulating readers is really a species of proselytizing. Pornography that is serious literature aims to "excite" in the same way that books which render an extreme form of religious experience aim to "convert."

3

Two French books recently translated into English, *Story of O* and *The Image*, conveniently illustrate some issues involved in this topic, barely explored in Anglo-American criticism, of pornography as literature.

Story of O by "Pauline Réage" appeared in 1954 and immediately became famous, partly due to the patronage of Jean Paulhan, who wrote the preface. It was widely believed that Paulhan himself had written the book—perhaps because of the precedent set by Bataille, who had contributed an essay (signed with his own name) to his *Madame Edwarda* when it was first published in 1937 under the pseudonym "Pierre Angelique," and also because the name Pauline suggested Paulhan. But Paulhan has always denied that he wrote *Story of O*, insisting that it was indeed written by a woman, someone previously unpublished and living in another part of France, who insisted on remaining unknown. While Paulhan's story did not halt speculation, the conviction that he was the author eventually faded. Over the years, a number of more ingenious hypotheses, attributing the book's authorship to other notables on the Paris literary scene, gained credence and then were dropped. The real identity of "Pauline Réage" remains one of the few well-kept secrets in contemporary letters.

The Image was published two years later, in 1956, also under a pseudonym, "Jean de Berg." To compound the mystery, it was dedicated to and had a preface by "Pauline Réage," who has not been heard from since. (The preface by "Réage" is terse and forgettable; the one by Paulhan is long and very interesting.) But gossip in Paris literary circles about the identity of "Jean de Berg" is more conclusive than the detective work on "Pauline Réage." One rumor only, which names the wife of an influential younger novelist, has swept the field.

It is not hard to understand why those curious enough to speculate about the two pseudonyms should incline toward some name from the established community of letters in France. For either of these books to be an amateur's one-shot seems scarcely conceivable. Different as they are from each other, *Story of O* and *The Image* both evince a quality that can't be ascribed simply to an abundance of the usual writerly endowments of sensibility, energy, and intelligence. Such gifts, very much in evidence, have themselves been processed through a dialogue of artifices. The somber self-consciousness of the narratives could hardly be further from the lack of control and craft usually considered the expression of obsessive lust. Intoxicating as is their subject (if the reader doesn't cut off and find it just funny or sinister), both narratives are more concerned with the "use" of erotic material than with the "expression" of it. And this use is preeminently—there is no other word for it—literary. The imagination pursuing its outrageous pleasures in *Story of O* and *The Image* remains firmly anchored to certain notions of the *formal* consummation of intense feeling, of procedures for exhausting an experience, that connect as much with literature and recent literary history as with the ahistorical domain of eros. And why not? Experiences aren't pornographic; only images and representations—structures of the imagination—are. That is why a pornographic book often can make the reader think of, mainly, other pornographic books, rather than sex unmediated—and this not necessarily to the detriment of his erotic excitement.

For instance, what resonates throughout *Story of O* is a voluminous body of pornographic or "libertine" literature, mostly trash, in both French and English, going back to the eighteenth century. The most obvious reference is to Sade. But here one must not think only of the writings of Sade himself, but of the reinterpretation of Sade by French literary intellectuals after World War II, a critical gesture perhaps comparable in its importance and influence upon educated literary taste and upon the actual direction of serious fiction in France to the reappraisal of James launched just before World War II in the United States, except that the French reappraisal has lasted longer and seems to have struck deeper roots. (Sade, of course, had never been forgotten. He was read enthusiastically by Flaubert, Baudelaire, and most of the other radical geniuses of French literature of the late nineteenth century. He was one of the patron saints of the Surrealist movement, and figures importantly in the thought of Breton. But it was the discussion of Sade after 1945 that really consolidated his position as an inexhaustible point of departure for radical thinking about the human condition. The well-known essay of Beauvoir, the indefatigable scholarly biography undertaken by Gilbert Lely, and writings as yet untranslated of Blanchot, Paulhan, Bataille, Klossowski, and Leiris are the most eminent documents of the postwar re-evaluation which secured this astonishingly hardy modification of French literary sensibility. The quality and theoretical density of the French interest in Sade remains virtually incomprehensible to English and American literary intellectuals, for whom Sade is perhaps an exemplary figure in the history of psychopathology, both individual and social, but inconceivable as someone to be taken seriously as a "thinker.")

But what stands behind *Story of O* is not only Sade, both the problems he raised and the ones raised in his name. The book is also rooted in the conventions of the "libertine" potboilers written in nineteenth-century France, typically situated in a fantasy England populated by brutal aristocrats with enormous sexual equipment and violent tastes, along the axis of sadomasochism, to match. The name of O's second lover-proprietor, Sir Stephen, clearly pays homage to this period fantasy, as does the figure of Sir Edmond of *Histoire de l'Oeil*. And it should be stressed that the allusion to a stock type of pornographic trash stands, as a literary reference, on exactly the same footing as the anachronistic setting of the main action, which is lifted straight from Sade's sexual theatre. The narrative opens in Paris (O joins her lover René in a car and is driven around) but most of the subsequent action is removed to more familiar if less plausible territory: that conveniently isolated château, luxuriously furnished and lavishly staffed with servants, where a clique of rich men congregate and to which women are brought as virtual slaves to be the objects, shared in common, of the men's brutal and inventive lust. There are whips and chains, masks worn by the men when the women are admitted to their presence, great fires burning in the hearth, unspeakable sexual indignities, floggings and more ingenious kinds of physical mutilation, several lesbian scenes when the excitement of the orgies in the great drawing room seems to flag. In short, the novel comes equipped with some of the creakiest items in the repertoire of pornography.

How seriously can we take this? A bare inventory of the plot might give the impression that *Story of O* is not so much pornography as meta-pornography, a brilliant parody. Something similar was urged in defense of *Candy* when it was published here several years ago, after some years of modest existence in Paris as a more or less official dirty book. *Candy* wasn't pornography, it was argued, but a spoof, a witty burlesque of the conventions of cheap pornographic narrative. My own view is that *Candy* may be funny, but it's still pornography. For pornography isn't a form that can parody itself. It is the nature of the pornographic imagination to prefer ready-made conventions of character, setting, and action. Pornography is a theatre of types, never of individuals. A parody of pornography, so far as it has any real competence, always remains pornography. Indeed, parody is one common form of pornographic writing. Sade himself often used it, inverting the moralistic fictions of Richardson in which female virtue always triumphs over male lewdness (either by saying no or by dying afterwards). With *Story of O*, it would be more accurate to speak of a "use" rather than of a parody of Sade.

The tone alone of *Story of O* indicates that whatever in the book might be read as parody or antiquarianism—a mandarin pornography?—is only one of several elements forming the narrative. (Although sexual situations encompassing all the expectable variations of lust are graphically described, the prose style is rather formal, the level of language dignified and almost chaste.) Features of the Sadean staging are used to shape the action, but the narrative's basic line differs fundamentally from anything Sade wrote. For one thing, Sade's work has a built-in open-endedness or principle of insatiability. His *120 Days of Sodom,* probably the most ambitious pornographic book ever conceived (in terms of scale), a kind of summa of the pornographic imagination; stunningly impressive and upsetting, even in the truncated form, part narrative and part scenario, in which it has survived. (The manuscript was accidentally rescued from the Bastille after Sade had been forced to leave it behind when he was transferred in 1789 to Charenton, but Sade believed until his death that his masterpiece had been destroyed when the prison was razed.) Sade's express train of outrages tears along an interminable but level track. His descriptions are too schematic to be sensuous. The fictional actions are illustrations, rather, of his relentlessly repeated ideas. Yet these polemical ideas themselves seem, on reflection, more like principles of a dramaturgy than a substantive theory. Sade's ideas—of the person as a "thing" or an "object," of the body as a machine and of the orgy as an inventory of the hopefully indefinite possibilities of several machines in collaboration with each other—seem mainly designed to make possible an endless, nonculminating kind of ultimately affectless activity. In contrast, *Story of O* has a definite movement; a logic of events, as opposed to Sade's static principle of the catalogue or encyclopedia. This plot movement is strongly abetted by the fact that, for most of the narrative, the author tolerates at least a vestige of "the couple" (O and René, O and Sir Stephen)—a unit generally repudiated in pornographic literature.

And, of course, the figure of O herself is different. Her feelings, however insistently they adhere to one theme, have some modulation and are carefully described. Although passive, O scarcely resembles those ninnies in Sade's tales who are detained in remote castles to be tormented by pitiless noblemen and satanic priests. And O is represented as active, too: literally active, as in the seduction of Jacqueline, and more important, profoundly active in her own passivity. O resembles her Sadean prototypes only superficially. There is no personal consciousness, except that of the author, in Sade's books. But O does possess a consciousness, from which vantage point her story is told. (Although written in the third person, the narrative never departs from O's point of view or understands more than she understands.) Sade aims to neutralize sexuality of all its personal associations, to represent a kind of impersonal—or pure—sexual encounter. But the narrative of "Pauline Réage" does show O reacting in quite different ways (including love) to different people, notably to René, to Sir Stephen, to Jacqueline, and to Anne-Marie.

Sade seems more representative of the major conventions of pornographic writing. So far as the pornographic imagination tends to make one person interchangeable with another and all people interchangeable with things, it's not functional to describe a person as O is described—in terms of a certain state of her will (which she's trying to discard) and of her understanding. Pornography is mainly populated by creatures like Sade's Justine, endowed with neither will nor intelligence nor even, apparently, memory. Justine lives in a perpetual state of astonishment, never learning anything from the strikingly repetitious violations of her innocence. After each fresh betrayal she gets in place for another round, as uninstructed by her experience as ever, ready to trust the next masterful libertine and have her trust rewarded by a renewed loss of liberty, the same indignities, and the same blasphemous sermons in praise of vice.

For the most part, the figures who play the role of sexual

objects in pornography are made of the same stuff as one
principal "humour" of comedy. Justine is like Candide, who is
also a cipher, a blank, an eternal naïf incapable of learning
anything from his atrocious ordeals. The familiar structure
of comedy which features a character who is a still center
in the midst of outrage (Buster Keaton is a classic image)
crops up repeatedly in pornography. The personages in pornography, like those of comedy, are seen only from the outside, behavioristically. By definition, they can't be seen in
depth, so as truly to engage the audience's feelings. In much
of comedy, the joke resides precisely in the *disparity* between
the understated or anesthetized feeling and a large outrageous
event. Pornography works in a similar fashion. The gain
produced by a deadpan tone, by what seems to the reader in
an ordinary state of mind to be the incredible *under*reacting of
the erotic agents to the situations in which they're placed, is not
the release of laughter. It's the release of a sexual reaction,
originally voyeuristic but probably needing to be secured by
an underlying direct identification with one of the participants
in the sexual act. The emotional flatness of pornography is
thus neither a failure of artistry nor an index of principled
inhumanity. The arousal of a sexual response in the reader
requires it. Only in the absence of directly stated emotions can
the reader of pornography find room for his own responses.
When the event narrated comes already festooned with the
author's explicitly avowed sentiments, by which the reader
may be stirred, it then becomes harder to be stirred by the
event itself.*

* This is very clear in the case of Genet's books, which, despite the
explicitness of the sexual experiences related, are not sexually arousing
for most readers. What the reader knows (and Genet has stated it
many times) is that Genet himself was sexually excited while writing
The Miracle of the Rose, Our Lady of the Flowers, etc. The reader
makes an intense and unsettling contact with Genet's erotic excitement, which is the energy that propels these metaphor-studded
narratives; but, at the same time, the author's excitement precludes
the reader's own. Genet was perfectly correct when he said that his
books were not pornographic.

Silent film comedy offers many illustrations of how the formal principle of continual agitation or perpetual motion (slapstick) and that of the deadpan really converge to the same end—a deadening or neutralization or distancing of the audience's emotions, its ability to identify in a "humane" way and to make moral judgments about situations of violence. The same principle is at work in all pornography. It's not that the characters in pornography cannot conceivably possess any emotions. They can. But the principles of underreacting and frenetic agitation make the emotional climate self-canceling, so that the basic tone of pornography is affectless, emotionless.

However, degrees of this affectlessness can be distinguished. Justine is the stereotype sex-object figure (invariably female, since most pornography is written by men or from the stereotyped male point of view): a bewildered victim, whose consciousness remains unaltered by her experiences. But O is an adept; whatever the cost in pain and fear, she is grateful for the opportunity to be initiated into a mystery. That mystery is the loss of the self. O learns, she suffers, she changes. Step by step she becomes more what she is, a process identical with the emptying out of herself. In the vision of the world presented by *Story of O*, the highest good is the transcendence of personality. The plot's movement is not horizontal, but a kind of ascent through degradation. O does not simply become identical with her sexual availability, but wants to reach the perfection of becoming an object. Her condition, if it can be characterized as one of dehumanization, is not to be understood as a by-product of her enslavement to René, Sir Stephen, and the other men at Roissy, but as the point of her situation, something she seeks and eventually attains. The terminal image for her achievement comes in the last scene of the book: O is led to a party, mutilated, in chains, unrecognizable, costumed (as an owl)—so convincingly no longer human that none of the guests thinks of speaking to her directly.

O's quest is neatly summed up in the expressive letter which serves her for a name. "O" suggests a cartoon of her sex, not her individual sex but simply woman; it also stands for a nothing. But what *Story of O* unfolds is a spiritual paradox, that of the full void and of the vacuity that is also a plenum. The power of the book lies exactly in the anguish stirred up by the continuing presence of this paradox. "Pauline Réage" raises, in a far more organic and sophisticated manner than Sade does with his clumsy expositions and discourses, the question of the status of human personality itself. But whereas Sade is interested in the obliteration of personality from the viewpoint of power and liberty, the author of *Story of O* is interested in the obliteration of personality from the viewpoint of happiness. (The closest statement of this theme in English literature: certain passages in Lawrence's *The Lost Girl*.)

For the paradox to gain real significance, however, the reader must entertain a view of sex different from that held by most enlightened members of the community. The prevailing view—an amalgam of Rousseauist, Freudian, and liberal social thought—regards the phenomenon of sex as a perfectly intelligible, although uniquely precious, source of emotional and physical pleasure. What difficulties arise come from the long deformation of the sexual impulses administered by Western Christianity, whose ugly wounds virtually everyone in this culture bears. First, guilt and anxiety. Then, the reduction of sexual capacities—leading if not to virtual impotence or frigidity, at least to the depletion of erotic energy and the repression of many natural elements of sexual appetite (the "perversions"). Then the spill-over into public dishonesties in which people tend to respond to news of the sexual pleasures of others with envy, fascination, revulsion, and spiteful indignation. It's from this pollution of the sexual health of the culture that a phenomenon like pornography is derived.

I don't quarrel with the historical diagnosis contained in this account of the deformations of Western sexuality. Nevertheless, what seems to me decisive in the complex of views held by most educated members of the community is a more questionable assumption—that human sexual appetite is, if untampered with, a natural pleasant function; and that "the obscene" is a convention, the fiction imposed upon nature by a society convinced there is something vile about the sexual functions and, by extension, about sexual pleasure. It's just these assumptions that are challenged by the French tradition represented by Sade, Lautréamont, Bataille, and the authors of *Story of O* and *The Image*. Their work suggests that "the obscene" is a primal notion of human consciousness, something much more profound than the backwash of a sick society's aversion to the body. Human sexuality is, quite apart from Christian repressions, a highly questionable phenomenon, and belongs, at least potentially, among the extreme rather than the ordinary experiences of humanity. Tamed as it may be, sexuality remains one of the demonic forces in human consciousness—pushing us at intervals close to taboo and dangerous desires, which range from the impulse to commit sudden arbitrary violence upon another person to the voluptuous yearning for the extinction of one's consciousness, for death itself. Even on the level of simple physical sensation and mood, making love surely resembles having an epileptic fit at least as much, if not more, than it does eating a meal or conversing with someone. Everyone has felt (at least in fantasy) the erotic glamour of physical cruelty and an erotic lure in things that are vile and repulsive. These phenomena form part of the genuine spectrum of sexuality, and if they are not to be written off as mere neurotic aberrations, the picture looks different from the one promoted by enlightened public opinion, and less simple.

One could plausibly argue that it is for quite sound reasons that the whole capacity for sexual ecstasy is inaccessible to most people—given that sexuality is something, like nuclear energy, which may prove amenable to domestication through scruple, but then again may not. That few people regularly, or perhaps ever, experience their sexual capacities at this unsettling pitch doesn't mean that the extreme is not authentic, or that the possibility of it doesn't haunt them anyway. (Religion is probably, after sex, the second oldest resource which human beings have available to them for blowing their minds. Yet among the multitudes of the pious, the number who have ventured very far into that state of consciousness must be fairly small, too.) There is, demonstrably, something incorrectly designed and potentially disorienting in the human sexual capacity—at least in the capacities of man-in-civilization. Man, the sick animal, bears within him an appetite which can drive him mad. Such is the understanding of sexuality —as something beyond good and evil, beyond love, beyond sanity; as a resource for ordeal and for breaking through the limits of consciousness—that informs the French literary canon I've been discussing.

The *Story of O*, with its project for completely transcending personality, entirely presumes this dark and complex vision of sexuality so far removed from the hopeful view sponsored by American Freudianism and liberal culture. The woman who is given no other name than O progresses simultaneously toward her own extinction as a human being and her fulfillment as a sexual being. It's hard to imagine how anyone would ascertain whether there exists truly, empirically, anything in "nature" or human consciousness that supports such a split. But it seems understandable that the possibility has always haunted man, as accustomed as he is to decrying such a split.

O's project enacts, on another scale, that performed by the existence of pornographic literature itself. What pornographic literature does is precisely to drive a wedge between one's existence as a full human being and one's existence as a sexual being—while in ordinary life a healthy person is one who prevents such a gap from opening up. Normally we don't experience, at least don't want to experience, our sexual fulfillment as distinct from or opposed to our personal fulfillment. But perhaps in part they are distinct, whether we like it or not. Insofar as strong sexual feeling does involve an obsessive degree of attention, it encompasses experiences in which a person can feel he is losing his "self." The literature that goes from Sade through Surrealism to these recent books capitalizes on that mystery; it isolates the mystery and makes the reader aware of it, invites him to participate in it.

This literature is both an invocation of the erotic in its darkest sense and, in certain cases, an exorcism. The devout, solemn mood of *Story of O* is fairly unrelieved; a work of mixed moods on the same theme, a journey toward the estrangement of the self from the self, is Buñuel's film *L'Age d'Or*. As a literary form, pornography works with two patterns —one equivalent to tragedy (as in *Story of O*) in which the erotic subject-victim heads inexorably toward death, and the other equivalent to comedy (as in *The Image*) in which the obsessional pursuit of sexual exercise is rewarded by a terminal gratification, union with the uniquely desired sexual partner.

4

The writer who renders a darker sense of the erotic, its perils of fascination and humiliation, than anyone else is Bataille. His *Histoire de l'Oeil* (first published in 1928) and *Madame Edwarda** qualify as pornographic texts insofar as their theme is an all-engrossing sexual quest that annihilates every consideration of persons extraneous to their roles in the sexual dramaturgy, and the fulfillment of this quest is depicted graphically. But this description conveys nothing of the extraordinary quality of these books. For sheer explicitness about sexual organs and acts is not necessarily obscene; it only becomes so when delivered in a particular tone, when it has acquired a certain moral resonance. As it happens, the sparse number of sexual acts and quasi-sexual defilements related in

---

* Unfortunately, the only translation available in English of what purports to be *Madame Edwarda*, that included in *The Olympia Reader*, pp. 662–672, published by Grove Press in 1965, just gives half the work. Only the *récit* is translated. But *Madame Edwarda* isn't a *récit* padded out with a preface also by Bataille. It is a two-part invention—essay and *récit*—and one part is almost unintelligible without the other.

Bataille's novellas can hardly compete with the interminable mechanistic inventiveness of the *120 Days of Sodom*. Yet because Bataille possessed a finer and more profound sense of transgression, what he describes seems somehow more potent and outrageous than the most lurid orgies staged by Sade.

One reason that *Histoire de l'Oeil* and *Madame Edwarda* make such a strong and upsetting impression is that Bataille understood more clearly than any other writer I know of that what pornography is really about, ultimately, isn't sex but death. I am not suggesting that every pornographic work speaks, either overtly or covertly, of death. Only works dealing with that specific and sharpest inflection of the themes of lust, "the obscene," do. It's toward the gratifications of death, succeeding and surpassing those of eros, that every truly obscene quest tends. (An example of a pornographic work whose subject is not the "obscene" is Louys' jolly saga of sexual insatiability, *Trois Filles de leur Mère*. *The Image* presents a less clear-cut case. While the enigmatic transactions between the three characters are charged with a sense of the obscene—more like a premonition, since the obscene is reduced to being only a constituent of voyeurism—the book has an unequivocally happy ending, with the narrator finally united with Claire. But *Story of O* takes the same line as Bataille, despite a little intellectual play at the end: the book closes ambiguously, with several lines to the effect that two versions of a final suppressed chapter exist, in one of which O received Sir Stephen's permission to die when he was about to discard her. Although this double ending satisfyingly echoes the book's opening, in which two versions "of the same beginning" are given, it can't, I think, lessen the reader's sense that O is death-bound, whatever doubts the author expresses about her fate.)

Bataille composed most of his books, the chamber music of pornographic literature, in *récit* form (sometimes accompanied by an essay). Their unifying theme is Bataille's own consciousness, a consciousness in an acute, unrelenting state of agony; but as an equally extraordinary mind in an earlier age might have written a theology of agony, Bataille has written an erotics of agony. Willing to tell something of the autobiographical sources of his narratives, he appended to *Histoire de l'Oeil* some vivid imagery from his own outrageously terrible childhood. (One memory: his blind, syphilitic, insane father trying unsuccessfully to urinate.) Time has neutralized these memories, he explains; after many years, they have largely lost their power over him and "can only come to life again, deformed, hardly recognizable, having in the course of this deformation taken on an obscene meaning." Obscenity, for Bataille, simultaneously revives his most painful experiences and scores a victory over that pain. The obscene, that is to say, the extremity of erotic experience, is the root of vital energies. Human beings, he says in the essay part of *Madame Edwarda,* live only through excess. And pleasure depends on "perspective," or giving oneself to a state of "open being," open to death as well as to joy. Most people try to outwit their own feelings; they want to be receptive to pleasure but keep "horror" at a distance. That's foolish, according to Bataille, since horror reinforces "attraction" and excites desire.

What Bataille exposes in extreme erotic experience is its subterranean connection with death. Bataille conveys this insight not by devising sexual acts whose consequences are lethal, thereby littering his narratives with corpses. (In the terrifying *Histoire de l'Oeil,* for instance, only one person dies; and the book ends with the three sexual adventurers, having debauched their way through France and Spain, acquiring a yacht in Gibraltar to pursue their infamies elsewhere.) His more effective method is to invest each action with a weight, a disturbing gravity, that feels authentically "mortal."

Yet despite the obvious differences of scale and finesse of execution, the conceptions of Sade and Bataille have some resemblances. Like Bataille, Sade was not so much a sensualist as someone with an intellectual project: to explore the scope of transgression. And he shares with Bataille the same ultimate identification of sex and death. But Sade could never have agreed with Bataille that "the truth of eroticism is tragic." People often die in Sade's books. But these deaths always seem unreal. They're no more convincing than those mutilations inflicted during the evening's orgies from which the victims recover completely the next morning following the use of a wondrous salve. From the perspective of Bataille, a reader can't help being caught up short by Sade's bad faith about death. (Of course, many pornographic books that are much less interesting and accomplished than those of Sade share this bad faith.)

Indeed, one might speculate that the fatiguing repetitiveness of Sade's books is the consequence of his imaginative failure to confront the inevitable goal or haven of a truly systematic venture of the pornographic imagination. Death is the only end to the odyssey of the pornographic imagination when it becomes systematic; that is, when it becomes focused on the pleasures of transgression rather than mere pleasure itself. Since he could not or would not arrive at his ending, Sade stalled. He multiplied and thickened his narrative; tediously reduplicated orgiastic permutations and combinations. And his fictional alter egos regularly interrupted a bout of rape or buggery to deliver to their victims his latest reworkings of lengthy sermons on what real "Enlightenment" means—the nasty truth about God, society, nature, individuality, virtue. Bataille manages to eschew anything resembling the counter-idealisms which are Sade's blasphemies (and which thereby perpetuate the banished idealism lying behind those fantasies); his blasphemies are autonomous.

Sade's books, the Wagnerian music dramas of pornographic literature, are neither subtle nor compact. Bataille achieves his effects with far more economical means: a chamber ensemble of non-interchangeable personages, instead of Sade's operatic multiplication of sexual virtuosi and career victims. Bataille renders his radical negatives through extreme compression. The gain, apparent on every page, enables his lean work and gnomic thought to go further than Sade's. Even in pornography, less can be more.

Bataille also has offered distinctly original and effective solutions to one perennial problem of pornographic narration: the ending. The most common procedure has been to end in a way that lays no claim to any internal necessity. Hence, Adorno could judge it the mark of pornography that it has neither beginning nor middle nor end. But Adorno is being unperceptive. Pornographic narratives do end—admittedly with abruptness and, by conventional novel standards, without motivation. This is not necessarily objectionable. (The discovery, midway in a science-fiction novel, of an alien planet may be no less abrupt or unmotivated.) Abruptness, an endemic facticity of encounters and chronically renewing encounters, is not some unfortunate defect of the pornographic narration which one might wish removed in order for the books to qualify as literature. These features are constitutive of the very imagination or vision of the world which goes into pornography. They supply, in many cases, exactly the ending that's needed.

But this doesn't preclude other types of endings. One notable feature of *Histoire de l'Oeil* and, to a lesser extent, *The Image,* considered as works of art, is their evident interest in more systematic or rigorous kinds of ending which still remain within the terms of the pornographic imagination—not seduced by the solutions of a more realistic or less abstract fiction. Their solution, considered very generally, is to construct a narrative that is, from the beginning, more rigorously controlled, less spontaneous and lavishly descriptive.

In *The Image* the narrative is dominated by a single metaphor, "the image" (though the reader can't understand the full meaning of the title until the end of the novel). At first, the metaphor appears to have a clear single application. "Image" seems to mean "flat" object or "two-dimensional surface" or "passive reflection"—all referring to the girl Anne whom Claire instructs the narrator to use freely for his own sexual purposes, making the girl into "a perfect slave." But the book is broken exactly in the middle ("Section V" in a short book of ten sections) by an enigmatic scene that introduces another sense of "image." Claire, alone with the narrator, shows him a set of strange photographs of Anne in obscene situations; and these are described in such a way as to insinuate a mystery in what has been a brutally straightforward, if seemingly unmotivated, situation. From this cæsura to the end of the book, the reader will have simultaneously to carry the awareness of the fictionally actual "obscene" situation being described and to keep attuned to hints of an oblique mirroring or duplication of that situation. That burden (the two perspectives) will be relieved only in the final pages of the book, when, as the title of the last section has it, "Everything Resolves Itself." The narrator discovers that Anne is not the erotic plaything of Claire donated gratuitously to him, but Claire's "image" or "projection," sent out ahead to teach the narrator how to love *her*.

The structure of *Histoire de l'Oeil* is equally rigorous, and more ambitious in scope. Both novels are in the first person; in both, the narrator is male, and one of a trio whose sexual interconnections constitute the story of the book. But the two narratives are organized on very different principles. "Jean de Berg" describes how something came to be known that was not known by the narrator; all the pieces of action are clues, bits of evidence; and the ending is a surprise. Bataille is describing an action that is really intrapsychic: three people sharing (without conflict) a single fantasy, the acting out of a collective perverse will. The emphasis in *The Image* is on behavior, which is opaque, unintelligible. The emphasis in *Histoire de l'Oeil* is on fantasy first, and then on its correlation with some spontaneously "invented" act. The development of the narrative follows the phases of acting out. Bataille is charting the stages of the gratification of an erotic obsession which haunts a number of commonplace objects. His principle of organization is thus a spatial one: a series of things, arranged in a definite sequence, are tracked down and exploited, in some convulsive erotic act. The obscene playing with or defiling of these objects, and of people in their vicinity, constitutes the action of the novella. When the last object (the eye) is used up in a transgression more daring than any preceding, the narrative ends. There can be no revelation or surprises in the story, no new "knowledge," only further intensifications of what is already known. These seemingly unrelated elements really are related; indeed, all versions of the same thing. The egg in the first chapter is simply the earliest version of the eyeball plucked from the Spaniard in the last.

Each specific erotic fantasy is also a generic fantasy—of performing what is "forbidden"—which generates a surplus atmosphere of excruciating restless sexual intensity. At times the reader seems to be witness to a heartless debauched fulfillment; at other times, simply in attendance at the remorseless progress of the negative. Bataille's works, better than any others I know of, indicate the aesthetic possibilities of pornography as an art form: *Histoire de l'Oeil* being the most accomplished artistically of all the pornographic prose fictions I've read, and *Madame Edwarda* the most original and powerful intellectually.

To speak of the aesthetic possibilities of pornography as an art form and as a form of thinking may seem insensitive or grandiose when one considers what acutely miserable lives people with a full-time specialized sexual obsession usually lead. Still, I would argue that pornography yields more than the truths of individual nightmare. Convulsive and repetitious as this form of the imagination may be, it does generate a vision of the world that can claim the interest (speculative, aesthetic) of those who are not erotomanes. Indeed, this interest resides in precisely what are customarily dismissed as the *limits* of pornographic thinking.

5

The prominent characteristics of all products of the pornographic imagination are their energy and their absolutism.

The books generally called pornographic are those whose primary, exclusive, and overriding preoccupation is with the depiction of sexual "intentions" and "activities." One could also say sexual "feelings," except that the word seems redundant. The feelings of the personages deployed by the pornographic imagination are, at any given moment, either identical with their "behavior" or else a preparatory phase, that of "intention," on the verge of breaking into "behavior" unless physically thwarted. Pornography uses a small crude vocabulary of feeling, all relating to the prospects of action: feeling one would like to act (lust); feeling one would not like to act (shame, fear, aversion). There are no gratuitous or non-functioning feelings; no musings, whether speculative or imagistic, which are irrelevant to the business at hand. Thus, the pornographic imagination inhabits a universe that is, however repetitive the incidents occurring within it, incomparably economical. The strictest possible criterion of relevance applies: everything must bear upon the erotic situation.

The universe proposed by the pornographic imagination is a total universe. It has the power to ingest and metamorphose and translate all concerns that are fed into it, reducing everything into the one negotiable currency of the erotic imperative. All action is conceived of as a set of sexual *exchanges*. Thus, the reason why pornography refuses to make fixed distinctions between the sexes or allow any kind of sexual preference or sexual taboo to endure can be explained "structurally." The bisexuality, the disregard for the incest taboo, and other similar features common to pornographic narratives function to multiply the possibilities of exchange. Ideally, it should be

possible for everyone to have a sexual connection with everyone else.

Of course the pornographic imagination is hardly the only
form of consciousness that proposes a total universe. Another
is the type of imagination that has generated modern symbolic
logic. In the total universe proposed by the logician's imagination, all statements can be broken down or chewed up to make
it possible to rerender them in the form of the logical language; those parts of ordinary language that don't fit are
simply lopped off. Certain of the well-known states of the
religious imagination, to take another example, operate in the
same cannibalistic way, engorging all materials made available
to them for retranslation into phenomena saturated with the
religious polarities (sacred and profane, etc.).

The latter example, for obvious reasons, touches closely on
the present subject. Religious metaphors abound in a good
deal of modern erotic literature—notably in Genet—and
in some works of pornographic literature, too. *Story of O*
makes heavy use of religious metaphors for the ordeal that O
undergoes. O "wanted to believe." Her drastic condition of
total personal servitude to those who use her sexually is repeatedly described as a mode of salvation. With anguish and
anxiety, she surrenders herself; and "henceforth there were no
more hiatuses, no dead time, no remission." While she has, to
be sure, entirely lost her freedom, O has gained the right to
participate in what is described as virtually a sacramental
rite.

> The word "open" and the expression "opening her legs" were,
> on her lover's lips, charged with such uneasiness and power
> that she could never hear them without experiencing a kind of
> internal prostration, a sacred submission, as though a god, and
> not he, had spoken to her.

Though she fears the whip and other cruel mistreatments before they are inflicted on her, "yet when it was over she was
happy to have gone through it, happier still if it had been

especially cruel and prolonged." The whipping, branding, and mutilating are described (from the point of view of *her* consciousness) as ritual ordeals which test the faith of someone being initiated into an ascetic spiritual discipline. The "perfect submissiveness" that her original lover and then Sir Stephen demand of her echoes the extinction of the self explicitly required of a Jesuit novice or Zen pupil. O is "that absent-minded person who has yielded up her will in order to be totally remade," to be made fit to serve a will far more powerful and authoritative than her own.

As might be expected, the straightforwardness of the religious metaphors in *Story of O* has evoked some correspondingly straight readings of the book. The novelist Mandiargues, whose preface precedes Paulhan's in the American translation, doesn't hesitate to describe *Story of O* as "a mystic work," and therefore "not, strictly speaking, an erotic book." What *Story of O* depicts "is a complete spiritual transformation, what others would call an *ascesis*." But the matter is not so simple. Mandiargues is correct in dismissing a psychiatric analysis of O's state of mind that would reduce the book's subject to, say, "masochism." As Paulhan says, "the heroine's ardor" is totally inexplicable in terms of the conventional psychiatric vocabulary. The fact that the novel employs some of the conventional motifs and trappings of the theatre of sadomasochism has itself to be explained. But Mandiargues has fallen into an error almost as reductive and only slightly less vulgar. Surely, the only alternative to the psychiatric reductions is not the religious vocabulary. But that only these two foreshortened alternatives exist testifies once again to the bone-deep denigration of the range and seriousness of sexual experience that still rules this culture, for all its much-advertised new permissiveness.

My own view is that "Pauline Réage" wrote an erotic book. The notion implicit in *Story of O* that eros is a sacrament is not the "truth" behind the literal (erotic) sense of the book—the lascivious rites of enslavement and degradation performed upon O—but, exactly, a metaphor for it. Why say something stronger, when the statement can't really *mean* anything stronger? But despite the virtual incomprehensibility to most educated people today of the substantive experience behind religious vocabulary, there is a continuing piety toward the grandeur of emotions that went into that vocabulary. The religious imagination survives for most people as not just the primary but virtually the only credible instance of an imagination working in a total way.

No wonder, then, that the new or radically revamped forms of the total imagination which have arisen in the past century—notably, those of the artist, the erotomane, the left revolutionary, and the madman—have chronically borrowed the prestige of the religious vocabulary. And total experiences, of which there are many kinds, tend again and again to be apprehended only as revivals or translations of the religious imagination. To try to make a fresh way of talking at the most serious, ardent, and enthusiastic level, heading off the religious encapsulation, is one of the primary intellectual tasks of future thought. As matters stand, with everything from *Story of O* to Mao reabsorbed into the incorrigible survival of the religious impulse, all thinking and feeling gets devalued. (Hegel made perhaps the grandest attempt to create a post-religious vocabulary, out of philosophy, that would command the treasures of passion and credibility and emotive appropriateness that were gathered into the religious vocabulary. But his most interesting followers steadily undermined the abstract meta-religious language in which he had bequeathed his thought, and concentrated instead on the specific social and practical applications of his revolutionary form of process-thinking, historicism. Hegel's failure lies like a gigantic disturbing hulk across the intellectual landscape. And no one has been big enough, pompous enough, or energetic enough since Hegel to attempt the task again.)

And so we remain, careening among our overvaried choices of kinds of total imagination, of species of total seriousness.

Perhaps the deepest spiritual resonance of the career of pornography in its "modern" Western phase under consideration here (pornography in the Orient or the Moslem world being something very different) is this vast frustration of human passion and seriousness since the old religious imagination, with its secure monopoly on the total imagination, began in the late eighteenth century to crumble. The ludicrousness and lack of skill of most pornographic writing, films, and painting is obvious to everyone who has been exposed to them. What is less often remarked about the typical products of the pornographic imagination is their pathos. Most pornography—the books discussed here cannot be excepted—points to something more general than even sexual damage. I mean the traumatic failure of modern capitalist society to provide authentic outlets for the perennial human flair for high-temperature visionary obsessions, to satisfy the appetite for exalted self-transcending modes of concentration and seriousness. The need of human beings to transcend "the personal" is no less profound than the need to be a person, an individual. But this society serves that need poorly. It provides mainly demonic vocabularies in which to situate that need and from which to initiate action and construct rites of behavior. One is offered a choice among vocabularies of thought and action which are not merely self-transcending but self-destructive.

6

But the pornographic imagination is not just to be understood as a form of psychic absolutism—some of whose products we might be able to regard (in the role of connoisseur, rather than client) with more sympathy or intellectual curiosity or aesthetic sophistication.

Several times before in this essay I have alluded to the possibility that the pornographic imagination says something worth listening to, albeit in a degraded and often unrecognizable form. I've urged that this spectacularly cramped form of the human imagination has, nevertheless, its peculiar access to some truth. This truth—about sensibility, about sex, about individual personality, about despair, about limits—can be shared when it projects itself into art. (Everyone, at least in dreams, has inhabited the world of the pornographic imagination for some hours or days or even longer periods of his life; but only the full-time residents make the fetishes, the trophies, the art.) That discourse one might call the poetry of transgression is also knowledge. He who transgresses not only breaks a rule. He goes somewhere that the others are not; and he knows something the others don't know.

Pornography, considered as an artistic or art-producing form of the human imagination, is an expression of what William James called "morbid-mindedness." But James was surely right when he gave as part of the definition of morbid-mindedness that it ranged over "a wider scale of experience" than healthy-mindedness.

What can be said, though, to the many sensible and sensitive people who find depressing the fact that a whole library of pornographic reading material has been made, within the last few years, so easily available in paperback form to the very young? Probably one thing: that their apprehension is justified, but may not be in scale. I am not addressing the usual complainers, those who feel that since sex after all *is* dirty, so are books reveling in sex (dirty in a way that a genocide screened nightly on TV, apparently, is not). There still remains a sizeable minority of people who object to or are repelled by pornography not because they think it's dirty but because they know that pornography can be a crutch for the psychologically deformed and a brutalization of the morally innocent. I feel an aversion to pornography for those reasons, too, and am uncomfortable about the consequences of its increasing availability. But isn't the worry somewhat misplaced? What's really at stake? A concern about the uses of knowledge itself. There's a sense in which *all* knowledge is dangerous, the reason being that not everyone is in the same condition as knowers or potential knowers. Perhaps most people don't need "a wider scale of experience." It may be that, without subtle and extensive psychic preparation, any widening of experience and consciousness is destructive for most people. Then we must ask what justifies the reckless unlimited confidence we have in the present mass availability of other kinds of knowledge, in our optimistic acquiescence in the transformation of and extension of human capacities by machines. Pornography is only one item among the many dangerous commodities being circulated in this society and, unattractive as it may be, one of the less lethal, the less costly to the community in terms of human suffering. Except perhaps in a small circle of writer-intellectuals in France, pornography is an inglorious and mostly despised department of the imagination. Its mean status is the very antithesis of the considerable spiritual prestige enjoyed by many items which are far more noxious.

In the last analysis, the place we assign to pornography depends on the goals we set for our own consciousness, our own experience. But the goal A espouses for his consciousness may *not* be one he's pleased to see B adopt, because he judges that B isn't qualified or experienced or subtle enough. And B may be dismayed and even indignant at A's adopting goals that he himself professes; when A holds them, they become presumptuous or shallow. Probably this chronic mutual suspicion of our neighbor's capacities—suggesting, in effect, a hierarchy of competence with respect to human consciousness—will never be settled to everyone's satisfaction. As long as the quality of people's consciousness varies so greatly, how could it be?

In an essay on the subject some years ago, Paul Goodman wrote: "The question is not *whether* pornography, but the quality of the pornography." That's exactly right. One could extend the thought a good deal further. The question is not *whether* consciousness or *whether* knowledge, but the quality of the consciousness and of the knowledge. And that invites consideration of the quality or fineness of the human subject—the most problematic standard of all. It doesn't seem inaccurate to say most people in this society who aren't actively mad are, at best, reformed or potential lunatics. But is anyone supposed to act on this knowledge, even genuinely live with it? If so many are teetering on the verge of murder, dehumanization, sexual deformity and despair, and we were to act on that thought, then censorship much more radical than the indignant foes of pornography ever envisage seems in order. For if that's the case, not only pornography but all forms of serious art and knowledge—in other words, all forms of truth—are suspect and dangerous.

(1967)

"*Thinking Against Oneself*": *Reflections on Cioran*

"What is the good of passing from one untenable position to another, of seeking justification always on the same plane?"

SAMUEL BECKETT

"Every now and then it is possible to have absolutely nothing; the possibility of nothing."

JOHN CAGE

Ours is a time in which every intellectual or artistic or moral event is absorbed by a predatory embrace of consciousness: historicizing. Any statement or act can be assessed as a necessarily transient "development" or, on a lower level, belittled as mere "fashion." The human mind possesses now, almost as second nature, a perspective on its own achievements that fatally undermines their value and their claim to truth. For over a century, this historicizing perspective has occupied the very heart of our ability to *understand* anything at all. Perhaps once a marginal tic of consciousness, it's now a gigantic, uncontrollable gesture—the gesture whereby man indefatigably patronizes himself.

We understand something by locating it in a multi-determined temporal continuum. Existence is no more than the precarious attainment of relevance in an intensely mobile flux of past, present, and future. But even the most relevant events carry within them the form of their obsolescence. Thus, a single work is eventually a contribution to a body of work; the details of a life form part of a life history; an individual life history appears unintelligible apart from social, economic, and cultural history; and the life of a society is the sum of "preceding conditions." Meaning drowns in a stream of becoming: the senseless and overdocumented rhythm of advent and supersession. The becoming of man is the history of the exhaustion of his possibilities.

Yet there is no outflanking the demon of historical consciousness by turning the corrosive historicizing eye on *it*. Unfortunately, that succession of exhausted possibilities (unmasked and discredited by thought and history itself) in which man now situates himself appears to be more than simply a mental "attitude"—which could be annulled by refocusing the mind. The best of the intellectual and creative speculation carried on in the West over the past hundred and fifty years seems incontestably the most energetic, dense, subtle, sheerly interesting, and *true* in the entire lifetime of man. And yet the equally incontestable result of all this genius is our sense of standing in the ruins of thought and on the verge of the ruins of history and of man himself. (Cogito ergo boom.) More and more, the shrewdest thinkers and artists are precocious archaeologists of these ruins-in-the-making, indignant or stoical diagnosticians of defeat, enigmatic choreographers of the complex spiritual movements useful for individual survival in an era of permanent apocalypse. The time of new collective visions may well be over: by now both the brightest and the gloomiest, the most foolish and the wisest, have been set down. But the need for individual spiritual counsel has never seemed more acute. *Sauve qui peut.*

The rise of historical consciousness is, of course, linked with the collapse, sometime in the early nineteenth century, of the venerable enterprise of philosophical system-building. Since the Greeks, philosophy (whether fused with religion or conceived as an alternative, secular wisdom) had been for the most part a collective or supra-personal vision. Claiming to give an account of "what is" in its various epistemological and ontological layers, philosophy secondarily insinuated an implicitly futuristic standard of how things "ought to be"—under the aegis of notions like order, harmony, clarity, intelligibility, and consistency. But the survival of these collective impersonal visions depends on philosophical statements being couched in such a way as to admit of multiple interpretations and applications, so that their bluff can't be called by unforeseen events. Renouncing the advantages of myth, which had developed a highly sophisticated *narrative* mode of accounting for change and for conceptual paradox, philosophy proliferated a new rhetorical mode: abstraction. Upon this abstract, atemporal discourse—with its claim to be able to describe the non-concrete "universals" or stable forms that underpin the mutable world—the authority of philosophy has always rested. More generally, the very possibility of the objective, formalized visions of Being and of human knowledge proposed by traditional philosophy depends on a particular relation between permanent structures and change in human experience, in which "nature" is the dominant theme and change is recessive. But this relation was upset—permanently?—around the time climaxed by the French Revolution, when "history" finally pulled up alongside "nature" and then took the lead.

At the point that history usurped nature as the decisive framework for human experience, man began to think historically about his experience, and the traditional ahistorical categories of philosophy became hollowed out. The only thinker to meet this awesome challenge head-on was Hegel, who thought he could salvage the philosophical enterprise from this radical reorientation of human consciousness by presenting philosophy as, in fact, no more and no less than the *history* of philosophy. Still, Hegel could not help presenting his own system as true—that is, as beyond history—because of its in-corporation of the historical perspective. So far as Hegel's system was true then, it ended philosophy. Only the last philosophical system was philosophy, truly conceived. So "the eternal" is reestablished once more, after all; and history comes (or will come) to an end. But history did not stop. Mere time proved Hegelianism bankrupt as a system, though not as a method. (As a method, proliferating into all the sciences of man, it confirmed and gave the largest single intellectual impetus to the consolidation of historical consciousness.)

After Hegel's effort, this quest for the eternal—once so glamorous and inevitable a gesture of consciousness—now stood exposed, as the root of philosophical thinking, in all its pathos and childishness. Philosophy dwindled into an outmoded fantasy of the mind, part of the provincialism of the spirit, the childhood of man. However firmly philosophical statements might cohere into an argument, there seemed no way of dispelling the radical question that had arisen as to the "value" of the terms composing the statements, no way of restoring a vast loss of confidence in the verbal currency in which philosophical arguments had been transacted. Confounded by the new surge of an increasingly secularized, drastically more competent and efficient human will bent on controlling, manipulating, and modifying "nature," its ventures into concrete ethical and political prescription badly lagging behind the accelerating historical change of the human landscape (among which changes must be counted the sheer accumulation of concrete empirical knowledge stored in printed books and documents), the leading words of philosophy came to seem excessively overdetermined. Or, what amounts to the same thing, they seem undernourished, emptied of meaning.

Subjected to the attritions of change on this unprecedented scale, philosophy's traditionally "abstract" leisurely procedures no longer appeared to address themselves to anything; they weren't substantiated any more by the sense that intelligent people had of their experience. Neither as a description of Being (reality, the world, the cosmos) nor, in the alternative conception (in which Being, reality, the world, the cosmos are taken as what lies "outside" the mind) that marks the first great retrenchment of the philosophical enterprise, as a description of mind only, did philosophy inspire much trust in its capacity to fulfill its traditional aspiration: that of providing the formal models for *understanding* anything. At the least, some kind of further retrenchment or relocation of discourse was felt to be necessary.

One response to the collapse of philosophical system building in the nineteenth century was the rise of ideologies—aggressively anti-philosophical systems of thought, taking the form of various "positive" or descriptive sciences of man. Comte, Marx, Freud, and the pioneer figures of anthropology, sociology, and linguistics immediately come to mind.

Another response to the debacle was a new kind of philosophizing: personal (even autobiographical), aphoristic, lyrical, anti-systematic. Its foremost exemplars: Kierkegaard, Nietzsche, Wittgenstein. Cioran is the most distinguished figure in this tradition writing today.

The starting point for this modern post-philosophic tradition of philosophizing is the awareness that the traditional forms of philosophical discourse have been broken. The leading possibilities that remain are mutilated, incomplete discourse (the aphorism, the note or jotting) or discourse that has risked metamorphosis into other forms (the parable, the poem, the philosophical tale, the critical exegesis).

Cioran has apparently chosen the essay form. Between 1949 and 1964, five collections have appeared: *Précis de Décomposition* (1949), *Syllogismes de l'Amertume* (1952), *Le Tentation d'Exister* (1956), *Histoire et Utopie* (1960), and *La Chute dans le Temps* (1964). But these are curious essays by ordinary standards—meditative, disjunctive in argument, essentially aphoristic in style. One recognizes, in this Roumanian-born writer who studied philosophy at the University of Bucharest and who has lived in Paris since 1937 and writes in French, the convulsive manner characteristic of German neophilosophical thinking, whose motto is: aphorism or eternity. (Examples: the philosophical aphorisms of Lichtenberg and Novalis; Nietzsche of course; passages in Rilke's *Duino Elegies;* and Kafka's *Reflections on Love, Sin, Hope, Death, the Way.*)

Cioran's method of broken argument is not the objective kind of aphoristic writing of La Rochefoucauld or Gracián, whose stopping and starting movement mirrors the disjunctive aspects of "the world," but rather bears witness to the impasse of the speculative mind, which moves outward only to be checked and broken off by the complexity of its own stance. For Cioran the aphoristic style is less a principle of reality than a principle of knowing: that it's the destiny of every profound idea to be quickly checkmated by another idea, which it itself has implicitly generated.

Still hoping to command something resembling its former prestige, philosophy now undertakes to give evidence incessantly of its own good faith. Though the existing range of conceptual tools for philosophy could no longer be felt to carry meaning in themselves, they might be recertified: through the passion of the thinker.

Philosophy is conceived as the personal task of the thinker. Thought becomes "thinking," and thinking—by a further turn of the screw—is redefined as worthless unless an extreme act, a risk. Thinking becomes confessional, exorcistic: an inventory of the most personal exacerbations of thinking.

Notice that the Cartesian leap is retained as the first move. Existence is still defined as thinking. The difference is that it's not any kind of cogitation, but only a certain kind of *difficult* thinking. Thought and existence are neither brute facts nor logical givens, but paradoxical, unstable situations. Hence, the possibility of conceiving the essay that gives the title to one of Cioran's books and to the first collection of his work in English, *The Temptation to Exist*. "To exist," Cioran says in that essay, "is a habit I do not despair of acquiring."

Cioran's subject: on being a *mind*, a consciousness tuned to the highest pitch of refinement. The final justification of his writings, if one may guess at it: something close to the thesis given its classical statement in Kleist's "On the Puppet Theatre." In that essay Kleist says that, however much we may long to repair the disorders in the natural harmony of man created by consciousness, this is not to be accomplished by a surrender of consciousness. There is no return, no going back to innocence. We have no choice but to go to the end of thought, there (perhaps), in total self-consciousness, to recover grace and innocence.

In Cioran's writings, therefore, the mind is a voyeur.

But not upon "the world." Upon itself. Cioran is, to a degree reminiscent of Beckett, concerned with the absolute integrity of thought. That is, with the reduction or circumscription of thought to thinking about thinking. "The only free mind," Cioran remarks, is "the one that, pure of all intimacy with being or objects, plies its own vacuity."

Yet, throughout, this act of mental disembowelment retains its "Faustian" or "Western" passionateness. Cioran will allow no possibility that anyone born into this culture can attain—as a way out of the trap—an "Eastern" abnegation of mind. (Compare Cioran's self-consciously futile longing for the East with Lévi-Strauss' affirmative nostalgia for "neolithic consciousness.)

Philosophy becomes tortured thinking. Thinking that devours itself—and continues intact and even flourishes, in spite (or perhaps because) of these repeated acts of self-cannibalism. In the passion play of thought, the thinker plays the roles of both protagonist and antagonist. He is both suffering Prometheus and the remorseless eagle who consumes his perpetually regenerated entrails.

Impossible states of being, unthinkable thoughts are Cioran's material for speculation. (Thinking against oneself, etc.) But he comes after Nietzsche, who set down almost the whole of Cioran's position a century ago. An interesting question: why does a subtle, powerful mind consent to say what has, for the most part, already been said? In order to make those ideas genuinely his own? Because, while they were true when originally set down, they have since become *more* true?

Whatever the answer, the "fact" of Nietzsche has undeniable consequences for Cioran. He must tighten the screws, make the argument denser. More excruciating. More rhetorical.

Characteristically, Cioran begins an essay where another writer would end it. Beginning with the conclusion, he goes on from there.

His kind of writing is meant for readers who in a sense already know what he says; they have traversed these vertiginous thoughts for themselves. Cioran doesn't make any of the usual efforts to "persuade," with his oddly lyrical chains of ideas, his merciless irony, his gracefully delivered allusions to nothing less than the whole of European thought since the Greeks. An argument is to be "recognized," and without too much help. Good taste demands that the thinker furnish only pithy glimpses of intellectual and spiritual torment. Hence, Cioran's tone—one of immense dignity, dogged, sometimes playful, often haughty. But despite all that may appear as arrogance, there is nothing complacent in Cioran, unless it be his very sense of futility and his uncompromisingly elitist attitude toward the life of the mind.

As Nietzsche wanted to will his moral solitude, Cioran wants to will the difficult. Not that the essays are hard to read, but their moral point, so to speak, is the unending disclosure of difficulty. The argument of a typical Cioran essay might be described as a network of proposals for thinking—along with dissipations of the grounds for continuing to hold these ideas, not to mention the grounds for "acting" on the basis of them. By his complex intellectual formulation of intellectual impasses, Cioran constructs a closed universe—of the difficult—that is the subject of his lyricism.

Cioran is one of the most *delicate* minds of real power writing today. Nuance, irony, and refinement are the essence of his thinking. Yet he declares in the essay "On a Winded Civilization": "Men's minds need a simple truth, an answer which delivers them from their questions, a gospel, a tomb. The moments of refinement conceal a death-principle: nothing is more fragile than subtlety."

A contradiction? Not exactly. It is only the familiar double standard of philosophy since its debacle: upholding one standard (health) for the culture at large, another (spiritual ambition) for the solitary philosopher. The first standard demands what Nietzsche called the sacrifice of the intellect. The second standard demands the sacrifice of health, of mundane happiness, often of participation in family life and other community institutions, perhaps even of sanity. The philosopher's aptitude for martyrdom is almost part of his good manners, in this tradition of philosophizing since Kierkegaard and Nietzsche. And one of the commonest indications of his good taste as a philosopher is an avowed contempt for philosophy. Thus, Wittgenstein's idea that philosophy is something like a disease and the job of the philosopher is to study philosophy as the physician studies malaria, not to pass it on but to cure people of it.

But whether such behavior is diagnosed as the self-hatred of the philosopher or as merely a certain coquetry of the void, more than inconsistency must be allowed here. In Cioran's case, his disavowals of mind are not less authentic because they're delivered by someone who makes such strenuous professional use of the mind. Consider the impassioned counsels in an essay of 1952, "Some Blind Alleys: A Letter"—in which Cioran, a steadily published writer in France, puts himself in the curious position of reproaching a friend about to become that "monster," an author, and violate his admirable "detachment, scorn, and silence" by describing them in a book. Cioran is not just displaying a facile ambivalence toward his own vocation, but voicing the painful, genuinely paradoxical experience that the free intellect can have of itself when it commits itself to writing and acquires an audience. Anyway, it is one thing to choose martyrdom and compromise for oneself; quite another, to advise a friend to do likewise. And since for Cioran the use of the mind is a martyrdom, using one's mind in public—more specifically, being a writer—becomes a problematic, partly shameful act; always suspect; in the last analysis, something obscene, socially as well as individually.

Cioran is another recruit to the melancholy parade of European intellectuals in revolt against the intellect—the rebellion of idealism against "idealism"—whose greatest figures are Nietzsche and Marx. A good part of his argument on this theme differs little from what has already been stated by countless poets and philosophers in the last century and this—not to mention the sinister, traumatic amplification of these charges against the intellect in the rhetoric and practice of fascism. But the fact that an important argument is not new doesn't mean that one is exempted from taking it seriously. And what could be more relevant than the thesis, reworked by Cioran, that the free use of the mind is ultimately anti-social, detrimental to the health of the community?

In a number of essays, but most clearly in "On a Winded Civilization" and "A Little Theory of Destiny," Cioran ranges himself firmly on the side of the critics of the Enlightenment. "Since the Age of the Enlightenment," he writes, "Europe has ceaselessly sapped her idols in the name of tolerance." But

these idols or "prejudices—organic fictions of a civilization—
assure its duration, preserve its physiognomy. It must respect them." Elsewhere in the first of the essays mentioned
above: "A minimum of unconsciousness is necessary if one
wants to stay inside history." Foremost among "the diseases
that undermine a civilization" is the hypertrophy of thought
itself, which leads to the disappearance of the capacity for
"inspired stupidity . . . fruitful exaltation, never compromised by a consciousness drawn and quartered." For any
civilization "vacillates as soon as it exposes the errors which
permitted its growth and its luster, as soon as it calls into
question its own truths." And Cioran goes on, all too famil-
iarly, to lament the suppression of the barbarian, of the non-
thinker, in Europe. "All his instincts are throttled by his
decency," is his comment on the Englishman. Protected from
ordeal, "sapped by nostalgia, that generalized ennui," the
average European is now monopolized and obsessed by "the
concept of *living well* (that mania of declining periods)." Already Europe has passed to "a provincial destiny." The new
masters of the globe are the less civilized peoples of America
and Russia and, waiting in the wings of history, the hordes of
violent millions from still less civilized "suburbs of the globe"
in whose hands the future resides.

Much of the old argument comes without transformation at
Cioran's hands. The old heroism, the denunciation of the mind
by the mind, served up once again in the name of the
antitheses: heart versus head, instinct versus reason. "Too
much lucidity" results in a loss of equilibrium. (One of the
arguments behind Cioran's expressed mistrust, in "Blind
Alleys" and "Style as Risk," of the book, the linguistic
communication, literature itself—at least in the present age.)

But at least one of the familiar antitheses—thought versus
action—is refined. In "On a Winded Civilization," Cioran
shares the standard view of the nineteenth-century romantics,
and is mainly concerned with the toll that the exercise of the
mind takes on the ability to act. "To act is one thing; to know

one is acting is another. When lucidity invests the action, insinuates itself into it, action is undone and, with it, prejudice, whose function consists, precisely, in subordinating, in enslaving consciousness to action." In "Thinking Against Oneself," however, the antithesis of thought and action is rendered in a more subtle and original manner. Thought is not simply that which impedes the direct, energetic performance of an act. Here, Cioran is more concerned with the inroads that action makes upon thought. Pointing out that "the sphere of consciousness shrinks in action," he supports the idea of a "liberation" from action as the only genuine mode of human freedom.

And even in the relatively simplistic argument of "On a Winded Civilization," when Cioran does invoke that exemplary European figure, "the tired intellectual," it's not simply to inveigh against the vocation of the intellectual, but to try to locate the exact difference between two states well worth distinguishing: being civilized and that mutilation of the organic person sometimes, tendentiously, called being "overcivilized." One may quarrel about the term, but the condition exists and is rampant—common among professional intellectuals, though scarcely confined to them. And, as Cioran correctly points out, a principal danger of being overcivilized is that one all too easily relapses, out of sheer exhaustion and the unsatisfied need to be "stimulated," into a vulgar and passive barbarism. Thus, "the man who unmasks his fictions" through an indiscriminate pursuit of the lucidity that is promoted by modern liberal culture "renounces his own resources and, in a sense, himself. Consequently, he will accept other fictions which will deny him, since they will not have cropped up from his own depths." Therefore, he concludes, "no man concerned with his own equilibrium may exceed a certain degree of lucidity and analysis."

Yet this counsel of moderation does not, in the end, limit Cioran's own enterprise. Saturated with a sense of the well-advertised and (in his belief) irreversible decline of European civilization, this model European thinker becomes, it would seem, emancipated from responsibility to his own health as well as his society's. For all his scorn for the enervated condition and the provincial destiny of the civilization of which he is a member, Cioran is also a gifted elegist of that civilization. Among the last, perhaps, of the elegists of the passing of "Europe"—of the European suffering, of European intellectual courage, of European vigor, of European overcomplexity. And determined, himself, to pursue that venture to its end.

His sole ambition: "to be abreast of the Incurable."

A doctrine of spiritual strenuousness. "Since every form of life betrays and corrupts Life, the man who is genuinely alive assumes a maximum of incompatibilities, works relentlessly at pleasure and pain alike. . . ." (I am quoting from "The Temptation to Exist.") And there can be no doubt in Cioran's thought that this most ambitious of all states of consciousness, while remaining truer to Life in the generic sense, to the full range of human prospects, is paid for dearly on the level of mundane existence. In terms of action, it means the acceptance of futility. Futility must be seen not as a frustration of one's hopes and aspirations, but as a prized and defended vantage point for the athletic leap of consciousness into its own complexity. It is of this desirable state that Cioran is speaking when he says: "Futility is the most difficult thing in the world." It requires that we "must sever our roots, must become metaphysically foreigners."

That Cioran conceives of this as being so formidable and difficult a task testifies perhaps to his own residual, unquenchable good health. It also may explain why his essay "A People of Solitaries" is, to my mind, one of the few things Cioran has ever written that falls well below his usual standard of brilliance and perspicacity. Writing on the Jews, who "represent the alienated condition par excellence" for Cioran no less than for Hegel and a host of intervening writers, Cioran displays a startling moral insensitivity to the contemporary aspects of his theme. Even without the example of Sartre's near-definitive treatment of the same subject in *Anti-Semite and Jew,* one could scarcely help finding Cioran's essay surprisingly cursory and highhanded.

A strange dialectic in Cioran: familiar elements fused in a complex mix. On the one hand, the traditional Romantic and vitalist contempt for "intellectuality" and for the hypertrophy of the mind at the expense of the body and the feelings and of the capacity for action. On the other hand, an exaltation of the life of the mind at the expense of body, feelings, and the capacity for action that could not be more radical and imperious.

The nearest model for this paradoxical attitude toward consciousness is the Gnostic-mystical tradition that, in Western Christianity, descends from Dionysius the Areopagite and the author of *The Cloud of Unknowing.*

And what Cioran says of the mystic applies perfectly to his own thought. "The mystic, in most cases, invents his adversaries . . . his thought asserts the existence of others by calculation, by artifice: it is a strategy of no consequence. His thought boils down, in the last instance, to a polemic with himself: he seeks to be, he becomes a crowd, even if it is only by making himself one new mask after the other, multiplying his faces: in which he resembles his Creator, whose histrionics he perpetuates."

Despite the irony in this passage, Cioran's envy of the mystics, whose enterprise so resembles his—"to find what escapes or survives the disintegration of his experiences: the residue of intemporality under the ego's vibrations"—is frank and unmistakable. Yet, like his master Nietzsche, Cioran remains nailed to the cross of an atheist spirituality. And his essays are best read as a manual of such an atheist spirituality. "Once we have ceased linking our secret life to God, we can ascend to ecstasies as effective as those of the mystics and conquer this world without recourse to the Beyond," is the opening sentence of the last paragraph of the essay "Dealing with the Mystics."

Politically, Cioran must be described as a conservative. Liberal humanism is for him simply not a viable or interesting option at all, and he regards the hope of radical revolution as something to be outgrown by the mature mind. (Thus, speaking of Russia in "A Little Theory of Destiny," he remarks: "The aspiration to 'save' the world is a morbid phenomenon of a people's youth.")

It may be relevant to recall that Cioran was born (in 1911) in Roumania, virtually all of whose distinguished expatriate intellectuals have been either apolitical or overtly reactionary; and that his only other book, besides the five collections of essays, is an edition of the writings of Joseph de Maistre (published in 1957), for which he wrote the introduction and selected the texts.* While he never develops anything like an explicit theology of counterrevolution in the manner of Maistre, those arguments seem close to Cioran's tacit position. Like Maistre, Donoso Cortés, and, more recently, Eric Voegelin, Cioran possesses what might be described—viewed from one angle—as a right-wing "Catholic" sensibility. The modern habit of fomenting revolutions against the established social order in the name of justice and equality is dismissed as a kind of childish fanaticism, much as an old cardinal might regard the activities of some uncouth millennarian sect. Within the same framework, one can locate Cioran's description of Marxism as "that sin of optimism," and his stand against the Enlightenment ideals of "tolerance" and freedom of thought. (It's perhaps worth noting, too, that Cioran is the son of a Greek Orthodox priest.)

Yet, while Cioran projects a recognizable political stance, though one present only implicitly in most of the essays, his

---

* He has also published an essay on Machiavelli and one on St.-John Perse—both as yet uncollected.

approach is not, in the end, grounded in a religious commitment. However much his political-moral sympathies have in common with the right-wing Catholic sensibility, Cioran himself, as I have already said, is committed to the paradoxes of an atheist theology. Faith alone, he argues, solves nothing.

Perhaps what prevents Cioran from making the commitment, even in a secular form, to something like the Catholic theology of order is that he understands too well and shares too many of the spiritual presuppositions of the Romantic movement. Critic of left-wing revolution that he may be, and a slightly snobbish analyst of the fact "that rebellion enjoys an undue privilege among us," Cioran cannot disavow the lesson that "almost all our discoveries are due to our violences, to the exacerbations of our instability." Thus, alongside the conservative implications of some of the essays, with their scornful treatment of the phenomenology of uprootedness, one must set the ironic-positive attitude toward rebellion expressed in "Thinking Against Oneself," an essay which concludes with the admonition that, "since the Absolute corresponds to a meaning we have not been able to cultivate, let us surrender to all rebellions: they will end by turning against themselves, against us. . . ."

Cioran is clearly unable to withhold admiration from what is extravagant, willful, extreme—one example of which is the extravagant, willful *ascesis* of the great Western mystics. Another is the fund of extremity stored up in the experience of the great madmen. "We derive our vitality from our store of madness," he writes in "The Temptation to Exist." Yet, in the essay on the mystics, he speaks of "our capacity to fling ourselves into a madness that is *not sacred*. In the unknown, we can go as far as the saints, without making use of their means. It will be enough for us to constrain reason to a long silence."

What makes Cioran's position not truly conservative in the modern sense is that his is, above all, an aristocratic stance.

See, for only one illustration of the resources of this stance, his essay, "Beyond the Novel," in which the novel is eloquently and persuasively condemned for its spiritual vulgarity—for its devotion to what Cioran calls "destiny in lower case."

Throughout Cioran's writings, what is being posed is the problem of *spiritual good taste*. Avoiding vulgarity and the dilution of the self is the prerequisite for the arduous double task of maintaining an intact self which one is able fully to affirm and yet, at the same time, transcend. Cioran can even defend the emotion of self-pity: for the person who can no longer complain or lament has ceased, by rejecting his miseries and relegating them "outside his nature and outside his voice . . . to communicate with his life, which he turns into an object." It may seem outrageous for Cioran to advocate, as he often does, resisting the vulgar temptation to be happy and of the "impasse of happiness." But such judgments seem far from an unfeeling affectation, once one grants him his impossible project: "to be *nowhere*, when no external condition obliges you to do so . . . to extricate oneself from the world—what a labor of abolition!"

More realistically, perhaps the best to be hoped for is a series of situations, a life, a milieu, which leave part of the venturesome consciousness free for its labors. One may recall Cioran's description of Spain in "A Little Theory of Destiny": "They live in a kind of melodious asperity, a *tragic non-seriousness*, which saves them from vulgarity, from happiness, and from success."

Certainly, Cioran's writings suggest, the role of the writer isn't likely to provide this kind of spiritual leverage. In "Advantages of Exile" and the brief "Verbal Demiurgy," he describes how the vocation of literature, particularly that of the poet, creates insurmountable conditions of inauthenticity. One may suffer, but when one deposits this suffering in literature, the result is "an accumulation of confusions, an inflation of horrors, of *frissons* that *date*. One cannot keep renewing Hell, whose very character is monotony. . . ."

Whether the vocation of the philosopher is any less compromised can hardly be proved. (Reason is dying, Cioran says in "Style as Risk," in both philosophy and art.) But at least philosophy, I imagine Cioran feels, maintains somewhat higher standards of decorum. Untempted by the same kind of fame or emotional rewards that can descend on the poet, the philosopher can perhaps better comprehend and respect the modesty of the inexpressible.

When Cioran describes Nietzsche's philosophy as "a sum of attitudes"—mistakenly scrutinized by scholars for the constants that the philosopher has rejected—it's clear that he accepts the Nietzschean standard, with its critique of "truth" as system and consistency, as his own.

In "Blind Alleys," Cioran speaks of "the stupidities inherent in the cult of truth." The implication, here and elsewhere, is that what the true philosopher says isn't something "true" but rather something necessary or liberating. For "the truth" is identified with depersonalization.

Once again, the line from Nietzsche to Cioran cannot be overemphasized. And for both writers, the critique of "truth" is intimately connected with the attitude toward "history."

Thus, one cannot understand Nietzsche's questioning of the value of truth in general and of the usefulness of historical truth in particular without grasping the link between the two notions. Nietzsche doesn't reject historical thinking because it is false. On the contrary, it must be rejected because it is true—a debilitating truth that has to be overthrown to allow a more inclusive orientation for human consciousness.

As Cioran says in "The Temptation to Exist": "History is merely an inessential mode of being, the most effective form of our infidelity to ourselves, a metaphysical refusal." And, in "Thinking Against Oneself," he refers to "history, man's aggression against himself."

Granted that the stamp of Nietzsche appears both on the form of Cioran's thinking and on his principal attitudes, where he most resembles Nietzsche is in his temperament. It's the temperament or personal style shared with Nietzsche that explains the connections, in Cioran's work, between such disparate materials as: the emphasis on the strenuousness of an ambitious spiritual life; the project of self-mastery through "thinking against oneself"; the recurrent Nietzschean thematics of strength versus weakness, health versus sickness; the savage and sometimes shrill deployment of irony (quite different from the near systematic, dialectical interplay of irony and seriousness to be found in Kierkegaard's writings); the preoccupation with the struggle against banality and boredom; the ambivalent attitude toward the poet's vocation; the seductive but always finally resisted lure of religious consciousness; and, of course, the hostility toward history and to most aspects of "modern" life.

What's missing in Cioran's work is anything comparable to Nietzsche's heroic effort to surmount nihilism (the doctrine of eternal recurrence).

And where Cioran most differs from Nietzsche is in not following Nietzsche's critique of Platonism. Contemptuous of history, yet haunted by time and mortality, Nietzsche still refused anything harking back to the rhetoric established by Plato for going beyond time and death, and indeed worked hard at exposing what he thought the essential fraud and bad faith involved in the Platonic intellectual transcendence. Cioran, apparently, hasn't been convinced by Nietzsche's arguments. All the venerable Platonic dualisms reappear in Cioran's writings, essential links of the argument, used with no more than an occasional hint of ironic reserve. One finds time versus eternity, mind versus body, spirit versus matter; and the more modern ones, too: life versus Life, and being versus existence. How seriously these dualisms are intended is hard to decide.

Could one regard the Platonist machinery in Cioran's thought as an aesthetic code? Or, alternatively, as a kind of moral therapy? But Nietzsche's critique of Platonism would still apply and still remain unanswered.

The only figure in the world of Anglo-American letters embarked on a theoretical enterprise comparable in intellectual power and scope to Cioran's is John Cage.

Also a thinker in the post- and anti-philosophical tradition of broken, aphoristic discourse, Cage shares with Cioran a revulsion against "psychology" and against "history" and a commitment to a radical transvaluation of values. But while comparable in range, interest, and energy to Cioran's, Cage's thought mainly offers the most radical contrast to it. From what must be assumed to be the grossest difference of temperament, Cage envisages a world in which most of Cioran's problems and tasks simply don't exist. Cioran's universe of discourse is occupied with the themes of sickness (individual and social), impasse, suffering, mortality. What his essays offer is diagnosis and, if not outright therapy, at least a manual of spiritual good taste through which one might be helped to keep one's life from being turned into an object, a thing. Cage's universe of discourse—no less radical and spiritually ambitious than Cioran's—refuses to admit these themes.

In contrast to Cioran's unrelenting elitism, Cage envisages a totally democratic world of the spirit, a world of "natural activity" in which "it is understood that everything is clean: there is no dirt." In contrast to Cioran's baroque standards of good and bad taste in intellectual and moral matters, Cage maintains there is no such thing as good or bad taste. In contrast to Cioran's vision of error and decline and (possible) redemption of one's acts, Cage proposes the perennial possibility of errorless behavior, if only we will allow it to be so. "Error is a fiction, has no reality in fact. Errorless music is written by not giving a thought to cause and effect. Any other kind of music always has mistakes in it. In other words there is no split between spirit and matter." And elsewhere in the same book from which these quotes are taken, *Silence:* "How can we speak of error when it is understood 'psychology never again'?" In contrast to Cioran's goal of infinite adaptability and intellectual agility (how to find the correct vantage point, the right place to stand in a treacherous world), Cage proposes for our experience a world in which it's never preferable to do other than we are doing or be elsewhere than we are. "It is only irritating," he says, "to think one would like to be somewhere else. Here we are now."

What becomes clear, in the context of this comparison, is how devoted Cioran is to the *will* and its capacity to transform the world. Compare Cage's: "Do you only take the position of doing nothing, and things will of themselves become transformed." What different views can follow the radical rejection of history is seen by thinking first of Cioran and then of Cage, who writes: "To be & be the present. Would it be a repetition? Only if we thought we owned it, but since we don't, it is free & so are we."

Reading Cage, one becomes aware how much Cioran is still confined within the premises of the historicizing consciousness; how inescapably he continues to repeat these gestures, much as he longs to transcend them. Of necessity then, Cioran's thought is halfway between anguished reprise of these gestures and a genuine transvaluation of them. Perhaps, for a unified transvaluation, one must look to those thinkers like Cage who—whether from spiritual strength or from spiritual insensitivity is a secondary issue—are able to jettison far more of the inherited anguish and complexity of this civilization. Cioran's fierce, tensely argued speculations sum up brilliantly the decaying urgencies of Western thought, but offer us no relief from them beyond the considerable satisfactions of the understanding. Relief, of course, is scarcely Cioran's intention. His aim is diagnosis. For relief, it may be that one must abandon the pride of knowing and feeling so much—a local pride that has cost everyone hideously by now.

Novalis wrote that "philosophy is properly home-sickness; the wish to be everywhere at home." If the human mind can be everywhere at home, it must in the end give up its local "European" pride and something else—that will seem strangely unfeeling and intellectually simplistic—must be allowed in. "All that is necessary," says Cage with his own devastating irony, "is an empty space of time and letting it act in its magnetic way."

(1967)

II

Theatre and Film

Does there exist an unbridgeable gap, even opposition, between the two arts? Is there something genuinely "theatrical," different in kind from what is genuinely "cinematic"?

Virtually all opinion holds that there is. A commonplace of discussion has it that film and theatre are distinct and even antithetical arts, each giving rise to its own standards of judgment and canons of form. Thus Erwin Panofsky argues in his celebrated essay "Style and Medium in the Motion Pictures" (1934, rewritten in 1956) that one of the criteria for evaluating a movie is its freedom from the impurities of theatricality, and that, to talk about film, one must first define "the basic nature of the medium." Those who think prescriptively about the nature of live drama, less confident in the future of that art than the *cinéphiles* in theirs, rarely take a comparably exclusivist line.

The history of cinema is often treated as the history of its emancipation from theatrical models. First of all from theatrical "frontality" (the unmoving camera reproducing the situation of the spectator of a play fixed in his seat), then from theatrical acting (gestures needlessly stylized, exaggerated—needlessly, because now the actor could be seen "close up"), then from theatrical furnishings (unnecessary distancing of the audience's emotions, disregarding the opportunity to immerse the audience in reality). Movies are regarded as advancing from theatrical stasis to cinematic fluidity, from theatrical artificiality to cinematic naturalness and immediateness. But this view is far too simple.

Such oversimplification testifies to the ambiguous scope of the camera eye. Because the camera *can* be used to project a relatively passive, unselective kind of vision—as well as the highly selective ("edited") vision generally associated with movies—cinema is a medium as well as an art, in the sense that it can encapsulate any of the performing arts and render it in a film transcription. (This "medium" or non-art aspect of film attained its routine incarnation with the advent of television. There, movies themselves became another performing art to be transcribed, miniaturized on film.) One *can* film a play or ballet or opera or sporting event in such a way that film becomes, relatively speaking, a transparency, and it seems correct to say that one is seeing the event filmed. But theatre is never a "medium." Thus, because one can make a movie of a play but not a play of a movie, cinema had an early but fortuitous connection with the stage. Some of the earliest films were filmed plays. Duse and Bernhardt are on film—marooned in time, absurd, touching; there is a 1913 British film of Forbes-Robertson playing Hamlet, a 1923 German film of *Othello* starring Emil Jannings. More recently, the camera has preserved Helene Weigel's performance of *Mother Courage* with the Berliner Ensemble, the Living Theatre production of *The Brig* (filmed by the Mekas brothers), and Peter Brook's staging of Weiss' *Marat/Sade*.

But from the beginning, even within the confines of the notion of film as a "medium" and the camera as a "recording" instrument, other events than those occurring in theatres were taken down. As with still photography, some of the events captured on moving photographs were staged but others were valued precisely because they were *not* staged—the camera being the witness, the invisible spectator, the invulnerable voyeuristic eye. (Perhaps public happenings, "news," constitute an intermediate case between staged and unstaged events; but film as "newsreel" generally amounts to using film as a "medium.") To create on film a *document* of a transient reality is a conception quite unrelated to the purposes of theatre. It only appears related when the "real event" being recorded happens to be a theatrical performance. In fact, the first use of the motion-picture camera was to make a documentary record of unstaged, casual reality; Lumière's films from the 1890's of crowd scenes in Paris and New York antedate any filming of plays.

The other paradigmatic non-theatrical use of film, which dates from the earliest period of movie-making with the celebrated work of Méliès, is the creation of illusion, the construction of fantasy. To be sure, Méliès (like many directors after him) conceived of the rectangle of the screen on analogy with the proscenium stage. And not only were the events staged; they were the very stuff of invention: impossible journeys, imaginary objects, physical metamorphoses. But this, even adding the fact that Méliès situated his camera in front of the action and hardly moved it, does not make his films theatrical in an invidious sense. In their treatment of persons as things (physical objects) and in their disjunctive presentation of time and space, Méliès' films are quintessentially "cinematic"—so far as there is such a thing.

If the contrast between theatre and films doesn't lie in the materials represented or depicted in a simple sense, this contrast survives in more generalized forms. According to some influential accounts, the boundary is virtually an ontological one. Theatre deploys artifice while cinema is committed to reality, indeed to an ultimately physical reality which is "redeemed," to use Siegfried Kracauer's striking word, by the camera. The aesthetic judgment that follows from this venture in intellectual map-making is that films shot in real-life settings are better (i.e., more cinematic) than those shot in a studio. Taking Flaherty and Italian neo-realism and the *cinéma-vérité* of Rouch and Marker and Ruspoli as preferred models, one would judge rather harshly the era of wholly studio-made films inaugurated around 1920 by *The Cabinet of Dr. Caligari*, films with ostentatiously artificial décor and landscapes, and applaud the direction taken at the same period in Sweden, where many films with strenuous natural settings were being shot on location. Thus, Panofsky attacks *Dr. Caligari* for "pre-stylizing reality," and urges upon cinema "the problem of manipulating and shooting unstylized reality in such a way that the result has style."

But there is no reason to insist on a single model for film. And it is helpful to notice how the apotheosis of realism in cinema, which gives the greatest prestige to "unstylized reality," covertly advances a definite political-moral position. Films have been rather too often acclaimed as the democratic art, the preeminent art of mass society. Once one takes this description seriously, one tends (like Panofsky and Kracauer) to wish that movies continue to reflect their origins in a vulgar level of the arts, to remain loyal to their vast unsophisticated audience. Thus, a vaguely Marxist orientation collaborates with a fundamental tenet of romanticism.

Cinema, at once high art and popular art, is cast as the art of the authentic. Theatre, by contrast, means dressing up, pretense, lies. It smacks of aristocratic taste and the class society. Behind the objection of critics to the stagy sets of *Dr. Caligari*, the improbable costumes and florid acting of Renoir's *Nana*, the talkiness of Dreyer's *Gertrud* as "theatrical" lay the judgment that such films were false, that they exhibited a sensibility both pretentious and reactionary which was out of step with the democratic and more mundane sensibility of modern life.

Anyway, whether aesthetic defect or no in the particular case, the synthetic "look" in films is not necessarily a misplaced theatricalism. From the beginning of film history, there were painters and sculptors who claimed that cinema's true future resided in artifice, construction. Not figurative narration or storytelling of any kind (either in a relatively realistic or in a "surrealistic" vein) but abstraction was film's true destiny. Thus, Theo van Doesburg in his essay of 1929, "Film as Pure Form," envisages film as the vehicle of "optical poetry," "dynamic light architecture," "the creation of a moving ornament." Films will realize "Bach's dream of finding an optical equivalent for the temporal structure of a musical composition." Though only a few film-makers—for example, Robert Breer—continue to pursue this conception of film, who can deny its claim to be cinematic?

Could anything be more alien to the nature of theatre than such a degree of abstraction? Let's not answer that question too quickly.

Panofsky derives the difference between theatre and film as a difference between the *formal* conditions of seeing a play and those of seeing a movie. In the theatre, "space is static, that is, the space represented on the stage, as well as the spatial relation of the beholder to the spectacle, is unalterably fixed," while in the cinema, "the spectator occupies a fixed seat, but

only physically, not as the subject of an aesthetic experience."
In the theatre, the spectator cannot change his angle of vision.
In the cinema, the spectator is "aesthetically . . . in permanent motion as his eye identifies with the lens of the camera,
which permanently shifts in distance and direction."

True enough. But the observation does not warrant a radical
dissociation of theatre and film. Like many critics, Panofsky
has a "literary" conception of the theatre. In contrast to
theatre, conceived of as basically dramatized literature (texts,
words), stands cinema, which he assumes to be primarily "a
visual experience." This means defining cinema by those
means perfected in the period of silent films. But many of the
most interesting movies today could hardly be described
adequately as images with sound added. And the most lively
work in the threatre is being done by people who envisage
theatre as more than, or different from, "plays" from Aeschylus
to Tennessee Williams.

Given his view, Panofsky is as eager to hold the line against
the infiltration of theatre by cinema as the other way around.
In the theatre, unlike movies, "the setting of the stage cannot
change during one act (except for such incidentals as rising
moons or gathering clouds and such illegitimate reborrowings
from film as turning wings or gliding backdrops)." Not only
does Panofsky assume that theatre means plays, but by the
aesthetic standard he tacitly proposes, the model play would
approach the condition of *No Exit,* and the ideal set would be
either a realistic living room or a blank stage. No less arbitrary
is his complementary view of what is illegitimate in film: all
elements not demonstrably subordinate to the image, more
precisely, the *moving* image. Thus Panofsky asserts: "Wherever a poetic emotion, a musical outburst, or a literary conceit
(even, I am grieved to say, some of the wisecracks of Groucho
Marx) entirely loses contact with visible movement, they strike
the sensitive spectator as, literally, out of place." What then of
the films of Bresson and Godard, with their allusive, thoughtful texts and their characteristic refusal to be primarily a visual

experience? How could one explain the extraordinary rightness of Ozu's relatively immobilized camera?

Part of Panofsky's dogmatism in decrying the theatrical taint in movies can be explained by recalling that the first version of his essay appeared in 1934 and undoubtedly reflects the recent experience of seeing a great many bad movies. Compared with the level that film reached in the late 1920's, it is undeniable that the average quality of films declined sharply in the early sound period. Although a number of fine, audacious films were made during the very first years of sound, the general decline had become clear by 1933 or 1934. The sheer dullness of most films of this period can't be explained simply as a regression to theatre. Still, it's a fact that film-makers in the 1930's did turn much more frequently to plays than they had in the preceding decade—filming stage successes such as *Outward Bound, Rain, Dinner at Eight, Blithe Spirit, Faisons un Rêve, Twentieth Century, Boudu Sauvé des Eaux,* the Pagnol trilogy, *She Done Him Wrong, Der Dreigroschen Oper, Anna Christie, Holiday, Animal Crackers, The Petrified Forest,* and many, many more. Most of these films are negligible as art; a few are first-rate. (The same can be said of the plays, though there is scant correlation between the merits of the movies and of the stage "originals.") However, their virtues and faults cannot be sorted out into a cinematic versus a theatrical element. Usually, the success of movie versions of plays is measured by the extent to which the script rearranges and displaces the action and deals less than respectfully with the spoken text—as do certain English films of plays by Wilde and Shaw, the Olivier Shakespeare films (at least *Henry V*), and Sjöberg's *Miss Julie.* But the basic disapproval of films which betray their origins in plays remains. (A recent example: the outrage and hostility which greeted Dreyer's masterly *Gertrud,* because of its blatant fidelity to the 1904 Danish play on which it is based, with characters conversing at length and quite formally, with little camera movement and most scenes filmed in medium shot.)

My own view is that films with complex or formal dialogue, films in which the camera is static or in which the action stays indoors, are not necessarily theatrical—whether derived from plays or not. *Per contra,* it is no more part of the putative "essence" of movies that the camera must rove over a large physical area than it is that the sound element in a film must always be subordinate to the visual. Though most of the action of Kurosawa's *The Lower Depths,* a fairly faithful transcription of Gorky's play, is confined to one large room, this film is just as cinematic as the same director's *Throne of Blood,* a very free and laconic adaption of *Macbeth.* The claustrophobic intensity of Melville's *Les Enfants Terribles* is as peculiar to the movies as the kinetic élan of Ford's *The Searchers* or the opening train journey in Renoir's *La Bête Humaine.*

A film does become theatrical in an invidious sense when the narration is coyly self-conscious. Compare Autant-Lara's *Occupe-toi d'Amélie,* a brilliant cinematic use of the conventions and materials of boulevard theatre, with Ophuls' clumsy use of similar conventions and materials in *La Ronde.*

In his book *Film and Theatre* (1936), Allardyce Nicoll argues that the difference between the two arts, both forms of dramaturgy, is that they use different kinds of characters. "Practically all effectively drawn stage characters are types [while] in the cinema we demand individualization . . . and impute greater power of independent life to the figures on the screen." (Panofsky, by the way, makes exactly the same contrast but in reverse: that the nature of films, unlike that of plays, requires flat or stock characters.)

Nicoll's thesis is not as arbitrary as it may at first appear. A little-remarked fact about movies is that the moments that are plastically and emotionally most successful, and the most effective elements of characterization, often consist precisely of "irrelevant" or unfunctional details. (One random example: the ping-pong ball the schoolmaster toys with in Ivory's

Shakespeare Wallah.) Movies thrive on the narrative equivalent of a technique familiar from painting and photography: off-centering. Hence, the pleasing disunity or fragmentariness of the characters of many of the greatest films, which is probably what Nicoll means by "individualization." In contrast, linear coherence of detail (the gun on the wall in the first act that must go off by the end of the third) is the rule in Occidental narrative theatre, and gives rise to the impression of the unity of the characters (a unity that may be equivalent to the construction of a "type").

But, even with these adjustments, Nicoll's thesis doesn't work so far as it rests on the idea that "when we go to the theatre, we expect theatre and nothing else." For what is this theatre-and-nothing-else if not the old notion of artifice? (As if art were ever anything else, some arts being artificial but others not.) According to Nicoll, when we sit in a theatre "in every way the 'falsity' of a theatrical production is borne in upon us, so that we are prepared to demand nothing save a theatrical truth." Quite a different situation obtains in the cinema, Nicoll holds. Every member of the movie audience, no matter how sophisticated, is on essentially the same level; we all believe that the camera cannot lie. As the film actor and his role are identical, the image cannot be dissociated from what is imaged. We experience what cinema gives us as the truth of life.

But couldn't theatre dissolve the distinction between the truth of artifice and the truth of life? Isn't that just what theatre as ritual seeks to do? Isn't that the aim of theatre conceived as an *exchange* with an audience?—something that films can never be.

Panofsky may be obtuse when he decries the theatrical taint in movies, but he is sound when he points out that, historically, theatre is only one of the arts feeding into cinema. As he remarks, it is apt that films came to be known popularly as moving pictures rather than as "photoplays" or "screen plays."

Cinema derives less from the theatre, from a performance art, an art that already moves, than it does from forms of art which were stationary. Nineteenth-century historical paintings, sentimental postcards, the museum of wax figures à la Madame Tussaud, and comic strips are the sources Panofsky cites. Another model, which he surprisingly fails to mention, is the early narrative uses of still photography—like the family photo album. The stylistics of description and scene-building developed by certain nineteenth-century novelists, as Eisenstein pointed out in his brilliant essay on Dickens, supplied still another prototype for cinema.

Movies are images (usually photographs) that move, to be sure. But the distinctive cinematic unit is not the image but the principle of connection between the images: the relation of a "shot" to the one that preceded it and the one that comes after. There is no peculiarly "cinematic" as opposed to "theatrical" mode of linking images.

If an irreducible distinction between theatre and cinema does exist, it may be this. Theatre is confined to a logical or *continuous* use of space. Cinema (through editing, that is, through the change of shot—which is the basic unit of film construction) has access to an alogical or *discontinuous* use of space.

In the theatre, actors are either in the stage space or "off." When "on," they are always visible or visualizable in contiguity with each other. In the cinema, no such relation is necessarily visible or even visualizable. (Example: the last shot of Paradjanov's *Shadows of Our Forgotten Ancestors*.) Some of the films considered objectionably theatrical are those which seem to emphasize spatial continuities, like Hitchcock's virtuoso *Rope* or the daringly anachronistic *Gertrud*. But closer analysis of both these films would show how complex their treatment of space is. The long takes increasingly favored in sound films are, in themselves, neither more nor less cinematic than the short takes characteristic of silents.

Thus, cinematic virtue does not reside in the fluidity of the movement of the camera or in the mere frequency of the change of shot. It consists in the arrangement of screen images and (now) of sounds. Méliès, for example, though he didn't go beyond the static positioning of his camera, had a very striking conception of how to *link* screen images. He grasped that editing offered an equivalent to the magician's sleight of hand—thereby establishing that one of the distinctive aspects of film (unlike theatre) is that anything can happen, that there is nothing that cannot be represented convincingly. Through editing, Méliès presents discontinuities of physical substance and behavior. In his films, the discontinuities are, so to speak, practical, functional; they accomplish a transformation of ordinary reality. But the continuous *re*invention of space (as well as the option of temporal indeterminacy) peculiar to film narration does not pertain only to the cinema's ability to fabricate "visions," to show the viewer a radically altered world. The most "realistic" use of the motion-picture camera also involves a discontinuous account of space, insofar as all film narration has a "syntax," composed of the rhythm of associations and disjunctions. (As Cocteau has written, "My primary concern in a film is to prevent the images from flowing, to oppose them to each other, to anchor them and join them without destroying their relief." But such a conception of film syntax need hardly entail, as Cocteau thinks, rejecting movies as "mere entertainment instead of a vehicle for thought.")

In marking the boundary between theatre and film, the issue of the continuity of space seems to me more fundamental than the obvious contrast between theatre as an organization of movement in three-dimensional space (like dance) and cinema as an organization of plane space (like painting). The theatre's capacities for manipulating space and time are simply much cruder and more labored than those of film. Theatre cannot equal the cinema's facilities for the strictly controlled repetition of images, for the duplication or matching of word and image, and for the juxtaposition and overlapping of images. (With advanced lighting techniques and an adept use of scrim, one can now "dissolve in" or "dissolve out" on the stage. But no technique could provide an equivalent on the stage of the "lap dissolve.")

Sometimes the division between theatre and film is located as the difference between the play and the film script. Theatre has been described as a mediated art, presumably because it usually consists of a preexistent play mediated by a particular performance which offers one of many possible interpretations of the play. Film, in contrast, is regarded as unmediated—because of its larger-than-life scale and more unrefusable impact on the eye, and because (in Panofsky's words) "the medium of the movies is physical reality as such" and the characters in a movie "have no aesthetic existence outside the actors." But there is an equally valid sense which shows movies to be the mediated art and theatre the unmediated one. We see what happens on the stage with our own eyes. We see on the screen what the camera sees.

In the cinema, narration proceeds by ellipsis (the "cut" or change of shot); the camera eye is a unified point of view that continually displaces itself. But the change of shot can provoke questions, the simplest of which is: from *whose* point of view is the shot seen? And the ambiguity of point of view latent in all cinematic narration has no equivalent in the theatre. Indeed, one should not underestimate the aesthetically positive role of *disorientation* in the cinema. Examples: Busby Berkeley dollying back from an ordinary-looking stage already established as some thirty feet deep to disclose a stage area three hundred feet square; Resnais panning from character X's point of view a full 360 degrees to come to rest upon X's face.

Much also may be made of the fact that, in its concrete existence, cinema is an *object* (a product, even) while theatre results in a *performance*. Is this so important? In a way, no. Art in all its forms, whether objects (like films or painting) or performances (like music or theatre), is first a mental act, a fact of consciousness. The object aspect of film and the performance aspect of theatre are only means—means to the experience which is not only "of" but "through" the film and the theatre event. Each subject of an aesthetic experience shapes it to his own measure. With respect to any *single* experience, it hardly matters that a film is identical from one projection of it to another while theatre performances are highly mutable.

The difference between object art and performance art underlies Panofsky's observation that "the screenplay, in contrast to the theatre play, has no aesthetic existence independent of its performance," so that characters in movies *are* the stars who enact them. It is because each film is an object, a totality that is set, that movie roles are identical with the actors' performances; while in the theatre (in the Occident, an artistic totality that is generally additive rather than organic) only the written play is "fixed," an object (literature) and therefore existing apart from any staging of it.

But these qualities of theatre and film are not, as Panofsky apparently thought, unalterable. Just as movies needn't necessarily be designed to be shown at all in theatre situations (they can be intended for more continuous and casual viewing: in the living room, in the bedroom, or on public surfaces like the façades of buildings), so a movie *may* be altered from one projection to the next. Harry Smith, when he runs off his films, makes each projection an unrepeatable performance. And, again, theatre is not just about preexisting plays which get produced over and over, well or badly. In Happenings, street or guerilla theatre, and certain other recent theatre events, the "plays" are identical with their productions in precisely the same sense as the screenplay is identical with the unique film made from it.

Despite these developments, however, a large difference still remains. Because films are objects, they are totally manipulable, totally calculable. Films resemble books, another portable art-object; making a film, like writing a book, means constructing an inanimate thing, every element of which is determinate. Indeed, this determinacy has or can have a quasi-mathematical form in films, as it does in music. (A shot lasts a certain number of seconds, "matching" two shots requires a change of angle of so many degrees.) Given the total determinacy of the result on celluloid (whatever the extent of the director's conscious intervention), it was inevitable that some film directors would want to devise schemas to make their intentions more exact. Thus, it was neither perverse nor primitive of Busby Berkeley to have used only one camera to shoot the whole of each of his mammoth dance numbers. Every "set-up" was designed to be shot from only one, exactly calculated angle. Working on a far more self-conscious level of artistry than Busby Berkeley, Bresson has declared that, for him, the director's task consists in finding the single way of doing each shot that is correct. No image is justified in itself, according to Bresson, but rather in the exactly specifiable relation it bears to the chronologically adjacent images—which relation constitutes its "meaning."

But theatre allows only the loosest approximation to this sort of formal concern and to this degree of aesthetic responsibility on the part of the director, which is why French critics justly speak of the director of a film as its "author." Because they are performances, events that are always "live," what takes place on a theatre stage is not subject to an equivalent degree of control and cannot admit a comparably exact integration of effects.

It would be foolish to conclude that superior films are those resulting from the greatest amount of conscious planning on the part of the director or those which objectify a complex plan (though the director may not have been aware of it, and proceeded in what seemed to him an intuitive or instinctive way). Plans may be faulty or ill-conceived or sterile. More important, the cinema admits of a number of quite different kinds of sensibility. One gives rise to the kind of formalized art to which cinema (unlike theatre) is naturally adapted. Another has produced an impressive body of "improvised" cinema. (This should be distinguished from the work of some film-makers, notably Godard, who have become fascinated with the "look" of improvised, documentary cinema, used for formalistic ends.)

Nevertheless, it seems indisputable that cinema, not only potentially but by its nature, is a more rigorous art than theatre. This capacity for formal rigor, combined with the accessibility of mass audiences, has given cinema an unquestioned prestige and attractiveness as an art form. Despite the extreme emotional resources of "pure theatre" demonstrated by Julian Beck and Judith Malina's Living Theatre and Jerzy Grotowski's Theatre Laboratory, theatre as an art form gives the general impression of having a problematic future.

More than a failure of nerve must account for the fact that theatre, this seasoned art, occupied since antiquity with all sorts of local offices—enacting sacred rites, reinforcing communal loyalty, guiding morals, provoking the therapeutic discharge of violent emotions, conferring social status, giving practical instruction, affording entertainment, dignifying celebrations, subverting established authority—is now on the defensive before movies, this brash art with its huge, amorphous, passive audience. But the fact is undeniable. Meanwhile, movies continue to maintain their astonishing pace of formal articulation. (Take the commercial cinema of Europe, Japan, and the United States since 1960, and consider what the audiences of these films in less than a decade have become habituated to in the way of increasingly elliptical storytelling and visualization.)

But note: this youngest of the arts is also the most heavily burdened with memory. Cinema is a time machine. Movies preserve the past, while theatres—no matter how devoted to the classics, to old plays—can only "modernize." Movies resurrect the beautiful dead; present, intact, vanished or ruined environments; embody without irony styles and fashions that seem funny today; solemnly ponder irrelevant or naïve problems. The historical particularity of the reality registered on celluloid is so vivid that practically all films older than four or five years are saturated with pathos. (The pathos I am describing is not simply that of old photographs, for it overtakes animated cartoons and drawn, abstract films as well as ordinary movies.) Films age (being objects) as no theatre event does (being always new). There is no pathos of mortality in theatre's "reality" as such, nothing in our response to a good performance of a Mayakovsky play comparable to the aesthetic role of the emotion of nostalgia when we see in 1966 a film by Pudovkin.

Also worth noting: compared with the theatre, innovations in cinema seem to be assimilated more efficiently, seem altogether more sharable—among other reasons, because new films are quickly and widely circulated. And, partly because virtually the entire body of accomplishment in film can be consulted in the present (in film libraries, of which the most celebrated is the Cinemathèque Française), most film-makers are more knowledgeable about the entire history of their art than most theatre directors are about even the very recent past of theirs.

The key word in most discussions of cinema is "possibility." There is a merely classifying use of the word, as in Panofsky's engaging judgment that "within their self-imposed limitations the early Disney films . . . represent, as it were, a chemically pure distillation of cinematic possibilities." But behind this relatively neutral usage lurks a more polemical sense of cinema's possibilities, in which what is regularly intimated is the obsolescence of theatre and its supersession by films.

Thus, Panofsky describes the mediation of the camera eye as opening "up a world of possibility of which the stage can never dream." Already in 1924, Artaud declared that motion pictures had made the theatre obsolete. Movies "possess a sort of virtual power which probes into the mind and uncovers undreamt-of possibilities . . . When this art's exhiliration has been blended in the right proportions with the psychic ingredient it commands, it will leave the theatre far behind and we will relegate the latter to the attic of our memories." (When sound came in, though, Artaud became disenchanted with films and returned to theatre.)

Meyerhold, facing the challenge head on, thought the only hope for theatre lay in a wholesale emulation of the cinema. "Let us 'cinematify' the theatre," he urged, meaning that the staging of plays should be "industrialized," theatres must accommodate audiences in the tens of thousands rather than in the hundreds. Meyerhold also seemed to find some relief in the idea that the coming of sound signaled the downfall of movies. Believing that the international appeal of films depended entirely on the fact that screen actors (unlike theatre actors) didn't have to speak any particular language, he was unable to imagine in 1930 that technology (dubbing, subtitling) could solve the problem.

Is cinema the successor, the rival, or the revivifyer of the theatre?

Sociologically, it is certainly the rival—one of many. Whether it is theatre's successor depends partly on how people understand and use the decline of theatre as an art form. One can't be sure that theatre is not in a state of irreversible decline, spurts of local vitality notwithstanding. And art forms *have* been abandoned (though not necessarily because they become "obsolete").

But why should theatre be rendered obsolete by movies? Predictions of obsolescence amount to declaring that a something has one particular task (which another something may do as well or better). But has theatre one particular task or aptitude? One which cinema is better able to perform?

Those who predict the demise of the theatre, assuming that cinema has engulfed its function, tend to impute a relation between films and theatre reminiscent of what was once said about photography and painting. If the painter's job really had been no more than fabricating likenesses, then the invention of the camera might indeed have made painting obsolete. But painting is hardly just "pictures," any more than cinema is just theatre democratized and made available to the masses (because it can be reproduced and distributed in portable standardized units).

In the naïve tale of photography and painting, painting was reprieved when it claimed a new task: abstraction. As the superior realism of photography was supposed to have liberated painting, allowing it to go abstract, cinema's superior power to represent (not merely to stimulate) the imagination may appear to have similarly emboldened the theatre, inviting the gradual obliteration of the conventional "plot."

This was how it was supposed to be, but not how it in fact turned out. Actually, painting and photography evidence parallel development rather than a rivalry or a supersession. And, at an uneven rate, so do theatre and film. The possibilities for theatre that lie in going beyond psychological realism, thereby achieving greater abstractness, are equally germane to the future of narrative films. Conversely, the idea of movies as witness to real life, testimony rather than invention or artifice, the treatment of collective historical situations rather than the depiction of imaginary personal "dramas," seems equally relevant to theatre. Alongside documentary films and their sophisticated heir, *cinéma-vérité*, one can place the new documentary theatre, the so-called "theatre of fact," exemplified in plays by Hochhuth, in Weiss' *The Investigation*, in Peter Brook's recent projects for a production called *US* with the Royal Skakespeare company in London.

Despite Panofsky's strictures, there seems no reason for theatre and film not to exchange with each other, as they have been doing right along.

The influence of the theatre upon films in the early years of cinema history is well known. According to Kracauer, the distinctive lighting of *Dr. Caligari* (and of many German films of the early 1920's) can be traced to an experiment with lighting that Max Reinhardt made shortly before on the stage in his production of Sorge's *The Beggar*. Even in this period, however, the impact was reciprocal. The accomplishments of the "expressionist film" were immediately absorbed by the expressionist theatre. Stimulated by the cinematic technique of the "iris-in," stage lighting took to singling out a lone player or some segment of the scene, masking out the rest of the stage. Rotating sets tried to approximate the instantaneous displacement of the camera eye. (More recently, reports have come of ingenious lighting techniques used by the Gorky Theatre in Leningrad, directed since 1956 by Georgy Tovstonogov, which allow for incredibly rapid scene changes taking place behind a horizontal curtain of light.)

Today traffic seems, with few exceptions, entirely one way: film to theatre. Particularly in France and in Central and Eastern Europe, the staging of many plays is inspired by the movies. The aim of adapting neo-cinematic devices for the stage (I exclude the outright use of films within the theatre production) seems mainly to tighten up the theatrical experience, to approximate the cinema's absolute control of the flow and location of the audience's attention. But the conception can be even more directly cinematic. An example is Josef Svoboda's production of *The Insect Play* by the Čapek brothers at the Czech National Theatre in Prague (recently seen in London), which frankly attempted to install a mediated vision upon the stage, equivalent to the discontinuous intensifications of the camera eye. According to a London critic's account, "the set consisted of two huge, faceted mirrors slung at an angle to the stage, so that they reflect whatever happens there defracted as if through a decanter stopper or the colossally magnified eye of a fly. Any figure placed at the base of their angle becomes multiplied from floor to proscenium; further out, and you find yourself viewing it not only face to face but from overhead, the vantage point of a camera slung to a bird or a helicopter."

Marinetti was perhaps the first to propose the use of films as one element in a theatre experience. Writing between 1910 and 1914, he envisaged the theatre as a final synthesis of all the arts; and as such it had to draw in the newest art form, movies. No doubt the cinema also recommended itself for inclusion because of the priority Marinetti gave to existing forms of popular entertainment, such as the variety theatre and the *café chantant*. (He called his projected total art form "the Futurist Variety Theatre.") And at that time scarcely anyone considered cinema anything but a vulgar art.

After World War I, similar ideas appear frequently. In the total-theatre projects of the Bauhaus group in the 1920's (Gropius, Piscator, etc.) film had an important place. Meyerhold insisted on its use in the theatre, describing his program as fulfilling Wagner's once "wholly utopian" proposals to "use all means available from the other arts." Alban Berg specified that a silent film of the developing story was to be projected in the middle of Act 2 of his opera *Lulu*. By now, the employment of film in theatre has a fairly long history which includes the "living newspaper" of the 1930's, "epic theatre," and Happenings. This year marked the introduction of a film sequence into Broadway-level theatre. In two successful musicals, London's *Come Spy with Me* and New York's *Superman*, both parodic in tone, the action is interrupted to lower a screen and run off a movie showing the pop-art hero's exploits.

But thus far the use of film within live theatre events has tended to be stereotyped. Film is often employed as *document*, supportive of or redundant to the live stage events (as in Brecht's productions in East Berlin). Its other principal use is as *hallucinant;* recent examples are Bob Whitman's Happenings, and a new kind of nightclub situation, the mixed-media discothèque (Andy Warhol's The Plastic Inevitable, Murray the

K's World). From the point of view of theatre, the interpolation of film into the theatre experience may be enlarging. But in terms of what cinema is capable of, it seems a reductive, monotonous use of film.

What Panofsky perhaps could not have realized when he wrote his essay is that much more than the "nature" of a specific art "medium" is at stake. The relation between film and theatre involves not simply a static definition of the two arts, but sensitivity to the possible course of their radicalization.

Every interesting aesthetic tendency now is a species of radicalism. The question each artist must ask is: What is *my* radicalism, the one dictated by *my* gifts and temperament? This doesn't mean all contemporary artists believe that art progresses. A radical position isn't necessarily a forward-looking position.

Consider the two principal radical positions in the arts today. One recommends the breaking down of distinctions between genres; the arts would eventuate in one art, consisting of many different kinds of behavior going on at the same time, a vast behavioral magma or synesthesia. The other position recommends the maintaining and clarifying of barriers between the arts, by the intensification of what each art distinctively is; painting must use only those means which pertain to painting, music only those which are musical, novels those which pertain to the novel and to no other literary form, etc. The two positions are, in a sense, irreconcilable—except that both are invoked to support the perennial modern quest for the definitive art form.

An art may be proposed as definitive because it is considered the most rigorous or most fundamental. For these reasons, Schopenhauer suggested and Pater asserted that all art aspires to the condition of music. More recently, the thesis that all the arts are leading toward one art has been advanced by enthusiasts of the cinema. The candidacy of film is founded on its being both so exact and, potentially, so complex a combination of music, literature, and the image.

Or, an art may be proposed as definitive because it is held to be most inclusive. This is the basis of the destiny for theatre held out by Wagner, Marinetti, Artaud, Cage—all of whom envisage theatre as a total art, potentially conscripting all the arts into its service. And as the ideas of synesthesia continue to proliferate among painters, sculptors, architects, and composers, theatre remains the favored candidate for the role of summative art. In this conception, theatre's role must disparage the claims of cinema. Partisans of theatre would argue that while music, painting, dance, cinema, and utterance can all converge on a "stage," the film object can only become bigger (multiple screens, 360 degree projection, etc.) or longer in duration or internally more articulated and complex. Theatre can be anything, everything; in the end, films can only be more of what they specifically (that is to say, cinematically) are.

Underlying the more grandiose apocalyptic expectations for both arts is a common animus. In 1923 Béla Bálacz, anticipating in great detail the thesis of Marshall McLuhan, described movies as the herald of a new "visual culture" which will give us back our bodies, and particularly our faces, which have been rendered illegible, soulless, unexpressive by the centuries-old ascendancy of "print." An animus against literature, against the printing press and its "culture of concepts," also informs most interesting thinking about the theatre in our time.

No definition or characterization of theatre and cinema can be taken for granted—not even the apparently self-evident observation that both cinema and theatre are temporal arts. In theatre and cinema, like music (and unlike painting), everything is *not* present all at once. But there are significant developments today pointing up the atemporal aspect of these forms. The allure of mixed-media forms in theatre suggests not only a more elongated and more complex "drama" (like Wagnerian opera) but also a more compact theatre experience which approaches the condition of painting. This prospect of compactness is broached by Marinetti; he calls it simultaneity, a leading notion of Futurist aesthetics. As the final synthesis of all the arts, theatre "would use the new twentieth century devices of electricity and the cinema; this would enable plays to be extremely short, since all these technical means would enable the theatrical synthesis to be achieved in the shortest possible space of time, as all the elements could be presented simultaneously."

The source of the idea of art as an act of violence pervading cinema and theatre is the aesthetics of Futurism and of Surrealism; its principal texts are, for theatre, the writings of Artaud and, for cinema, two films of Luis Buñuel, *L'Age d'Or* and *Un Chien Andalou*. (More recent examples: the early plays of Ionesco, at least as conceived; the "cinema of cruelty" of Hitchcock, Clouzot, Franju, Robert Aldrich, Polanski; work by the Living Theatre; some of the neo-cinematic light shows in experimental theatres and discothèques; the sound of late Cage and LaMonte Young.) The relation of art to an audience understood to be passive, inert, surfeited, can only be assault. Art becomes identical with aggression.

However understandable and valuable this theory of art as an assault on the audience is today (like the complementary notion of art as ritual), one must continue to question it, particularly in the theatre. For it can become as much a convention as anything else and end, like all theatrical conventions, by reinforcing rather than challenging the deadness of the audience. (As Wagner's ideology of a total theatre played its role in confirming the philistinism of German culture.)

Moreover, the depth of the assault must be assessed honestly. In the theatre, this means not "diluting" Artaud. Artaud's writings express the demand for a totally open (therefore flayed, self-cruel) consciousness of which theatre would be one adjunct or instrument. No work in the theatre has yet amounted to this. Thus, Peter Brook has astutely and forthrightly disclaimed that his company's work in the "Theatre of Cruelty," which culminated in his celebrated production of *Marat/Sade*, is genuinely Artaudian. It is Artaudian, he says, in a trivial sense only. (Trivial from Artaud's point of view, not from ours.)

For some time, all useful ideas in art have been extremely sophisticated. Take, for example, the idea that everything is what it is and not another thing: a painting is a painting; sculpture is sculpture; a poem is a poem, not prose. Or the complementary idea: a painting can be "literary" or sculptural, a poem can be prose, theatre can emulate and incorporate cinema, cinema can be theatrical.

We need a new idea. It will probably be a very simple one. Will we be able to recognize it?

(1966)

Bergman's *Persona*

One impulse is to take Bergman's masterpiece for granted. Since 1960 at least, with the breakthrough into new narrative forms propagated with most notoriety (if not greatest distinction) by *Last Year in Marienbad,* film audiences have continued to be educated by the elliptical and complex. As Resnais' imagination was subsequently to surpass itself in *Muriel,* a succession of ever more difficult and accomplished films have turned up in recent years. But such good fortune releases nobody who cares about films from acclaiming work as original and triumphant as *Persona.* It is depressing that this film has received only a fraction of the attention it deserves since it opened in New York, London, and Paris.

To be sure, some of the paltriness of the critics' reaction may be more a response to the signature that *Persona* carries than to the film itself. That signature has come to mean a prodigal, tirelessly productive career; a rather facile, often merely beautiful, by now (it seemed) almost oversize body of work; a lavishly inventive, sensual, yet melodramatic talent, employed with what appeared to be a certain complacency, and prone to embarrassing displays of intellectual bad taste. From the Fellini of the North, exacting filmgoers could hardly be blamed for not expecting, ever, a truly great film. But *Persona* happily forces one to put aside such dismissive preconceptions about its author.

The rest of the neglect of *Persona* may be set down to emotional squeamishness; the film, like much of Bergman's recent work, bears an almost defiling charge of personal agony. This is particularly true of *The Silence*—most accomplished, by far, of the films Bergman has made before this one. And *Persona* draws liberally on the themes and schematic cast established in *The Silence*. (The principal characters in both films are two women bound together in a passionate agonized relationship, one of whom has a pitiably neglected small son. Both films take up the themes of the scandal of the erotic; the polarities of violence and powerlessness, reason and unreason, language and silence, the intelligible and the unintelligible.) But Bergman's new film ventures at least as much beyond *The Silence* as that film is an advance, in its emotional power and subtlety, over all his previous work.

That achievement gives, for the present moment, the measure of a work which is undeniably "difficult." *Persona* is bound to trouble, perplex, and frustrate most filmgoers—at least as much as *Marienbad* did in its day. Or so one would suppose. But, heaping imperturbability upon indifference, critical reaction to *Persona* has shied away from associating anything very baffling with the film. The critics have allowed, mildly, that the latest Bergman is unnecessarily obscure. Some add that this time he's overdone the mood of unremitting bleakness. It's intimated that with this film he has ventured out of his depth, exchanging art for artiness. But the difficulties and rewards of *Persona* are much more formidable than such banal objections would suggest.

Of course, evidence of these difficulties is available anyway —even in the absence of more pertinent controversy. Why else all the discrepancies and just plain misrepresentations in the accounts given by critics of what actually happens during the film? Like *Marienbad*, *Persona* seems defiantly obscure. Its general look has nothing of the built-in, abstract evocativeness of the château in Resnais' film; the space and furnishings of *Persona* are anti-romantic, cool, mundane, clinical (in one sense, literally so), and bourgeois-modern. But no less of a mystery is lodged in this setting. Actions and dialogue are given which the viewer is bound to find puzzling, being unable to decipher whether certain scenes take place in the past, present, or future; and whether certain images and episodes belong to reality or fantasy.

One common approach to a film presenting difficulties of this now familiar sort is to treat such distinctions as irrelevant and rule that the film is actually all of one piece. This usually means situating the action of the film in a merely (or wholly) mental universe. But this approach only covers over the difficulty, it seems to me. *Within* the structure of what is shown, the elements continue being related to each other in the ways that originally suggested to the viewer that some events were realistic while others were visionary (whether fantasy, dream, hallucination, or extra-worldly visitation). Causal connections observed in one portion of the film are still being flouted in another part; the film still gives several equally persuasive but mutually exclusive explanations of the same event. These discordant internal relations only get transposed, intact, but not reconciled, when the whole film is relocated in the mind. I should argue that it is no more helpful to describe *Persona* as a wholly subjective film—an action taking place within a single character's head—than it was (how easy to see that now) in elucidating *Marienbad*, a film whose disregard for conventional chronology and a clearly delineated border between fantasy and reality could scarcely have constituted more of a provocation than *Persona*.

But neither is it any sounder to approach this film in search of an objective narrative, ignoring the fact that *Persona* is strewn with signs that cancel each other. Even the most skillful attempt to arrange a single, plausible anecdote out of the film must leave out or contradict some of its key sections, images, and procedures. Attempted less skillfully, it has led to the flat, impoverished, and partly inaccurate account of Bergman's film promulgated by most reviewers and critics.

According to this account, *Persona* is a psychological chamber drama which chronicles the relation between two women. One is a successful actress, evidently in her mid-thirties, named Elizabeth Vogler (Liv Ullman), now suffering from an enigmatic mental collapse whose chief symptoms are muteness and a near-catatonic lassitude. The other is the pretty young nurse of twenty-five named Alma (Bibi Andersson) charged with caring for Elizabeth—first at the mental hospital and then at the beach cottage loaned to them for this purpose by the woman psychiatrist at the hospital who is Elizabeth's doctor and Alma's supervisor. What happens in the course of the film, according to the critics' consensus, is that, through some mysterious process, the two women exchange identities. The ostensibly stronger one, Alma, becomes weaker, gradually assuming the problems and confusions of her patient, while the sick woman felled by despair (or psychosis) eventually regains her power of speech and returns to her former life. (We don't see this exchange consummated. What is shown at the end of *Persona* looks like an agonized stalemate. But it was reported that the film, until shortly before it was released, contained a brief closing scene that showed Elizabeth on the stage again, apparently completely recovered. From this, presumably, the viewer could infer that the nurse was now mute and had taken on the burden of Elizabeth's despair.)

Proceeding from this constructed version, half "story" and

half "meaning," critics have read off a number of further meanings. Some regard the transaction between Elizabeth and Alma as illustrating an impersonal law that operates intermittently in human affairs; no ultimate responsibility pertains to either of them. Others posit a conscious cannibalism of the innocent Alma by the actress—and thus read the film as a parable of the predatory, demonic energies of the artist, incorrigibly scavenging life for raw material.* Other critics move quickly to an even more general plane, extracting from *Persona* a diagnosis of the contemporary dissociation of personality, a demonstration of the inevitable failure of good will and trust, and predictable correct views on such matters as the alienated affluent society, the nature of madness, psychiatry and its limitations, the American war on Vietnam, the Western legacy of sexual guilt, and the Six Million. (Then the critics often go on, as Michel Cournot did several months ago in *Le Nouvel Observateur,* to chide Bergman for this vulgar didacticism which they have imputed to him.)

But even when turned into a story, I think, this prevailing account of *Persona* grossly oversimplifies and misrepresents. True, Alma does seem to grow progressively more insecure, more vulnerable; in the course of the film she is reduced to fits

* For example, Richard Corliss in the Summer 1967 *Film Quarterly:* "Slowly Alma comes to understand that she is just another of Elizabeth's 'props.'" True, in the sense that Alma, after reading a letter Elizabeth writes to the psychiatrist does entertain this bitter idea of what Elizabeth is up to. Not true, though, in the sense that the viewer lacks the evidence for coming to any definite conclusions about what's really going on. Yet this is precisely what Corliss does assume, so that he can then go on to make a statement about Elizabeth which isn't backed up by anything said or shown in the film. "The actress had borne a child to help her 'live the part' of a mother, but was disgusted by the boy's determination to stay alive after the role was completed. Now she wants to toss Alma away like an old prompt book."
The same point about Elizabeth as an exemplar of the parasitical, unscrupulous energies of the artist is made by Vernon Young in his unfavorable notice of the film in the Summer 1967 *Hudson Review.* Both Corliss and Young point out that Elizabeth shares the same last name, Vogler, with the magician-artist in *The Magician.*

of hysteria, cruelty, anxiety, childish dependence, and (probably) delusion. It's also true that Elizabeth gradually becomes stronger, that is, more active, more responsive; though her change is far subtler and, until virtually the end, she still refuses to speak. But all this is hardly tantamount to the "exchange" of attributes and identities that critics have glibly spoken of. Nor is it established, as most critics have assumed, that Alma, however much she does come with pain and longing to identify herself with the actress, takes on Elizabeth's dilemmas, whatever those may be. (They're far from made clear.)

My own view is that the temptation to invent more story ought to be resisted. Take, for instance, the scene that starts with the abrupt presence of a middle-aged man wearing dark glasses (Gunnar Björnstrand) near the beach cottage where Elizabeth and Alma have been living in isolation. All we see is that he approaches Alma, addressing her and continuing to call her, despite her protests, by the name Elizabeth; that he tries to embrace her, ignoring her struggle to free herself; that throughout this scene Elizabeth's impassive face is never more than a few inches away; that Alma suddenly yields to his embraces, saying, "Yes, I am Elizabeth" (Elizabeth is still watching intently), and goes to bed with him amid a torrent of endearments. Then we see the two women together (shortly after?); they are alone, behaving as if nothing has happened. This sequence can be taken as illustrating Alma's growing identification with Elizabeth, and gauging the extent of the process by which Alma is learning (really? in her imagination?) to become Elizabeth. While Elizabeth has perhaps voluntarily renounced being an actress by becoming mute, Alma is involuntarily and painfully engaged in becoming that Elizabeth Vogler, the performer, who no longer exists. Still, nothing we see justifies describing this scene as a real event—something happening in the course of the plot on the same level as the initial removal of the two women to the beach cottage.* But neither can we be absolutely sure that this, or something like it, isn't taking place. After all, we do see it happening. (And it's the nature of cinema to confer on all events, without indications to the contrary, an equivalent degree of reality: everything shown on the screen is *there*, present.)

The difficulty of *Persona* stems from the fact that Bergman withholds the kind of clear signals for sorting out fantasies from reality offered, for example, by Buñuel in *Belle de Jour*. Buñuel puts in the clues; he wants the viewer to be able to decipher his film. The insufficiency of the clues Bergman has planted must be taken to indicate that he intends the film to remain partly encoded. The viewer can only move toward, but never achieve, certainty about the action. However, so far as the distinction between fantasy and reality is of any use in understanding *Persona*, I should argue that much more than the critics have allowed of what happens in and around the beach cottage is most plausibly understood as Alma's fantasy. One prime bit of evidence for this thesis is a sequence occurring soon after the two women arrive at the seaside. It's the sequence in which, after we have seen Elizabeth enter Alma's room and stand beside her and stroke her hair, we see Alma, pale, troubled, asking Elizabeth the next morning, "Did you come to my room last night?" and Elizabeth, slightly quizzical, anxious, shaking her head no. Now, there seems no reason to doubt Elizabeth's answer. The viewer isn't given any evidence of a malevolent plan on Elizabeth's part to undermine Alma's confidence in her own sanity; nor any evidence for doubting Elizabeth's memory or sanity in the ordinary

* Which is what most critics have done with this scene: assume that it's a real event and insert it into the "action" of the film. Richard Corliss disposes of the matter, without a touch of uncertainty, thus: "When Elizabeth's blind husband visits, he mistakes Alma for his wife [and] they make love." But the only evidence for the husband being blind is that the man we see wears dark glasses—plus the critic's wish to find a "realistic" explanation for such implausible goings-on.

sense. But if that is the case, two important points have been established early in the film. One is that Alma is hallucinating —and, presumably, will continue doing so. The other is that hallucinations or visions will appear on the screen with the same rhythms, the same look of objective reality as something "real." (However, some clues, too complex to describe here, are given in the lighting of certain scenes.) And once these points are granted, it seems highly plausible to take at least the scene with Elizabeth's husband as Alma's fantasy, as well as several scenes which depict a charged, trancelike physical contact between the two women.

But sorting out what is fantasy from what is real in *Persona* (i.e., what Alma imagines from what may be taken as really happening) is a minor achievement. And it quickly becomes a misleading one, unless subsumed under the larger issue of the form of exposition or narration employed by the film. As I have already suggested, *Persona* is constructed according to a form that resists being reduced to a story—say, the story about the relation (however ambiguous and abstract) between two women named Elizabeth and Alma, a patient and a nurse, a star and an ingenue, *alma* (soul) and *persona* (mask). Such reduction to a story means, in the end, a reduction of Bergman's film to the single dimension of psychology. Not that the psychological dimension isn't there. It is. But to understand *Persona,* the viewer must go beyond the psychological point of view.

This seems mandatory because Bergman allows the audience to interpret Elizabeth's mute condition in several different ways—as involuntary mental breakdown and as voluntary moral decision leading either toward a self-purification or toward suicide. But whatever the background of her condition, Bergman wishes to involve the viewer much more in the sheer fact of it than in its causes. In *Persona,* muteness is first of all a fact with a certain psychic and moral weight, a fact which initiates its own kind of psychic and moral causality upon an "other."

I am inclined to impute a privileged status to the speech made by the psychiatrist to Elizabeth before she departs with Alma to the beach cottage. The psychiatrist tells the silent, stony-faced Elizabeth that she has understood her case. She has grasped that Elizabeth wants to be sincere, not to play a role, not to lie; to make the inner and the outer come together. And that, having rejected suicide as a solution, she has decided to be mute. The psychiatrist concludes by advising Elizabeth to bide her time and live her experience through, predicting that eventually the actress will renounce her muteness and return to the world . . . But even if one treats this speech as setting forth a privileged view, it would be a mistake to take it as the key to *Persona;* or even to assume that the psychiatrist's thesis wholly explains Elizabeth's condition. (The doctor could be wrong, or, at the least, be simplifying the matter.) By placing this speech so early in the film (even earlier, a superficial account of Elizabeth's symptoms is addressed to Alma when the doctor first assigns her to the case), and by never referring explicitly to this "explanation" again, Bergman has, in effect, both taken account of psychology and dispensed with it. Without ruling out psychological explanation, he consigns to a relatively minor place any consideration of the role the actress's *motives* have in the action.

Persona takes a position beyond psychology—as it does, in an analogous sense, beyond eroticism. It certainly contains the materials of an erotic subject, such as the "visit" of Elizabeth's husband that ends with his going to bed with Alma while Elizabeth looks on. There is, above all, the connection between the two women themselves which, in its feverish proximity, its caresses, its sheer passionateness (avowed by Alma in word, gesture, and fantasy) could hardly fail, it would seem, to suggest a powerful, if largely inhibited, sexual involvement. But, in fact, what might be sexual in feeling is largely transposed into something beyond sexuality, beyond eroticism even. The most purely sexual episode in the film is the scene in which Alma, sitting across the room from Elizabeth, tells the story of an impromptu beach orgy; Alma speaks, transfixed, reliving the memory and at the same time consciously delivering up this shameful secret to Elizabeth as her greatest gift of love. Entirely through discourse and without any resort to images (through a flashback), a violent sexual atmosphere is generated. But this sexuality has nothing to do with the "present" of the film, and the relationship between the two women. In this respect, *Persona* makes a remarkable modification of the structure of *The Silence*. In the earlier film, the love-hate relationship between the two sisters projected an unmistakable sexual energy—particularly the feelings of the older sister (Ingrid Thulin). In *Persona*, Bergman has achieved a more interesting situation by delicately excising or transcending the possible sexual implications of the tie between the two women. It is a remarkable feat of moral and psychological poise. While maintaining the indeterminacy of the situation (from a psychological point of view), Bergman does not give the impression of evading the issue, and presents nothing that is psychologically improbable.

The advantages of keeping the psychological aspects of *Persona* indeterminate (while internally credible) are that Bergman can do many other things besides tell a story. Instead of a full-blown story, he presents something that is, in one sense, cruder and, in another, more abstract: a body of material, a subject. The function of the subject or material may be as much its opacity, its multiplicity, as the ease with which it yields itself to being incarnated in a determinate action or plot.

In a work constituted along these principles, the action would appear intermittent, porous, shot through intimations of absence, of what could not be univocally said. This doesn't mean that the narration has forfeited "sense." But it does mean that sense isn't necessarily tied to a determinate plot. Alternatively, there is the possibility of an extended narration composed of events that are not (wholly) explicated but are, nevertheless, possible and may even have taken place. The forward movement of such a narrative might be measured by reciprocal relations between its parts—e.g., displacements—rather than by ordinary realistic (mainly psychological) causality. There might exist what could be called a dormant plot. Still, critics have better things to do than ferret out the story line as if the author had—through mere clumsiness or error or frivolity or lack of craft—concealed it. In such narratives, it is a question not of a plot that has been mislaid but of one that has been (at least in part) annulled. That intention, whether conscious on the artist's part or merely implicit in the work, should be taken at face value and respected.

Take the matter of information. One tactic upheld by traditional narrative is to give "full" information (by which I mean all that is needed, according to the standard of relevance set up in the "world" proposed by the narrative), so that the ending of the viewing or reading experience coincides, ideally, with full satisfaction of one's desire to know, to understand what happened and why. (This is, of course, a highly manipulated quest for knowledge. The business of the artist is to convince his audience that what they haven't learned at the end they *can't* know, or shouldn't *care* about knowing.) In contrast, one of the salient features of new narratives is a deliberate, calculated frustration of the desire to know. Did anything happen last year at Marienbad? What did become of the girl in *L'Avventura?* Where is Alma going when she boards a bus alone toward the close of *Persona?*

Once it is conceived that the desire to know may be (in part) systematically thwarted, the old expectations about plotting no longer hold. Such films (or comparable works of prose fiction) can't be expected to supply many of the familiar satisfactions of traditional narrations, such as being "dramatic." At first it may seem that a plot still remains, only it's being related at an oblique, uncomfortable angle, where vision is obscured. Actually, the plot isn't there at all in the old sense; the point of these new works is not to tantalize but to involve the audience more directly in other matters, for instance, in the very processes of knowing and seeing. (An eminent precursor of this concept of narration is Flaubert; the persistent use of off-center detail in the descriptions in *Madame Bovary* is one instance of the method.)

The result of the new narration, then, is a tendency to dedramatize. *Journey to Italy*, for example, tells what is ostensibly a story. But it is a story which proceeds by omissions. The audience is being haunted, as it were, by the sense of a lost or absent meaning to which even the artist himself has no access. The avowal of agnosticism on the artist's part may look like frivolity or contempt for the audience. Antonioni enraged many people by saying that he didn't know himself what happened to the missing girl in *L'Avventura*—whether she had, for instance, committed suicide or run away. But this attitude should be taken with the utmost seriousness. When the artist declares that he "knows" no more than the audience does, he is saying that all the meaning resides in the work itself, that there is nothing "behind" it. Such works seem to lack sense or meaning only to the extent that entrenched critical attitudes have established as a dictum for the narrative arts (cinema as well as prose literature) that meaning resides solely in this surplus of "reference" outside the work—to the "real world" or to the artist's "intention." But this is, at best, an arbitrary ruling. The meaning of a narration is not identical with a paraphrase of the values associated by an ideal audience with the "real-life" equivalents or sources of the plot elements, or with the attitudes projected by the artist toward these elements. Neither is meaning (whether in films, fiction, or theatre) a function of a determinate plot. Other kinds of narration are possible besides those based on a story, in which the fundamental problem is the treatment of the plot line and the construction of characters. For instance, the material can be treated as a *thematic resource,* one from which different (and perhaps concurrent) narrative structures are derived as variations. But inevitably, the formal mandates of such a construction must differ from those of a story (or even a set of parallel stories). The difference will probably appear most striking in the treatment of time.

A story involves the audience in what happens, how a situation comes out. Movement is decisively linear, whatever the meanderings and digressions. One moves from A to B, then to look forward to C, even as C (if the affair is satisfactorily managed) points one's interest in the direction of D. Each link in the chain is, so to speak, self-abolishing—once it has served its turn. In contrast, the development of a theme-and-variation narrative is much less linear. The linear movement can't be altogether suppressed, since the experience of the work remains an event in time (the time of viewing or reading). But this forward movement can be sharply qualified by a competing retrograde principle, which could take the form, say, of continual backward- and cross-references. Such a work would invite reexperiencing, multiple viewing. It would ask the spectator or reader ideally to position himself simultaneously at several different points in the narrative.

Such a demand, characteristic of theme-and-variation narratives, obviates the necessity of establishing a conventional chronological scheme. Instead, time may appear in the guise of a perpetual present; or events may form a conundrum which makes it impossible to distinguish exactly between past, present, and future. *Marienbad* and Robbe-Grillet's *L'Immortelle* are stringent examples of the latter procedure. In *Persona*, Bergman uses a mixed approach. While the treatment of time sequence in the body of the film seems roughly realistic or chronological, at the beginning and close of the film distinctions of "before" and "after" are drastically bleached out, almost indecipherable.

In my own view, the construction of *Persona* is best described in terms of this variations-on-a-theme form. The theme is that of *doubling;* the variations are those that follow from the leading possibilities of that theme (on both a formal and a psychological level) such as duplication, inversion, reciprocal exchange, unity and fission, and repetition. The action cannot be univocally paraphrased. It's correct to speak of *Persona* in terms of the fortunes of two characters named Elizabeth and Alma who are engaged in a desperate duel of identities. But it is equally pertinent to treat *Persona* as relating the duel between two mythical parts of a single self: the corrupted person who acts (Elizabeth) and the ingenuous soul (Alma) who founders in contact with corruption.

A sub-theme of doubling is the contrast between hiding and showing forth. The Latin word *persona*, from which the English "person" derives, means the mask worn by an actor. To be a person, then, is to possess a mask; and in *Persona*, both women wear masks. Elizabeth's mask is her muteness. Alma's mask is her health, her optimism, her normal life (she is engaged; she likes and is good at her work, etc.) But in the course of the film, both masks crack.

To summarize this drama by saying that the violence that the actress has done to herself is transferred to Alma is too simple. Violence and the sense of horror and impotence are, more truly, the residual experiences of consciousness subjected to an ordeal. By not just telling a "story" about the psychic ordeal of two women, Bergman is using that ordeal as a constituent element of his main theme. And that theme of doubling appears to be no less a formal idea than a psychological one. As I have already stressed, Bergman has withheld enough information about the story of the two women to make it impossible to determine clearly the main outlines, much less all, of what passes between them. Further, he has introduced a number of reflections about the nature of representation (the status of the image, of the word, of action, of the film medium itself). *Persona* is not just a representation of transactions between the two characters, Alma and Elizabeth, but a meditation on the film which is "about" them.

The most explicit parts of this meditation are the opening and closing sequences, in which Bergman tries to create the film as an object: a finite object, a made object, a fragile, perishable object, and therefore something existing in space as well as time.

Persona begins with darkness. Then two points of light gradually gain in brightness, until we see that they're the two carbons of the arc lamp; after this, a portion of the leader flashes by. Then follows a suite of rapid images, some barely identifiable—a chase scene from a slapstick silent film; an erect penis; a nail being hammered into the palm of a hand; a view from the rear of a stage of a heavily made-up actress declaiming to the footlights and darkness beyond (we see this image soon again and know that it's Elizabeth playing her last role, that of Electra); the self-immolation of a Buddhist monk in South Vietnam; assorted dead bodies in a morgue. All these images go by very rapidly, mostly too fast to see; but gradually they slow down, as if consenting to adjust to the duration in which the viewer can comfortably perceive. Then follow the final set of images—run off at normal speed. We see a thin, unhealthy-looking boy around eleven lying prone under a sheet on a hospital cot against the wall of a bare room; the viewer at first is bound to associate to the corpses just shown. But the boy stirs, awkwardly kicks off the sheet, turns on his stomach, puts on a pair of large round glasses, takes out a book, and begins to read. Then we see before him an indecipherable blur, very faint, but on its way to becoming an image, the larger-than-life but never very distinct face of a beautiful woman. Slowly, tentatively, as in a trance, the boy reaches up and begins to caress the image. (The surface he touches suggests a movie screen, but also a portrait and a mirror.)

Who is that boy? Most people have assumed he is Elizabeth's son, because we learn later that she does have a son (whose snapshot she tears up when her husband sends it to her in the hospital) and because they think the face on the screen is the actress's face. Actually, it isn't. Not only is the image far from clear (this is obviously deliberate) but Bergman modulates the image back and forth between Elizabeth's face and Alma's. If only for this reason, it seems facile to assign the boy a literal identity. Rather, I think, his identity is something we shouldn't expect to know.

In any case, the boy is not seen again until the close of the film when more briefly, after the action is finished, there is a complementary montage of fragmented images, ending with the child again reaching caressingly toward the huge blurry blow-up of a woman's face. Then Bergman cuts to the shot of the incandescent arc lamp, showing the reverse of the phenomenon which opens the film. The carbons begin to fade; slowly the light goes out. The film dies, as it were, before our eyes. It dies as an object or a thing does, declaring itself to be used up, and thereby virtually independent of the volition of the maker.

Any account which leaves out or dismisses as incidental how *Persona* begins and ends hasn't been talking about the film that Bergman made. Far from being extraneous or pretentious, as many reviewers found it, the so-called frame of *Persona* is, it seems to me, a central statement of the motif of aesthetic self-reflexiveness that runs through the entire film. The element of self-reflexiveness in *Persona* is anything but an arbitrary concern, one superadded to the dramatic action. For one thing, it is the most explicit statement on the formal level of the theme of doubling or duplication present on a psychological level in the transactions between Alma and Elizabeth. The formal "doublings" in *Persona* are the largest extension of the theme of doubling which furnishes the material of the film.

Perhaps the most striking single episode, in which the formal and psychological resonances of the double theme are played out most starkly, is Alma's long description of Elizabeth's maternity and her relation to her son. This monologue is repeated twice in its entirety, the first time showing Elizabeth as she listens, the second time showing Alma as she speaks. The sequence ends spectacularly, with the close-up of a double or composite face, half Elizabeth's and half Alma's.

Here Bergman is pointing up the paradoxical promise of film—namely, that it always gives the illusion of a voyeuristic access to an untampered reality, a neutral view of things as they are. What is filmed is always, in some sense, a "document." But what contemporary film-makers more and more often show is the process of seeing itself, giving grounds or evidence for several different ways of seeing the same thing, which the viewer may entertain concurrently or successively.

Bergman's use of this idea in *Persona* is strikingly original, but the larger intention is a familiar one. In the ways that Bergman made his film self-reflexive, self-regarding, ultimately self-engorging, we should recognize not a private whim but the expression of a well-established tendency. For it is precisely the energy for this sort of "formalist" concern with the nature and paradoxes of the medium itself which was unleashed when the nineteenth-century formal structures of plot and characters (with their presumption of a much less complex reality than that envisaged by the contemporary consciousness) were demoted. What is commonly patronized as an overexquisite self-consciousness in contemporary art, leading to a species of auto-cannibalism, can be seen—less pejoratively—as the liberation of new energies of thought and sensibility.

This, for me, is the promise behind the familiar thesis that locates the difference between traditional and new cinema in the altered status of the camera. In the aesthetic of traditional films, the camera tried to remain unperceived, to efface itself before the spectacle it was rendering. In contrast, what counts as new cinema can be recognized, as Pasolini has remarked, by the "felt presence of the camera." (Needless to say, new cinema doesn't mean just cinema of this last decade. To cite only two predecessors, recall Vertov's *The Man with the*

Camera [1929], with its Pirandellian playfulness with the contrast between film as a physical object and film as the live image, and Benjamin Christensen's *Häxan* [1921], with its leap back and forth between fiction and journalistic documentary.) But Bergman goes beyond Pasolini's criterion, inserting into the viewer's consciousness the felt present of the film as an object. This happens not only at the beginning and end but in the middle of *Persona*, when the image—a shot of Alma's horrified face—cracks, like a mirror, then burns. When the next scene begins immediately afterward (as if nothing had happened), the viewer has not only an almost indelible after-image of Alma's anguish but a sense of added shock, a formal-magical apprehension of the film, as if it had collapsed under the weight of registering such drastic suffering and then had been, as it were, magically reconstituted.

Bergman's intention, in the beginning and end of *Persona* and in this terrifying caesura in the middle, is quite different from—indeed, it is the romantic opposite of—Brecht's intention of alienating the audience by supplying continual reminders that what they are watching is theatre. Bergman seems only marginally concerned with the thought that it might be salutary for audiences to be reminded that they are watching a film (an artifact, something made), not reality. Rather, he is making a statement about the complexity of what can be represented, an assertion that the deep, unflinching knowledge of anything will in the end prove destructive. A character in Bergman's films who perceives something intensely eventually consumes what he knows, uses it up, is forced to move on to other things.

This principle of intensity at the root of Bergman's sensibility determines the specific ways in which he uses new narrative forms. Anything like the vivacity of Godard, the intellectual innocence of *Jules and Jim*, the lyricism of Bertolucci's *Before the Revolution* and Skolimowski's *Le Départ* are outside his range. Bergman's work is characterized by slowness, deliberateness of pacing—something like the heaviness of Flaubert. Hence, the excruciatingly unmodulated quality of *Persona* (and of *The Silence* before it), a quality only very superficially described as pessimism. It is not that Bergman is pessimistic about life and the human situation—as if it were a question of certain opinions—but rather that the quality of his sensibility, when he is faithful to it, has only a single subject: the depths in which consciousness drowns. If the maintenance of personality requires safeguarding the integrity of masks, and the truth about a person always means his unmasking, cracking the mask, then the truth about life as a whole is the shattering of the whole façade—behind which lies an absolute cruelty.

It is here, I think, that one must locate the ostensibly political allusions in *Persona*. Bergman's references to Vietnam and the Six Million are quite different from the references to the Algerian War, Vietnam, China in the films of Godard. Unlike Godard, Bergman is not a topical or historically oriented filmmaker. Elizabeth watching a newsreel on TV of a bonze in Saigon immolating himself, or staring at the famous photograph of a little boy from the Warsaw Ghetto being led off to be slaughtered, are, for Bergman, above all, images of total violence, of unredeemed cruelty. They occur in *Persona* as images of what cannot be imaginatively encompassed or digested, rather than as occasions for right political and moral thoughts. In their function, these images don't differ from the earlier flashbacks of a palm into which a nail is being hammered or of the anonymous bodies in a morgue. History or politics enters *Persona* only in the form of pure violence. Bergman makes an "aesthetic" use of violence—far from ordinary left-liberal propaganda.

The subject of *Persona* is the violence of the spirit. If the two women violate each other, each can be said to have at least as profoundly violated herself. In the final parallel to this theme, the film itself seems to be violated—to emerge out of and descend back into the chaos of "cinema" and film-as-object.

Bergman's film, profoundly upsetting, at moments terrifying, relates the horror of the dissolution of personality: Alma crying out to Elizabeth at one point, "I'm not you!" And it depicts the complementary horror of the theft (whether voluntary or involuntary is left unclear) of personality, which mythically is rendered as vampirism: we see Elizabeth kissing Alma's neck; at one point, Alma sucks Elizabeth's blood. Of course, the theme of the vampiristic exchanges of personal substance needn't be treated as a horror story. Think of the very different emotional range of this material in Henry James' *The Sacred Fount*. The most obvious difference between James' treatment and Bergman's is in the degree of felt suffering that is represented. For all their undeniably disagreeable aura, the vampiristic exchanges between the characters in James' late novel are represented as partly voluntary and, in some obscure way, just. Bergman rigorously excludes the realm of justice (in which characters get what they "deserve"). The spectator is not furnished, from some reliable outside point of view, with any idea of the true moral standing of Elizabeth and Alma; their enmeshment is a given, not the result of some prior situation we are allowed to understand; the mood is one of desperation, in which all attributions of voluntariness seem superficial. All we are given is a set of compulsions or gravitations, in which the two women founder, exchanging "strength" and "weakness."

But perhaps the main difference between Bergman's and James' treatment of this theme derives from their contrasting position with respect to language. As long as discourse continues in the James novel, the texture of the person continues. The continuity of language constitutes a bridge over the abyss of the loss of personality, the foundering of the personality in absolute despair. But in *Persona*, it is precisely language—its continuity—which is put in question. (Bergman is the more modern artist, and cinema is the natural home of those who suspect language, a ready vehicle for the vast weight of suspicion lodged in the contemporary sensibility against "the word." As the purification of language has become the particular task of modernist poetry and of prose writers like Stein, Beckett, and Robbe-Grillet, much of the new cinema has become a vehicle for those wishing to demonstrate the futility and duplicities of language.) The theme had already appeared in *The Silence,* with the incomprehensible language into which the translator sister descends, unable to communicate with the old porter who attends her when at the end of the film she lies dying in the empty hotel in the imaginary garrison city. But Bergman does not take the theme beyond the fairly banal range of the "failure of communication" of the soul isolated in pain, and the "silence" of abandonment and death. In *Persona,* the theme of the burden and the failure of language is developed in a much more complex way.

Persona takes the form of a virtual monologue. Besides Alma, there are only two other speaking characters: the psychiatrist and Elizabeth's husband; they appear very briefly. For most of the film we are with the two women, in isolation at the beach—and only one of them, Alma, is talking, talking shyly but incessantly. Since the actress has renounced speech as some sort of contaminating activity, the nurse has moved in to demonstrate the harmlessness and utility of speech. Though the verbalization of the world in which Alma is engaged always has something uncanny about it, it is at the beginning a wholly generous act, conceived for the benefit of her patient. But this soon changes. The actress's silence becomes a provocation, a temptation, a trap. What Bergman unfolds is a situation reminiscent of Strindberg's one-act play *The Stronger,* a duel between two people, one of whom is aggressively silent. And, as in the Strindberg play, the one who talks, who spills her soul, turns out to be weaker than the one who keeps silent. For the quality of that silence alters continually, becoming more and more potent: the mute woman keeps changing.

Each of Alma's gestures—of trustful affection, of envy, of hostility—is voided by Elizabeth's relentless silence. Alma is also betrayed by speech itself. Language is presented as an instrument of fraud and cruelty (the glaring sounds of the newscast; Elizabeth's painful letter to the psychiatrist, which Alma reads); as an instrument of unmasking (the psychiatrist's explanation of why Elizabeth has "chosen" silence; Alma's excoriating portrait of the secrets of Elizabeth's motherhood); as an instrument of self-revelation (Alma's confessional narrative of the impromptu beach orgy); and as art and artifice (the lines of Electra Elizabeth is delivering on stage when she suddenly goes silent; the radio drama Alma switches on in Elizabeth's hospital room that makes the actress smile). *Persona* demonstrates the lack of an appropriate language, a language that is genuinely full. All that remains is a language of lacunae, appropriate to a narrative strung along a set of gaps in the "explanation." In *Persona* these absences of utterance become more potent than words: the person who places uncritical faith in words is brought down from relative composure and self-confidence to hysterical anguish.

Here, indeed, is the most powerful instance of the motif of exchange. The actress creates a void by her silence. The nurse, by speaking, falls into it—depleting herself. Sickened at the vertigo opened up by the absence of language, Alma at one point begs Elizabeth just to repeat nonsense words and phrases that she hurls at her. But during all the time at the shore, despite every kind of tact, cajoling, and finally frantic pleading by Alma, Elizabeth refuses (obstinately? cruelly? helplessly?) to speak. She has only two lapses. Once when Alma, in a fury, threatens her with a pot of scalding water, the terrified Elizabeth backs against the wall and screams, "No, don't hurt me!" For the moment Alma is triumphant; having made her point, she puts down the pot. But Elizabeth becomes entirely silent again, until late in the film—here, the time sequence is indeterminate—in a brief sequence in the bare hospital room, which shows Alma bending over Elizabeth's bed, begging the actress to say one word. Impassively, Elizabeth complies. The word is "Nothing."

Bergman's treatment of the theme of language in *Persona* also suggests a comparison with films of Godard, particularly *Deux ou Trois Choses* (the café scene). Another example is the recent short film, *Anticipation,* a story of anti-utopia, set in a future world extrapolated from our own which is ruled by the system of "spécialisation intégrale"; in this world there are two kinds of prostitutes, one representing physical love ("gestes sans paroles") and the other representing sentimental love ("paroles sans gestes"). Compared with Bergman's narrative context, the mode of science-fiction fantasy in which Godard has cast his theme permits him both a greater abstraction and the possibility of a resolution of the problem (the divorce between language and love, mind and body) posed so abstractly, so "aesthetically," in the film. At the end of *Anticipation,* the talking prostitute learns to make love and the interplanetary traveler's broken speech is mended; and the fourfold bleached-out color streams merge into full color. The mode of *Persona* is more complex, and far less abstract. There is no happy ending. At the close of the film, mask and person, speech and silence, actor and "soul" remain divided—however parasitically, even vampiristically, they are shown to be intertwined.

(1967)

Godard

"It may be true that one has to choose between ethics and
aesthetics, but it is no less true that whichever one chooses, one will
always find the other at the end of the road. For the very definition of
the human condition should be in the mise-en-scène itself."

Godard's work has been more passionately debated in recent
years than that of any other contemporary film-maker. Though
he has a good claim to being ranked as the greatest director,
aside from Bresson, working actively in the cinema today, it's
still common for intelligent people to be irritated and frustrated by his films, even to find them unbearable. Godard's
films haven't yet been elevated to the status of classics or
masterpieces—as have the best of Eisenstein, Griffith, Gance,
Dreyer, Lang, Pabst, Renoir, Vigo, Welles, etc.; or, to take
some nearer examples, *L'Avventura* and *Jules and Jim*. That is,
his films aren't yet embalmed, immortal, unequivocally (and
merely) "beautiful." They retain their youthful power to
offend, to appear "ugly," irresponsible, frivolous, pretentious,

empty. Film-makers and audiences are still learning from Godard's films, still quarreling with them.

Meanwhile Godard (partly by turning out a new film every few months) manages to keep nimbly ahead of the inexorable thrust of cultural canonization; extending old problems and abandoning or complicating old solutions—offending veteran admirers in numbers almost equal to the new ones he acquires. His thirteenth feature, *Deux ou Trois Choses que je sais d'elle* (1966), is perhaps the most austere and difficult of all his films. His fourteenth feature, *La Chinoise* (1967), opened in Paris last summer and took the first Special Jury Prize at the Venice Film Festival in September; but Godard didn't come from Paris to accept it (his first major film festival award) because he had just begun shooting his next film, *Weekend*, which was playing in Paris by January of this year.

To date, fifteen feature films have been completed and re-leased, the first being the famous *A Bout de Souffle* (*Breath-less*) in 1959. The succeeding films, in order, are:

> *Le Petit Soldat* (1960)
> *Une Femme est une Femme* (*A Woman Is a Woman*) (1961)
> *Vivre sa Vie* (*My Life to Live*) (1962)
> *Les Carabiniers* (1963)
> *Le Mépris* (*Contempt*) (1963)
> *Bande à Part* (*Band of Outsiders*) (1964)
> *Une Femme Mariée* (*A Married Woman*) (1964)
> *Alphaville* (1965)
> *Pierrot le Fou* (1965)
> *Masculin Féminin* (1966)
> *Made in U.S.A.* (1966)

plus the last three I have already mentioned. In addition, five shorts were made between 1954 and 1958, the most interesting of these being the two from 1958, "Charlotte et son Jules" and "Une Histoire d'Eau." There are also seven "sketches": the first, "La Paresse," was one of the episodes in *Les Septs Pechés Capitaux* (1961); the most recent three were all made in

1967—"Anticipation," in *Le Plus Vieux Métier du Monde;* a section of *Far From Vietnam,* the corporate film edited by Chris Marker; and an episode in the still unreleased, Italian-produced *Gospel 70.* Considering that Godard was born in 1930, and that he has made all his films within the commercial cinema industry, it's an astonishingly large body of work. Unfortunately, many of the films have not been seen at all in the United States (among the major gaps, *Pierrot le Fou* and *Deux ou Trois Choses*) or have never been released for art-house distribution (like *Le Petit Soldat* and *Les Carabiniers*) or have been granted no more than a brief, token run in New York City only. Though, of course, not all the films are equally fine, these lacunae matter. Godard's work—unlike that of most film directors, whose artistic development is much less personal and experimental—deserves, ultimately demands, to be seen in its entirety. One of the most modern aspects of Godard's artistry is that each of his films derives its final value from its place in a larger enterprise, a life work. Each film is, in some sense, a fragment—which, because of the stylistic continuities of Godard's work, sheds light on the others.

Indeed, practically no other director, with the exception of Bresson, can match Godard's record of making *only* films that are unmistakably and uncompromisingly their author's. (Contrast Godard on this score with two of his most gifted contemporaries: Resnais, who, after making the sublime *Muriel,* was able to descend to *La Guerre est Finie,* and Truffaut, who could follow *Jules and Jim* with *La Peau Douce*—for each director, only his fourth feature.) That Godard is indisputably the most influential director of his generation surely owes much to his having demonstrated himself incapable of adulterating his own sensibility, while still remaining manifestly unpredictable. One goes to a new film by Bresson fairly confident of being treated to another masterpiece. One goes to the latest Godard prepared to see something both achieved and chaotic, "work in progress" which resists easy admiration. The qualities that make Godard, unlike Bresson, a culture hero (as well as, like Bresson, one of the major artists of the age) are precisely his prodigal energies, his evident risk-taking, the quirky individualism of his mastery of a corporate, drastically commercialized art.

But Godard is not merely an intelligent iconoclast. He is a deliberate "destroyer" of cinema—hardly the first cinema has known, but certainly the most persistent and prolific and timely. His approach to established rules of film technique like the unobtrusive cut, consistency of point of view, and clear story line is comparable to Schoenberg's repudiation of the tonal language prevailing in music around 1910 when he entered his atonal period or to the challenge of the Cubists to such hallowed rules of painting as realistic figuration and three-dimensional pictorial space.

The great culture heroes of our time have shared two qualities: they have all been ascetics in some exemplary way, and also great destroyers. But this common profile has permitted two different, yet equally compelling attitudes toward "culture" itself. Some—like Duchamp, Wittgenstein, and Cage—bracket their art and thought with a disdainful attitude toward high culture and the past, or at least maintain an ironic posture of ignorance or incomprehension. Others—like Joyce, Picasso, Stravinsky, and Godard—exhibit a hypertrophy of appetite for culture (though often more avid for cultural debris than for museum-consecrated achievements); they proceed by voraciously scavenging in culture, proclaiming that nothing is alien to their art.

From cultural appetite on this scale comes the creation of work that is on the order of a subjective compendium: casually encyclopedic, anthologizing, formally and thematically eclectic, and marked by a rapid turnover of styles and forms. Thus, one of the most striking features of Godard's work is its daring efforts at hybridization. Godard's insouciant mixtures of tonalities, themes, and narrative methods suggest something like the union of Brecht and Robbe-Grillet, Gene Kelly and Francis Ponge, Gertrude Stein and David Riesman, Orwell and Robert Rauschenberg, Boulez and Raymond Chandler, Hegel and rock 'n' roll. Techniques from literature, theatre, painting, and television mingle freely in his work, alongside witty, impertinent allusions to movie history itself. The elements often seem contradictory—as when (in the recent films) what Richard Roud calls "a fragmentation/collage method of narration"* drawn from advanced painting and poetry is combined with the bare, hard-staring, neo-realist aesthetic of television (cf. the interviews, filmed in frontal close-up and medium shot, in *A Married Woman, Masculine Feminine,* and *Deux ou Trois Choses*); or when Godard uses highly stylized visual compositions (such as the recurrent blues and reds in *A Woman Is a Woman, Contempt, Pierrot le Fou, La Chinoise,* and *Weekend*) at the same time that he seems eager to promote the look of improvisation and to conduct an unremitting search for the "natural" manifestations of personality before the truth-exacting eye of the camera. But, however jarring these mergers are in principle, the results Godard gets from them turn out to be something harmonious, plastically and ethically engaging, and emotionally tonic.

The consciously reflective—more precisely, reflexive—aspect of Godard's films is the key to their energies. His work constitutes a formidable meditation on the *possibilities* of cinema, which is to restate what I have already argued, that he enters the history of film as its first consciously destructive figure. Put otherwise, one might note that Godard is probably the first major director to enter the cinema on the level of commercial production with an explicitly critical intention. "I'm still as much of a critic as I ever was during the time of *Cahiers du Cinéma*," he has declared. (Godard wrote regularly for that magazine between 1956 and 1959, and still occasionally contributes to it.) "The only difference is that instead of writing criticism, I now film it." Elsewhere, he describes *Le Petit*

---

* In his excellent book *Godard* (New York: Doubleday and Co., 1968), the first full-length study of Godard in English.

Soldat as an "auto-critique," and that word, too, applies to all of Godard's films.

But the extent to which Godard's films speak in the first person, and contain elaborate and often humorous reflections on the cinema as a means, is not a private whim but one elaboration of a well-established tendency of the arts to become more self-conscious, more self-referring. Like every important body of work in the canon of modern culture, Godard's films are simply what they are and also events that push their audience to reconsider the meaning and scope of the art form of which they are instances; they're not only works of art, but meta-artistic activities aimed at reorganizing the audience's entire sensibility. Far from deploring the tendency, I believe that the most promising future of films as an art lies in this direction. But the manner in which films continue into the end of the twentieth century as a serious art, becoming more self-regarding and critical, still permits a great deal of variation. Godard's method is far removed from the solemn, exquisitely conscious, self-annihilating structures of Bergman's great film *Persona*. Godard's procedures are much more lighthearted, playful, often witty, sometimes flippant, sometimes just silly. Like any gifted polemicist (which Bergman is not), Godard has the courage to simplify himself. This simplistic quality in much of Godard's work is as much a kind of generosity toward his audience as an aggression against them; and, partly, just the overflow of an inexhaustibly vivacious sensibility.

The attitude that Godard brings to the film medium is often called, disparagingly, "literary." What's usually meant by this charge, as when Satie was accused of composing literary music or Magritte of making literary painting, is a preoccupation with ideas, with conceptualization, at the expense of the sensual integrity and emotional force of the work—more generally, the habit (a kind of bad taste, it's supposed) of violating the essential unity of a given art form by introducing alien elements into it. That Godard has boldly addressed the task of

representing or embodying abstract ideas as no other film-
maker has done before him is undeniable. Several films even
include guest intellectual appearances: a fictional character
falls in with a real philosopher (the heroine of *My Life to Live*
interrogates Brice Parain in a café about language and sincerity; in *La Chinoise*, the Maoist girl disputes with Francis
Jeanson on a train about the ethics of terrorism); a critic and
film-maker delivers a speculative soliloquy (Roger Leenhardt
on intelligence, ardent and compromising, in *A Married
Woman*); a grand old man of film history has a chance to
reinvent his own somewhat tarnished personal image (Fritz
Lang as himself, a chorus figure meditating on German poetry,
Homer, movie-making, and moral integrity, in *Contempt*). On
their own, many of Godard's characters muse aphoristically to
themselves or engage their friends on such topics as the difference between the Right and the Left, the nature of cinema, the
mystery of language, and the spiritual void underlying the
satisfactions of the consumer society. Moreover, Godard's films
are not only idea-ridden, but many of his characters are ostentatiously literate. Indeed, from the numerous references to
books, mentions of writers' names, and quotations and longer
excerpts from literary texts scattered throughout his films,
Godard gives the impression of being engaged in an unending
agon with the very fact of literature—which he attempts to
settle partially by incorporating literature and literary identities into his films. And, apart from his original use of it as a
cinematic object, Godard is concerned with literature both as a
model for film and as the revival and alternative to film. In
interviews and in his own critical writings, the relation between cinema and literature is a recurrent theme. One of the
differences Godard stresses is that literature exists "as art from
the very start" but cinema doesn't. But he also notes a potent
similarity between the two arts: that "we novelists and film-
makers are condemned to an analysis of the world, of the real;
painters and musicians aren't."

By treating cinema as above all an exercise in intelligence,

Godard rules out any neat distinction between "literary" and "visual" (or cinematic) intelligence. If film is, in Godard's laconic definition, the "analysis" of something "with images and sounds," there can be no impropriety in making literature a subject for cinematic analysis. Alien to movies as this kind of material may seem, at least in such profusion, Godard would no doubt argue that books and other vehicles of cultural consciousness are part of the world; therefore they belong in films. Indeed, by putting on the same plane the fact that people read and think and go seriously to the movies and the fact that they cry and run and make love, Godard has disclosed a new vein of lyricism and pathos for cinema: in bookishness, in genuine cultural passion, in intellectual callowness, in the misery of someone strangling in his own thoughts. (An instance of Godard's original way with a more familiar subject, the poetry of loutish illiteracy, is the twelve-minute sequence in *Les Carabiniers* in which the soldiers unpack their picture-postcard trophies.) His point is that no material is inherently unassimilable. But what's required is that literature indeed undergo its transformation into material, just like anything else. All that can be given are literary extracts, shards of literature. In order to be absorbed by cinema, literature must be dismantled or broken into wayward units; then Godard can appropriate a portion of the intellectual "content" of any book (fiction or non-fiction), borrow from the public domain of culture any contrasting tone of voice (noble or vulgar), invoke in an instant any diagnosis of contemporary malaise that is thematically relevant to his narrative, no matter how inconsistent it may be with the psychological scope or mental competence of the characters as already established.

Thus, so far as Godard's films are "literary" in some sense, it seems clear that his alliance with literature is based on quite different interests from those which linked earlier experimental film-makers to the advanced writing of their time. If Godard envies literature, it is not so much for the formal innovations carried out in the twentieth century as for the heavy burden of explicit ideation accommodated within prose literary forms. Whatever notions Godard may have gotten from reading Faulkner or Beckett or Mayakovsky for formal inventions in cinema, his introduction of a pronounced literary taste (his own?) into his films serves mainly as a means for assuming a more public voice or elaborating more general statements. While the main tradition of avant-garde film-making has been a "poetic" cinema (films, like those made by the Surrealists in the 1920's and 1930's, inspired by the emancipation of modern poetry from storylike narrative and sequential discourse to the direct presentation and sensuous, polyvalent association of ideas and images), Godard has elaborated a largely anti-poetic cinema, one of whose chief literary models is the prose essay. Godard has even said: "I consider myself an essay writer. I write essays in the form of novels, or novels in the form of essays."

Notice that Godard has here made the novel interchangeable with film—apt in a way, since it is the tradition of the novel that weighs most heavily upon cinema, and the example of what the novel has recently become that spurs Godard.* "I've found an idea for a novel," mumbles the hero of *Pierrot le Fou* at one point, in partial self-mockery assuming the quavering voice of Michel Simon. "Not to write the life of a man, but only life, life itself. What there is between people, space . . . sound and colors. . . . There must be a way of achieving that; Joyce tried, but one must, must be able . . . to do better." Surely, Godard is here speaking for himself as a

---

* Speaking historically, it would seem that modern literature has been much more heavily influenced by cinema than vice versa. But the matter of influence is complex. For example, the Czech director Vera Chytilova has said that her model for the diptych form of her brilliant first feature, *Something Else,* was the alternating narratives of *The Wild Palms;* but then a good case could be made out for the powerful influence of cinematic techniques upon Faulkner's mature methods of narrative construction. And Godard at one point, inspired by the same Faulkner book, wanted to have the two films he shot in the summer of 1966, *Made in U.S.A.* and *Deux ou Trois Choses,* projected together, with a reel of one alternating with a reel of the other.

film-maker, and he appears confident that film can accomplish
what literature cannot, literature's incapacity being partly due
to the less favorable *critical* situation into which each important literary work is deposited. I have spoken of Godard's
work as consciously destructive of old cinematic conventions.
But this task of demolition is executed with the élan of someone working in an art form experienced as young, on the
threshhold of its greatest development rather than at its end.
Godard views the destruction of old rules as a constructive
effort—in contrast to the received view of the current destiny
of literature. As he has written, "literary critics often praise
works like *Ulysses* or *Endgame* because they exhaust a certain
genre, they close the doors on it. But in the cinema we are
always praising works which *open* doors."

The relation to models offered by literature illuminates a
major part of the history of cinema. Film, both protected and
patronized by virtue of its dual status as mass entertainment
and as art form, remains the last bastion of the values of the
nineteenth-century novel and theatre—even to many of the
same people who have found accessible and pleasurable such
post-novels as *Ulysses, Between the Acts, The Unnameable,
Naked Lunch,* and *Pale Fire,* and the corrosively de-drama-
tized dramas of Beckett, Pinter, and the Happenings. Hence,
the standard criticism leveled against Godard is that his plots
are undramatic, arbitrary, often simply incoherent; and that
his films generally are emotionally cold, static except for a
busy surface of senseless movements, top-heavy with undram-
atized ideas, unnecessarily obscure. What his detractors
don't grasp, of course, is that Godard doesn't want to do what
they reproach him for not doing. Thus, audiences at first took
the jump cuts in *Breathless* to be a sign of amateurishness, or a
perverse flouting of self-evident rules of cinematic technique;
actually, what looks as though the camera had stopped inadvertently for a few seconds in the course of a shot and then
started up again was an effect Godard deliberately obtained in

the cutting room, by snipping pieces out of perfectly smooth takes. (If one sees *Breathless* today, however, the once obtrusive cutting and the oddities of the hand-held camera are almost invisible, so widely imitated are these techniques now.) No less deliberate is Godard's disregard for the formal conventions of film narration based on the nineteenth-century novel— cause-and-effect sequences of events, climactic scenes, logical denouements. At the Cannes Film Festival several years ago, Godard entered into debate with Georges Franju, one of France's most talented and idiosyncratic senior film-makers. "But surely, Monsieur Godard," the exasperated Franju is reported to have said, "you do at least acknowledge the necessity of having a beginning, middle, and end in your films." "Certainly," Godard replied. "But not necessarily in that order."

Godard's insouciance seems to me quite justified. For what is truly surprising is that film directors have not for some time, by exploiting the fact that whatever is "shown" (and heard) in the film experience is unremittingly *present,* made themselves more independent of what are essentially novelistic notions of narrative. But, as I have indicated, until now the only well-understood alternative has been to break completely with the formal structures of prose fiction, to dispense altogether with "story" and "characters." This alternative, practiced entirely outside the commercial cinema industries, resulted in the "abstract" film or the "poetic" film based on the association of images. In contrast, Godard's method is still a narrative one, though divorced from the literalism and reliance on psychological explanation that most people associate with the serious novel. Because they modify, rather than make a complete rupture with, the conventions of prose fiction underlying the main tradition of cinema, Godard's films strike many as more puzzling than the forthright "poetic" or "abstract" films of the official cinematic avant-garde.

Thus, it is precisely the presence, not the absence, of story in Godard's films that gives rise to the standard criticism of them. Unsatisfactory as his plots may be to many people, it would hardly be correct to describe Godard's films as plot-less—like, say, Djiga Vertov's *The Man with the Camera*, the two silent films of Buñuel (*L'Age d'Or*, *Un Chien Andalou*), or Kenneth Anger's *Scorpio Rising*, films in which a story line has been completely discarded as the narrative framework. Like all ordinary feature films, Godard's films show an inter-related group of fictional characters located in a recognizable, consistent environment: in his case, usually contemporary and urban (Paris). But while the sequence of events in a Godard film suggests a fully articulated story, it doesn't add up to one; the audience is presented with a narrative line that is partly erased or effaced (the structural equivalent of the jump cut). Disregarding the traditional novelist's rule of explaining things as fully as they seem in need of explanation, Godard provides simplistic motives or frequently just leaves the motives un-explained; actions are often opaque, and fail to issue into con-sequences; occasionally the dialogue itself is not entirely audi-ble. (There are other films, like Rossellini's *Journey to Italy* and Resnais' *Muriel*, that employ a comparably "unrealistic" system of narration in which the story is decomposed into disjunct objectified elements; but Godard, the only director with a whole body of work along these lines, has suggested more of the diverse routes for "abstracting" from an ostensibly realistic narrative than any other director. It is important, too, to distinguish various structures of abstracting—as, for in-stance, between the systematically "indeterminate" plot of Bergman's *Persona* and the "intermittent" plots of Godard's films.)

Although Godard's narrative procedures apparently owe less to cinematic models than to literary ones (at least, he never mentions the avant-garde past of cinema in interviews and statements but often mentions as models the work of Joyce, Proust, and Faulkner), he has never attempted, nor does it seem conceivable that he will attempt in the future, a transpo-sition into film of any of the serious works of contemporary post-novelistic fiction. On the contrary, like many directors,

Godard prefers mediocre, even sub-literary material, finding that easier to dominate and transform by the *mise-en-scène*. "I don't really like telling a story," Godard has written, somewhat simplifying the matter. "I prefer to use a kind of tapestry, a background on which I can embroider my own ideas. But I generally do need a story. A conventional one serves as well, perhaps even best." Thus, Godard has ruthlessly described the novel on which his brilliant *Contempt* was based, Moravia's *Ghost at Noon*, as "a nice novel for a train journey, full of old-fashioned sentiments. But it is with this kind of novel that one can make the best films." Although *Contempt* stays close to Moravia's story, Godard's films usually show few traces of their literary origins. (At the other extreme and more typical is *Masculine Feminine*, which bears no recognizable relation to the stories by Maupassant, "La Femme de Paul" and "La Signe," from which Godard drew his original inspiration.)

Whether text or pretext, most of the novels that Godard has chosen as his point of departure are heavily plotted action stories. He has a particular fondness for American kitsch: *Made in U.S.A.* was based on *The Jugger* by Richard Stark, *Pierrot le Fou* on *Obsession* by Lionel White, and *Band of Outsiders* on Dolores Hitchens' *Fool's Gold*. Godard resorts to popular American narrative conventions as a fertile, solid base for his own anti-narrative inclinations. "The Americans know how to tell stories very well; the French not at all. Flaubert and Proust don't know how to narrate; they do something else." Although that something else is plainly what Godard is after too, he has discerned the utility of starting from crude narrative. One allusion to this strategy is the memorable dedication of *Breathless:* "To Monogram Pictures." (In its original version, *Breathless* had no credit titles whatever, and the first image of the film was preceded only by this terse salute to Hollywood's most prolific purveyors of low-budget, quickie action pictures during the 1940s and early 1950s.) Godard wasn't being impudent or flippant here—or only a little bit. Melodrama is one of the integral resources of his plotting.

Think of the comic-strip quest of *Alphaville*; the gangster-movies romanticism of *Breathless*, *Band of Outsiders*, and *Made in U.S.A.*; the spy-thriller ambiance of *Le Petit Soldat* and *Pierrot le Fou*. Melodrama—which is characterized by the exaggeration, the frontality, the opaqueness of "action"—provides a framework for both intensifying and transcending traditional realistic procedures of serious film narrative, but in a way which isn't necessarily condemned (as the Surrealist films were) to seeming esoteric. By adapting familiar, second-hand, vulgar materials—popular myths of action and sexual glamour—Godard gains a considerable freedom to "abstract" without losing the possibility of a commercial theatre audience.

That such familiar materials do lend themselves to this kind of abstracting treatment—even contain the germ of it—had been amply demonstrated by one of the first great directors, Louis Feuillade, who worked in the debased form of the crime serial (*Fantomas, Les Vampires, Judex, Ti Minh*). Like the sub-literary model from which he drew, these serials (the greatest of which were done between 1913 and 1916) grant little to the standards of verisimilitude. Devoid of any concern for psychology, which was already beginning to make its appearance in films in the work of Griffith and De Mille, the story is populated by largely interchangeable characters and so crammed with incident that it can be followed only in a general way. But these are not the standards by which the films should be judged. What counts in Feuillade's serials is their formal and emotional values, which are produced by a subtle juxtaposition of the realistic and the highly improbable. The realism of the films lies in their look (Feuillade was one of the first European directors to do extensive location shooting); the implausibility comes from the wild nature of the actions inscribed on this physical space and the unnaturally speeded-up rhythms, formal symmetries, and repetitiveness of the action. In the Feuillade films, as in certain early Lang and early Hitchcock films, the director has carried the melodramatic narrative to absurd extremes, so that the action takes on a hallucinatory quality. Of course, this degree of abstraction of realistic material into the logic of fantasy requires a generous use of ellipsis. If time patterns and space patterns and the abstract rhythms of action are to predominate, the action itself must be "obscure." In one sense, such films clearly have stories—of the most direct, action-packed kind. But in another sense, that of the continuity and consistency and ultimate intelligibility of incidents, the story has no importance at all. The loss of the sparse intertitles on some of the Feuillade films which have survived in only a single print seems hardly to matter, just as the formidable impenetrability of the plots of Hawks' *The Big Sleep* and Aldrich's *Kiss Me Deadly* doesn't matter either, indeed seems quite satisfying. Such film narratives attain their emotional and aesthetic weight precisely through this incomprehensibility, as the "obscurity" of certain poets (Mallarmé, Roussel, Stevens, Empson) isn't a deficiency in their work but an important technical means for accumulating and compounding relevant emotions and for establishing different levels and units of "sense." The obscurity of Godard's plots (*Made in U.S.A.* ventures furthest in this direction) is equally functional, part of the program of abstracting his materials.

Yet at the same time, these materials being what they are, Godard retains some of the vivacity of his simplistic literary and film models. Even as he employs the narrative conventions of the Série Noire novels and the Hollywood thrillers, transposing them into abstract elements, Godard has responded to their casual, sensuous energy and has introduced some of that into his own work. One result is that most of his films give the impression of speed, verging sometimes on haste. By comparison, Feuillade's temperament seems more dogged. On a few essentially limited themes (like ingenuity, ruthlessness, physical grace), Feuillade's films present a seemingly inexhaustible number of formal variations. His choice of the open-ended serial form is thus entirely appropriate. After the twenty episodes of *Les Vampires,* nearly seven hours of projection time, it's clear there was no necessary end to the exploits of the stupendous Musidora and her gang of masked bandits, any more than the exquisitely matched struggle between arch-criminal and arch-detective in *Judex* need ever terminate. The rhythm of incident Feuillade establishes is subject to indefinitely prolonged repetition and embellishment, like a sexual fantasy elaborated in secret over a long period of time. Godard's films move to a quite different rhythm; they lack the unity of fantasy, along with its obsessional gravity and its tireless, somewhat mechanistic repetitiveness.

The difference may be accounted for by the fact that the hallucinatory, absurd, abstracted action tale, while a central resource for Godard, doesn't control the form of his films as it did for Feuillade. Although melodrama remains one term of Godard's sensibility, what has increasingly emerged as the opposing term is the resources of fact. The impulsive, dissociated tone of melodrama contrasts with the gravity and controlled indignation of the sociological exposé (note the recurrent theme of prostitution that appears in what is virtually Godard's first film, the short "Une Femme Coquette," which he made in 1955, and continues in *My Life to Live, A Married Woman, Deux ou Trois Choses,* and *Anticipation*) and the even cooler tones of straight documentary and quasi-sociology (in *Masculine Feminine, Deux ou Trois Choses, La Chinoise*).

Though Godard has toyed with the idea of the serial form, as in the end of *Band of Outsiders* (which promises a sequel, never made, relating further adventures of its hero and heroine in Latin America) and in the general conception of *Alphaville* (proposed as the latest adventure of a French serial hero, Lemmy Caution), Godard's films don't relate unequivocally to any single genre. The open-endedness of Godard's films doesn't mean the hyperexploitation of some particular genre, as in Feuillade, but the successive devouring of genres. The countertheme to the restless activity of the characters in

Godard's films is an expressed dissatisfaction with the limits or stereotyping of "actions." Thus, in *Pierrot le Fou*, Marianne's being bored or fed up moves what there is of a plot; at one point, she says directly to the camera: "Let's leave the Jules Verne novel and go back to the *roman policier* with guns and so on." The emotional statement depicted in *A Woman Is a Woman* is summed up in the wish expressed by Belmondo's Alfredo and Anna Karina's Angela to be Gene Kelly and Cyd Charisse in a late 1940's Hollywood musical choreographed by Michael Kidd. Early in *Made in U.S.A.* Paula Nelson comments: "Blood and mystery already. I have the feeling of moving about in a Walt Disney film starring Humphrey Bogart. Therefore it must be a political film." But this remark measures the extent to which *Made in U.S.A.* both is and is not a political film. That Godard's characters occasionally look out of the "action" to locate themselves as actors in a film genre is only partly a piece of nostalgic first-person wit on the part of Godard the film-maker; mainly it's an ironic disavowal of commitment to any one genre or way of regarding an action.

If the organizing principle of Feuillade's films is serial repetitiveness and obsessional elaboration, that of Godard's is the juxtaposition of contrary elements of unpredictable length and explicitness. While Feuillade's work implicitly conceives art as the gratification and prolongation of fantasy, Godard's work implies a quite different function for art: sensory and conceptual dislocation. Each of Godard's films is a totality that undermines itself, a de-totalized totality (to borrow Sartre's phrase).

Instead of a narration unified by the coherence of events (a "plot") and a consistent tone (comic, serious, oneiric, affectless, or whatever), the narrative of Godard's films is regularly broken or segmented by the incoherence of events and by abrupt shifts in tone and level of discourse. Events appear to the spectator partly as converging toward a story, partly as a succession of independent tableaux.

The most obvious way Godard segments the forward-moving sequence of narration into tableaux is by explicitly theatricalizing some of his material, once more laying to rest the lively prejudice that there is an essential incompatibility between the means of theatre and those of film. The conventions of the Hollywood musical, with songs and stage performances interrupting the story, supply one precedent for Godard—inspiring the general conception of *A Woman Is a Woman,* the dance trio in the café in *Band of Outsiders,* the song sequences and Vietnam protest skit performed outdoors in *Pierrot le Fou,* the singing telephone call in *Weekend.* His other model is, of course, the non-realistic and didactic theatre expounded by Brecht. An aspect of Godard Brechtianizing is his distinctive style of constructing political micro-entertainments: in *La Chinoise,* the home political theatre-piece acting out the American aggression in Vietnam; or the Feiffer dialogue of the two ham radio operators that opens *Deux ou Trois Choses.* But the more profound influence of Brecht resides in those formal devices Godard uses to counteract ordinary plot development and complicate the emotional involvement of the audience. One device is the direct-to-camera declarations by the characters in many films, notably *Deux ou Trois Choses, Made in U.S.A.,* and *La Chinoise.* ("One should speak as if one were quoting the truth," says Marina Vlady at the beginning of *Deux ou Trois Choses,* quoting Brecht. "The actors must quote.") Another frequently used technique derived from Brecht is the dissection of the film narrative into short sequences: in *My Life to Live,* in addition, Godard puts on the screen prefatory synopses to each scene which describe the action to follow. The action of *Les Carabiniers* is broken into short brutal sections introduced by long titles, most of which represent cards sent home by Ulysses and Michelangelo; the titles are handwritten, which makes them a little harder to read and brings home to the movie audience the fact that it is being asked to read. Another, simpler device is the relatively arbitrary subdivision of action into numbered sequences, as when the credits of *Masculine Feminine* announce a film consisting of "fifteen precise actions" (*quinze faits précis*). A minimal device is the ironic, pseudo-quantitative statement of something, as in *A Married Woman*, with the brief monologue of Charlotte's little son explaining how to do an unspecified something in exactly ten steps: or in *Pierrot le Fou*, when Ferdinand's voice announces at the beginning of a scene: "Chapter Eight. We cross France." Another example: the very title of one film, *Deux ou Trois Choses*—the lady about whom surely more than two or three things are known being the city of Paris. And, in support of these tropes of the rhetoric of disorientation, Godard practices many specifically sensorial techniques that serve to fragment the cinematic narrative. In fact, most of the familiar elements of Godard's visual and aural stylistics—rapid cutting, the use of unmatched shots, flash shots, the alternation of sunny takes with gray ones, the counterpoint of prefabricated images (signs, paintings, billboards, picture postcards, posters), the discontinuous music—function in this way.

Apart from the general strategy of "theatre," perhaps Godard's most striking application of the dissociative principle is his treatment of ideas. Certainly ideas are not developed in Godard's films systematically, as they might be in a book. They aren't meant to be. In contrast to their role in Brechtian theatre, ideas are chiefly formal elements in Godard's films, units of sensory and emotional stimulation. They function at least as much to dissociate and fragment as they do to indicate or illuminate the "meaning" of the action. Often the ideas, rendered in blocks of words, lie at a tangent to the action. Nana's reflections on sincerity and language in *My Life to Live*, Bruno's observations about truth and action in *Le Petit Soldat*, the articulate self-consciousness of Charlotte in *A Married Woman* and of Juliette in *Deux ou Trois Choses*, Lemmy Caution's startling aptitude for cultivated literary allusions in *Alphaville* are not functions of the realistic psychology of these characters. (Perhaps the only one of Godard's intellectually reflective protagonists who still seems "in character" when ruminating is Ferdinand in *Pierrot le Fou*.) Although Godard proposes film discourse as constantly open to ideas, ideas are only one element in a narrative form which posits an intentionally ambiguous, open, playful relation of *all* the parts to the total scheme.

Godard's fondness for interpolating literary "texts" in the action, which I have already mentioned, is one of the main variants on the presence of ideas in his films. Among the many instances: the Mayakovsky poem recited by the girl about to be executed by a firing squad in *Les Carabiniers;* the excerpt from the Poe story read aloud in the next-to-last episode in *My Life to Live;* the lines from Dante, Hölderlin, and Brecht that Lang quotes in *Contempt;* the oration from Saint-Just by a character dressed as Saint-Just in *Weekend;* the passage from Elie Faure's *History of Art* read aloud by Ferdinand to his young daughter in *Pierrot le Fou;* the lines from *Romeo and Juliet* in French translation dictated by the English teacher in *Band of Outsiders;* the scene from Racine's *Bérénice* rehearsed by Charlotte and her lover in *A Married Woman;* the quote from Fritz Lang read aloud by Camille in *Contempt;* the passages from Mao declaimed by the FLN agent in *Le Petit Soldat;* the antiphonal recitations from the little red book in *La Chinoise*. Usually someone makes an announcement before beginning to declaim, or can be seen taking up a book and reading from it. Sometimes, though, these obvious signals for the advent of a text are lacking—as with the excerpts from *Bouvard and Pecuchet* spoken by two customers in a café in *Deux ou Trois Choses,* or the long extract from *Death on the Installment Plan* delivered by the maid ("Madame Celine") in *A Married Woman*. (Although usually literary, the text may be a film: like the excerpt from Dreyer's *Jeanne d'Arc* that Nana watches in *My Life to Live,* or a minute of film shot by Godard in Sweden, reputed to be a parody of Bergman's *The Silence,* that Paul and the two girls see in *Masculine Feminine*.) These texts introduce psycho-

logically dissonant elements into the action; they supply
rhythmical variety (temporarily slowing down the action);
they interrupt the action and offer ambiguous comment on it;
and they also vary and extend the point of view represented in
the film. The spectator is almost bound to be misled if he
regards these texts simply, either as opinions of characters in
the film or as samples of some unified point of view advocated
by the film which presumably is dear to the director. More
likely, just the opposite is or comes to be the case. Aided by
"ideas" and "texts," Godard's film narratives tend to consume
the points of view presented in them. Even the political ideas
expressed in Godard's work—part Marxist and part anarchist
in one canonical style of the postwar French intelligentsia—
are subject to this rule.

Like the ideas, which function partly as divisive elements,
the fragments of cultural lore embedded in Godard's films
serve in part as a form of mystification and a means for refract-
ing emotional energy. (In *Le Petit Soldat,* for instance, when
Bruno says of Veronica the first time he sees her that she
reminds him of a Giraudoux heroine, and later wonders
whether her eyes are Renoir gray or Velásquez gray, the main
impact of these references is their unverifiability by the audience.) Inevitably, Godard broaches the menace of the bastard-
ization of culture, a theme most broadly stated in *Contempt* in
the figure of the American producer with his booklet of
proverbs. And, laden as his films are with furnishings of high
culture, it's perhaps inevitable that Godard should also invoke
the project of laying down the burden of culture—as Ferdinand does in *Pierrot le Fou* when he abandons his life in Paris
for the romantic journey southward carrying only a book of
old comics. In *Weekend,* Godard posits against the petty
barbarism of the car-owning urban bourgeoisie the possibly
cleansing violence of a rebarbarized youth, imagined as a
hippy-style liberation army roaming the countryside whose
principal delights seem to be contemplation, pillage, jazz, and
cannibalism. The theme of cultural disburdenment is treated

most fully and ironically in *La Chinoise*. One sequence shows the young cultural revolutionaries purging their shelves of all their books but the little red one. Another brief sequence shows just a blackboard at first, filled with the neatly listed names of several dozen stars of Western culture from Plato to Shakespeare to Sartre; these are then erased one by one, thoughtfully, with Brecht the last to go. The five pro-Chinese students who live together want to have only one point of view, that of Chairman Mao; but Godard shows, without insulting anyone's intelligence, how chimerical and inadequate to reality (and yet how appealing) this hope actually is. For all his native radicalism of temperament, Godard himself still appears a partisan of that other cultural revolution, ours, which enjoins the artist-thinker to maintain a multiplicity of points of view on any material.

All the devices Godard employs to keep shifting the point of view within a film can be looked at another way—as adjuncts to a positive strategy, that of overlaying a number of narrative voices, for effectively bridging the difference between first-person and third-person narration. Thus *Alphaville* opens with three samples of first-person discourse: first, a prefatory statement spoken off-camera by Godard, then a declaration by the computer-ruler Alpha 60, and only then the usual soliloquizing voice, that of the secret-agent hero, shown grimly driving his big car into the city of the future. Instead of, or in addition to, using "titles" between scenes as narrative signals (for example: *My Life to Live, A Married Woman*), Godard seems now more to favor installing a narrative voice in the film. This voice may belong to the main character: Bruno's musings in *Le Petit Soldat*, Charlotte's free associating subtext in *A Married Woman*, Paul's commentary in *Masculine Feminine*. It may be the director's, as in *Band of Outsiders* and "Le Grand Escroc," the sketch from *Les Plus Belles Escroqueries du Monde* (1963). What's most interesting is when there are two voices, as in *Deux ou Trois Choses,* throughout which both Godard (whispering) and the heroine comment on the action. *Band of Outsiders* introduces the notion of a narrative intelligence which can "open a parenthesis" in the action and directly address the audience, explaining what Franz, Odile, and Arthur are really feeling at that moment; the narrator can intervene or comment ironically on the action or on the very fact of seeing a movie. (Fifteen minutes into the film, Godard off-camera says, "For the latecomers, what's happened so far is . . .") Thereby two different but concurrent times are established in the film—the time of the action shown, and the time of the narrator's reflection on what's shown—in a way which allows free passage back and forth between the first-person narration and the third-person presentation of the action.

Although the narrating voice already has a major role in some of his earliest work (for instance, the virtuoso comic monologue of the last of the pre-*Breathless* shorts, *Une Histoire d'Eau*), Godard continues to extend and complicate the task of oral narration, arriving at such recent refinements as the beginning of *Deux ou Trois Choses,* when from off-camera he introduces his leading actress, Marina Vlady, by name and then describes her as the character she will play. Such procedures tend, of course, to reinforce the self-reflexive and self-referring aspect of Godard's films, for the ultimate narrative presence is simply the fact of cinema itself; from which it follows that, for the sake of truth, the cinematic medium must be made to manifest itself before the spectator. Godard's methods for doing this range from the frequent ploy of having an actor make rapid playful asides to the camera (i.e., to the audience) in mid-action, to the use of a bad take—Anna Karina fumbles a line, asks if it's all right, then repeats the line—in *A Woman Is a Woman. Les Carabiniers* only gets underway after we hear first some coughing and shuffling and an instruction by someone, perhaps the composer or a sound technician, on the set. In *La Chinoise,* Godard makes the point about its being a movie by, among other devices, flashing the clapper board on the screen from time to time, and by briefly cutting to Raoul Coutard, the cameraman on this as on most of Godard's films, seated behind his apparatus. But then one immediately imagines some underling holding another clapper while that scene was shot, and someone else who had to be there behind another camera to photograph Coutard. It's impossible ever to penetrate behind the final veil and experience cinema unmediated by cinema.

I have argued that one consequence of Godard's disregard for the aesthetic rule of having a fixed point of view is that he dissolves the distinction between first-person and third-person narration. But perhaps it would be more accurate to say that Godard proposes a new conception of point of view, thereby staking out the possibility of making films in the first person. By this, I don't mean simply that his films are subjective or personal; so is the work of many other directors, particularly the cinematic avant-garde and underground. I mean something stricter, which may indicate the originality of his achievement: namely, the way in which Godard, especially in his recent films, has built up a narrative presence, that of the film-maker, who is the central *structural* element in the cinematic narrative. This first-person film-maker isn't an actual character within the film. That is, he is not to be seen on the screen (except in the episode in *Far from Vietnam*, which shows only Godard at a camera talking, intercut with snippets from *La Chinoise*), though he is heard from time to time and one is increasingly aware of his presence just off-camera. But this off-screen persona is not a lucid, authorial intelligence, like the detached observer-figure of many novels cast in the first person. The ultimate first person in Godard's movies, his particular version of the film-maker, is the person responsible for the film who stands outside it as a mind beset by more complex, fluctuating concerns than any single film can represent or incarnate. The most profound drama of a Godard film arises from the clash between this restless, wider consciousness of the director and the determinate, limited argument of the particular film he's engaged in making. Therefore each film is, simultaneously, a creative activity and a destructive one. The director virtually uses up his models, his sources, his ideas, his latest moral and artistic enthusiasms—and the shape of the film consists of various means for letting the audience know that's what is happening. This dialectic has reached its furthest development so far in *Deux ou Trois Choses,* which is more radically a first-person film than any Godard has made.

The advantage of the first-person mode for cinema is presumably that it vastly augments the liberty of the film-maker while at the same time providing incentives for greater formal rigor—the same goals espoused by all the serious post-novelists of this century. Thus Gide has Edouard, the author-protagonist of *The Counterfeiters,* condemn all previous novels because their contours are "defined," so that, however perfect, what they contain is "captive and lifeless." He wanted to write a novel that would "run freely" because he'd chosen "not to foresee its windings." But the liberation of the novel turned out to consist in writing a novel about writing a novel: presenting "literature" within literature. In a different context, Brecht discovered "theatre" within theatre. Godard has discovered "cinema" within cinema. However loose or spontaneous-looking or personally self-expressive his films may appear, what must be appreciated is that Godard subscribes to a severely alienated conception of his art: a cinema that eats cinema. Each film is an ambiguous event that must be simultaneously promulgated and destroyed. Godard's most explicit statement of this theme is the painful monologue of self-interrogation which was his contribution to *Far from Vietnam.* Perhaps his wittiest statement of this theme is a scene in *Les Carabiniers* (similar to the end of an early Mack Sennett two-reeler, *Mabel's Dramatic Career*) in which Michelangelo takes time off from the war to visit a movie theatre, apparently for the first time, since he reacts as audiences did sixty years ago when movies first began to be shown. He follows the movements of the actors on the screen with his whole body, ducks under the seat when a train appears, and at last, driven wild by the sight of a girl taking a bath in the film within a film, bolts from his seat and rushes up to the stage. After first standing on tiptoe to try to look into the tub, then feeling tentatively for the girl along the surface of the screen, he finally tries to grab her—ripping away part of the screen within the screen, and revealing the girl and the bathroom to be a projection on a filthy wall. Cinema, as Godard says in *Le Grand Escroc*, "is the most beautiful fraud in the world."

Though all his distinctive devices serve the fundamental aim of breaking up the narrative or varying the perspective, Godard doesn't aim at a systematic variation of points of view. Sometimes, to be sure, he does elaborate a strong plastic conception—like the intricate visual patterns of the couplings of Charlotte with her lover and her husband in *A Married Woman;* and the brilliant formal metaphor of the monochromatic photography in three "political colors" in *Anticipation*. Still, Godard's work characteristically lacks formal rigor, a quality preeminent in all the work of Bresson and Jean-Marie Straub and in the best films of Welles and Resnais.

The jump cuts in *Breathless*, for instance, are not part of any strict overall rhythmic scheme, an observation that's confirmed by Godard's account of their rationale. "I discovered in *Breathless* that when a discussion between two people became boring and tedious one could just as well cut between the speeches. I tried it once, and it went very well, so I did the same thing right through the film." Godard may be exaggerating the casualness of his attitude in the cutting room, but his reliance upon intuition on the set is well known. For no film has a full shooting script been prepared in advance, and many films have been improvised day by day throughout large parts of the shooting; in the recent films shot with direct sound, Godard has the actors wear tiny earphones so that while they are on camera he can speak to each of them privately, feeding them their lines or posing questions which they're to answer (direct-to-camera interviews). And, though he generally uses professional actors, Godard has been increasingly open to incorporating accidental presences. (Examples: in *Deux ou Trois Choses*, Godard, off camera, interviewing a young girl who worked in the beauty parlor which he'd taken over for a day of filming; Samuel Fuller talking, as himself, to Ferdinand, played by Belmondo, at a party at the beginning of *Pierrot le Fou*, because Fuller, an American director Godard admires, happened to be in Paris at the time and was visiting Godard on the set.) When using direct sound, Godard also generally keeps any natural or casual noises picked up on the soundtrack, even those unrelated to the action. While the results of this permissiveness are not interesting in every case, some of Godard's happiest effects have been last-minute inventions or the result of accident. The church bells tolling when Nana dies in *My Life to Live* just happened to go off, to everyone's surprise, during the shooting. The stunning scene in negative in *Alphaville* turned out that way because at the last moment Coutard told Godard there wasn't enough equipment on the set to light the scene properly (it was night); Godard decided to go ahead anyway. Godard has said that the spectacular ending of *Pierrot le Fou*, Ferdinand's suicide by self-dynamiting, "was invented on the spot, unlike the beginning, which was organized. It's a sort of Happening, but one that was controlled and dominated. Two days before I began I had nothing, absolutely nothing. Oh well, I did have the book. And a certain number of locations." Godard's conviction that it is possible to absorb chance, using it as an additional tool for developing new structures, extends beyond making only minimal preparations for a film and keeping the conditions of shooting flexible to the editing itself. "Sometimes I have shots that were badly filmed, because I lacked time or money," Godard has said. "Putting them together creates a different impression; I don't reject this; on the contrary, I try to do my best to bring out this new idea."

Godard's openness to the aleatoric miracle is supported by his predilection for shooting on location. In his work to date—

features, shorts, and sketches all included—only his third feature, *A Woman Is a Woman*, was shot in a studio; the rest were done in "found" locations. (The small hotel room in which *Charlotte et son Jules* takes place was where Godard was then living; the apartment in *Deux ou Trois Choses* belonged to a friend; and the apartment in *La Chinoise* is where Godard lives now.) Indeed, one of the most brilliant and haunting aspects of Godard's science-fiction fables—the sketch from *RoGoPag* (1962), "Le Nouveau Monde," *Alphaville*, and *Anticipation*—is that they were filmed entirely in unretouched sites and buildings existing around the Paris of the mid-1960's like Orly Airport and the Hotel Scribe and the new Electricity Board building. This, of course, is exactly Godard's point. The fables about the future are at the same time essays about today. The streak of movie-educated fantasy that runs strong through Godard's work is always qualified by the ideal of documentary truth.

From Godard's penchant for improvisation, for incorporating accidents, and for location shooting, one might infer a lineage from the neo-realist aesthetic made famous by Italian films of the last twenty-five years, starting with Visconti's *Ossessione* and *La Terra Trema* and reaching its apogee in the postwar films of Rossellini and the recent debut of Olmi. But Godard, although a fervent admirer of Rossellini, is not even a neo-neo-realist, and hardly aims to expel the artifice from art. What he seeks is to conflate the traditional polarities of spontaneous mobile thinking and finished work, of the casual jotting and the fully premeditated statement. Spontaneity, casualness, lifelikeness are not values in themselves for Godard, who is rather interested in the *convergence* of spontaneity with the emotional discipline of abstraction (the dissolution of "subject matter"). Naturally, the results are far from tidy. Although Godard achieved the basis of his distinctive style very quickly (by 1958), the restlessness of his temperament and his intellectual voracity impel him to adopt an essentially exploratory posture in relation to film-making, in which he may answer a problem raised but not resolved in one film by starting on another. Still, viewed as a whole, Godard's work is much closer in problems and scope to the work of a radical purist and formalist in film like Bresson than to the work of the neo-realists—even though the relation with Bresson must also be drawn largely in terms of contrasts.

Bresson also achieved his mature style very quickly, but his career has throughout consisted of thoroughly premeditated, independent works conceived within the limits of his personal aesthetic of concision and intensity. (Born in 1910, Bresson has made eight feature films, the first in 1943 and the most recent in 1967.) Bresson's art is characterized by a pure, lyric quality, by a naturally elevated tone, and by a carefully constructed unity. He has said, in an interview conducted by Godard (*Cahiers du Cinèma* #178, May 1966), that for him "improvisation is at the base of creation in the cinema." But the look of a Bresson film is surely the antithesis of improvisation. In the finished film, a shot must be both autonomous and necessary; which means that there's only one ideally correct way of composing each shot (though it may be arrived at quite intuitively) and of editing the shots into a narrative. For all their great energy, Bresson's films project an air of formal deliberateness, of having been organized according to a relentless, subtly calculated rhythm which required their having had everything inessential cut from them. Given his austere aesthetic, it seems apt that Bresson's characteristic subject is a person either literally imprisoned or locked within an excruciating dilemma. Indeed, if one does accept narrative and tonal unity as a primary standard for film, Bresson's asceticism—his maximal use of minimal materials, the meditative "closed" quality of his films—seems to be the only truly rigorous procedure.

Godard's work exemplifies an aesthetic (and, no doubt, a temperament and sensibility) the opposite of Bresson's. The moral energy informing Godard's film-making, while no less powerful than Bresson's, leads to a quite different asceticism:

the labor of endless self-questioning, which becomes a constitutive element in the artwork. "More and more with each
film," he said in 1965, "it seems to me the greatest problem in
filming is to decide where and why to begin a shot and why to
end it." The point is that Godard cannot envisage anything but
arbitrary solutions to his problem. While each shot is autonomous, no amount of thinking can make it necessary. Since film
for Godard is preeminently an open structure, the distinction
between what's essential and inessential in any given film becomes senseless. Just as no absolute, immanent standards can
be discovered for determining the composition, duration, and
place of a shot, there can be no truly sound reason for excluding anything from a film. This view of film as an assemblage
rather than a unity lies behind the seemingly facile character-
izations Godard has made of many of his recent films. "*Pierrot
le Fou* isn't really a film, it's an attempt at cinema." About
Deux ou Trois Choses: "In sum, it's not a film, it's an attempt
at a film and is presented as such." *A Married Woman* is
described in the main titles: "Fragments of a Film Shot in
1964"; and *La Chinoise* is subtitled "A Film in the Process of
Being Made." In claiming to offer no more than "efforts" or
"attempts," Godard acknowledges the structural openness or
arbitrariness of his work. Each film remains a fragment in the
sense that its possibilities of elaboration can never be used up.
For granted the acceptability, even desirability, of the method
of juxtaposition ("I prefer simply putting things side by
side"), which assembles contrary elements without reconciling
them, there can indeed be no internally necessary end to a
Godard film, as there is to a Bresson film. Every film must
either seem broken off abruptly or else ended arbitrarily—
often by the violent death in the last reel of one or more of the
main characters, as in *Breathless, Le Petit Soldat, My Life to
Live, Les Carabiniers, Contempt, Masculine Feminine,* and
Pierrot le Fou.

Predictably, Godard has supported these views by pressing
the relationship (rather than the distinction) between "art"

and "life." Godard claims never to have had the feeling as he worked, which he thinks a novelist must have, "that I am differentiating between life and creation." The familiar mythical terrain is occupied once again: "cinema is somewhere between art and life." Of *Pierrot le Fou*, Godard has written: "Life is the subject, with 'Scope and color as its attributes. . . . Life on its own as I would like to capture it, using pan shots on nature, *plans fixes* on death, brief shots, long takes, soft and loud sounds, the movements of Anna and Jean-Paul. In short, life filling the screen as a tap fills a bathtub that is simultaneously emptying at the same rate." This, Godard claims, is how he differs from Bresson, who, when shooting a film, has "an idea of the world" that he is "trying to put on the screen or, which comes to the same thing, an idea of the cinema" he's trying "to apply to the world." For a director like Bresson, "cinema and the world are moulds to be filled, while in *Pierrot* there is neither mould nor matter."

Of course Godard's films aren't bathtubs; and Godard harbors his complex sentiments about the world and his art to the same extent and in much the same way as Bresson. But despite Godard's lapse into a disingenuous rhetoric, the contrast with Bresson stands. For Bresson, who was originally a painter, it is the austerity and rigor of cinematic means which make this art (though very few movies) valuable to him. For Godard, it's the fact that cinema is so loose, promiscuous, and accommodating a medium which gives movies, even many inferior ones, their authority and promise. Film can mix forms, techniques, points of view; it can't be identified with any single leading ingredient. Indeed, what the film-maker must show is that nothing is excluded. "One can put everything in a film," says Godard. "One must put everything in a film."

A film is conceived of as a living organism: not so much an object as a presence or an encounter—a fully historical or contemporary event, whose destiny it is to be transcended by future events. Seeking to create a cinema which inhabits the real present, Godard regularly puts into his films references to current political crises: Algeria, de Gaulle's domestic politics, Angola, the Vietnam war. (Each of his last four features includes a scene in which the main characters denounce the American aggression in Vietnam, and Godard has declared that until that war ends he'll put such a sequence into every film he makes.) The films may include even more casual references and off-the-cuff sentiments—a dig at André Malraux; a compliment to Henri Langlois, director of the Cinemathèque Française; an attack on irresponsible projectionists who show 1:66 films in Cinemascope ratio; or a plug for the unreleased movie of a fellow director and friend. Godard welcomes the opportunity to use the cinema topically, "journalistically." Using the interview style of *cinéma-vérité* and TV documentary, he can canvas characters for their opinions about the pill or the significance of Bob Dylan. Journalism can provide the basis for a film: Godard, who writes the scripts for all his movies, lists "Documentation from 'Ou en est la prostitution?' by Marcel Sacotte" as a source for *My Life to Live;* the story of *Deux ou Trois Choses* was suggested by a feature story, published in *Le Nouvel Observateur,* about housewives in new low-income apartment projects becoming part-time prostitutes to augment the family income.

As photography, cinema has always been an art which records temporality; but up to now this has been an inadvertent aspect of feature fiction films. Godard is the first major director who deliberately incorporates certain contingent aspects of the particular social moment when he's shooting a film—sometimes making these the frame of the film. Thus, the frame of *Masculine Feminine* is a report on the situation of French youth during three politically critical months of winter 1965, between the first presidential election and the run-off; and *La Chinoise* analyzes the faction of Communist students in Paris inspired by the Maoist cultural revolution in the summer of 1967. But of course Godard does not intend to supply facts in a literal sense, the sense which denies the relevance of imagination and fantasy. In his view, "you can start either with fiction or documentary. But whichever you start with, you will inevitably find the other." Perhaps the most interesting development of his point is not the films which have the form of reportage but those which have the form of fables. The timeless universal war which is the subject of *Les Carabiniers* is illustrated by World War II documentary footage, and the squalor in which the mythic protagonists (Michelangelo, Ulysses, Cleopatra, Venus) live is concretely France today. *Alphaville* is, in Godard's words, "a fable on a realistic ground," because the intergalactic city is also, literally, Paris now.

Unworried by the issue of impurity—there are no materials unusable for film—Godard is, nevertheless, involved in an extremely purist venture: the attempt to devise a structure for films which speaks in a purer present tense. His effort is to make movies which live in the actual present, and not to tell something from the past, relate something that's already taken place. In this, of course, Godard is following a direction already taken in literature. Fiction, until recently, was the art of the past. Events told in an epic or novel are, when the reader starts the book, already (as it were) in the past. But in much of the new fiction, events pass before us as if in a present coexisting with the time of the narrative voice (more accurately, with the time in which the reader is being addressed by the narrative voice). Events exist, therefore, in the present—at least as much of the present as the reader himself inhabits. It is for this reason that such writers as Beckett, Stein, Burroughs, and Robbe-Grillet prefer actually to use the present tense, or its equivalent. (Another strategy: to make the distinction between past, present, and future time within the narration an explicit conundrum, and an insoluble one—as, for example, in certain tales of Borges and Landolfi and in *Pale Fire*.) But if the development is feasible for literature, it would seem even more apt for film to make a comparable move since, in a way, film narration knows *only* the present tense. (Everything shown is equally present, no matter when it takes place.) For film to exploit its natural liberty what was necessary was to have a much looser, less literal attachment to telling a "story." A story in the traditional sense—something that's already taken place—is replaced by a segmented situation in which the suppression of certain explicative connections between scenes creates the impression of an action continually beginning anew, unfolding in the present tense.

And, of necessity, this present tense must appear as a somewhat behaviorist, external, anti-psychological view of the human situation. For psychological understanding depends on holding in mind simultaneously the dimensions of past, present, and future. To see someone psychologically is to lay out temporal coordinates in which he is situated. An art which aims at the present tense cannot aspire to this kind of "depth" or innerness in the portrayal of human beings. The lesson is already clear from the work of Stein and Beckett; Godard demonstrates it for film.

Godard explicitly alludes to this choice only once, in connection with *My Life to Live*, which, he says, he "built . . . in tableaux to accentuate the theatrical side of the film. Besides, this division corresponded to the external view of things which best allowed me to give a feeling of what was going on inside. In other words, a contrary procedure to that used by Bresson in *Pickpocket*, in which the drama is seen from within. How can one render the 'inside'? I think, by staying prudently outside." But though there are obvious advantages to staying "outside"—flexibility of form, freedom from superimposed limiting solutions—the choice is not so clear-cut as Godard suggests. Perhaps one never goes "inside" in the sense Godard attributes to Bresson—a procedure considerably different from the reading off of motives and summing up of a character's interior life promoted by nineteenth-century novelistic realism. Indeed, by those standards, Bresson is himself considerably "outside" his characters; for instance, more involved in their somatic presence, the rhythm of their movements, the heavy weight of inexpressible feeling which they bear.

Still, Godard is right in saying that, compared with Bresson, he is "outside." One way he stays outside is by constantly shifting the point of view from which the film is told, by the juxtaposition of contrasting narrative elements: realistic alongside implausible aspects of the story, written signs interposed between images, "texts" recited aloud interrupting dialogue, static interviews as against rapid actions, interpolation of a narrator's voice explaining or commenting on the action, and so forth. A second way is by his rendering of "things" in a strenuously neutralized fashion, in contrast with Bresson's thoroughly intimate vision of things as objects used, disputed, loved, ignored, and worn out by people. Things in Bresson's films, whether a spoon, a chair, a piece of bread, a pair of shoes, are always marked by their human use. The point is *how* they are used—whether skillfully (as the prisoner uses his spoon in *Un Condamné à Mort*, and the heroine of *Mouchette* uses the saucepan and bowls to make breakfast coffee) or clumsily. In Godard's films, things display a wholly alienated character. Characteristically, they are used with indifference, neither skillfully nor clumsily; they are simply there. "Objects exist," Godard has written, "and if one pays more attention to them than to people, it is precisely because they exist more than these people. Dead objects are still alive. Living people are often already dead." Whether things can be the occasion for visual gags (like the suspended egg in *A Woman Is a Woman*, and the movie posters in the warehouse in *Made in U.S.A.*) or can introduce an element of great plastic beauty (as do the Pongeist studies in *Deux ou Trois Choses* of the burning end of a cigarette and of bubbles separating and coming together on the surface of a hot cup of coffee), they always occur in a context of, and serve to reinforce, emotional dissociation. The most noticeable form of Godard's dissociated rendering of things is his ambivalent immersion in the allure of pop imagery and his only partly ironic display of the symbolic currency of urban capitalism—pinball machines, boxes of detergent, fast cars, neon signs, billboards, fashion magazines. By extension, this fascination with alienated things dictates the settings of most of Godard's films: highways, airports, anonymous hotel rooms or soulless modern apartments, brightly lit modernized cafés, movie theatres. The furniture and settings of Godard's films are the landscape of alienation—whether he is displaying the pathos in the mundane facticity of the actual life of dislocated, urban persons such as petty hoodlums, discontented housewives, left-wing students, prostitutes (the everyday present) or presenting anti-utopian fantasies about the cruel future.

A universe experienced as fundamentally dehumanized or dissociated is also one conducive to rapid "associating" from one ingredient in it to another. Again, the contrast can be made with Bresson's attitude, which is rigorously non-associative and therefore concerned with the depth in any situation; in a Bresson film there are certain organically derived and mutually relevant exchanges of personal energy that flourish or exhaust themselves (either way, unifying the narrative and supplying it with an organic terminus). For Godard, there are no genuinely organic connections. In the landscape of pain, only three strictly unrelated responses of real interest are possible; violent action, the probe of "ideas," and the transcendence of sudden, arbitrary, romantic love. But each of these possibilities is understood to be revocable, or artificial. They are not acts of personal fulfillment; not so much solutions as dissolutions of a problem. It has been noted that many of Godard's films project a masochistic view of women, verging on misogyny, and an indefatigable romanticism about "the couple." It's an odd but rather familiar combination of attitudes. Such contradictions are psychological or ethical analogues to Godard's fundamental formal presuppositions. In work conceived of as open-ended, associative, composed of "fragments," constructed by the (partly aleatoric) juxtaposition of contrary elements, any principle of action or any decisive emotional resolution is bound to be an artifice (from an ethical point of view) or ambivalent (from a psychological point of view).

Each film is a provisional network of emotional and intellectual impasses. With the probable exception of his view on Vietnam, there is no attitude Godard incorporates in his films that is not simultaneously being bracketed, and therefore criticized, by a dramatization of the gap between the elegance and seductiveness of ideas and the brutish or lyrical opaqueness of the human condition. The same sense of impasse characterizes Godard's moral judgments. For all the use made of the metaphor and the fact of prostitution to sum up contemporary miseries, Godard's films can't be said to be "against" prostitution and "for" pleasure and liberty in the unequivocal sense that Bresson's films directly extol love, honesty, courage, and dignity and deplore cruelty and cowardice.

From Godard's perspective, Bresson's work is bound to appear "rhetorical," whereas Godard is bent on destroying rhetoric by a lavish use of irony—the familiar outcome when a restless, somewhat dissociated intelligence struggles to cancel an irrepressible romanticism and tendency to moralize. In many of his films Godard deliberately seeks the framework of parody, of irony as contradiction. For instance, *A Woman Is a Woman* proceeds by putting an ostensibly serious theme (a woman frustrated both as wife and as would-be mother) in an ironically sentimental framework. "The subject of *A Woman Is a Woman*," Godard has said, "is a character who succeeds in resolving a certain situation, but I conceived this subject within the framework of a neo-realistic musical: an *absolute contradiction*, but that is precisely why I wanted to make the film." Another example is the lyrical treatment of a rather nasty scheme of amateur gangsterism in *Band of Outsiders*, complete with the high irony of the "happy ending" in which Odile sails away with Franz to Latin America for further romantic adventures. Another example: the nomenclature of

Alphaville, a film in which Godard takes up some of his most serious themes, is a collection of comic-strip identities (characters have names like Lemmy Caution, the hero of a famous series of French thrillers; Harry Dickson; Professor Leonard Nosferatu, alias von Braun; Professor Jeckyll) and the lead is played by Eddie Constantine, the expatriate American actor whose mug has been a cliché of 'B' French detective films for two decades; indeed, Godard's original title for the film was "Tarzan versus IBM." Still another example: the film Godard decided to make on the double theme of the Ben Barka and Kennedy murders, *Made in U.S.A.,* was conceived as a parodic remake of *The Big Sleep* (which had been revived at an art house in Paris in the summer of 1966), with Bogart's role of the trench-coated detective embroiled in an insoluble mystery now played by Anna Karina. The danger of such lavish use of irony is that ideas will be expressed at their point of self-caricature, and emotions only when they are mutilated. Irony intensifies what is already a considerable limitation on the emotions in the films that results from the insistence on the pure presentness of cinema narration, in which situations with less deep affect will be disproportionately represented—at the expense of vividly depicted states of grief, rage, profound erotic longing and fulfillment, and physical pain. Thus, while Bresson, at his almost unvarying best, is able to convey deep emotions without ever being sentimental, Godard, at his less effective, devises turns of plot that appear either hardhearted or sentimental (at the same time seeming emotionally flat).

Godard "straight" seems to me more successful—whether in the rare pathos he has allowed in *Masculine Feminine,* or in the hard coolness of such directly passionate films as *Les Carabiniers, Contempt, Pierrot le Fou,* and *Weekend.* This coolness is a pervasive quality of Godard's work. For all their violence of incident and sexual matter-of-factness, the films have a muted, detached relation to the grotesque and painful as well as to the seriously erotic. People are sometimes tortured and often die in Godard's films, but almost casually.

(He has a particular predilection for automobile accidents: the end of *Contempt*, the wreck in *Pierrot le Fou*, the landscape of affectless highway carnage in *Weekend*.) And people are rarely shown making love, though if they are, what interests Godard isn't the sensual communion but what sex reveals "about the spaces between people." The orgiastic moments come when young people dance together or sing or play games or run—people run beautifully in Godard movies—not when they make love.

"Cinema is emotion," says Samuel Fuller in *Pierrot le Fou*, a thought one surmises that Godard shares. But emotion, for Godard, always comes accompanied by some decoration of wit, some transmuting of feeling that he clearly puts at the center of the art-making process. This accounts for part of Godard's preoccupation with language, both heard and seen on the screen. Language functions as a means of emotional distancing from the action. The pictorial element is emotional, immediate; but words (including signs, texts, stories, sayings, recitations, interviews) have a lower temperature. While images invite the spectator to identify with what is seen, the presence of words makes the spectator into a critic.

But Godard's Brechtian use of language is only one aspect of the matter. Much as Godard owes to Brecht, his treatment of language is more complex and equivocal and relates rather to the efforts of certain painters who use words actively to undermine the image, to rebuke it, to render it opaque and unintelligible. It's not simply that Godard gives language a place that no other film director has before him. (Compare the verbosity of Godard's films with Bresson's verbal severity and austerity of dialogue.) He sees nothing in the film medium that prevents one of the subjects of cinema from being language itself—as language has become the very subject of much contemporary poetry and, in a metaphoric sense, of some important painting, such as that of Jasper Johns. But it seems that language can become the subject of cinema only at that point when a film-maker is obsessed by the problematic character of language—as Godard so evidently is. What other directors have regarded mainly as an adjunct of greater "realism" (the advantage of sound films as compared with silents) becomes in Godard's hands a virtually autonomous, sometimes subversive instrument.

I have already noted the varied ways in which Godard uses language as speech—not only as dialogue, but as monologue, as recited discourse, including quotation, and in off-screen comment and interrogation. Language is as well an important visual or plastic element in his films. Sometimes the screen is entirely filled with a printed text or lettering, which becomes the substitute for or counterpoint to a pictorial image. (Just a few examples: the stylishly elliptical credits that open each film; the postcard messages from the two soldiers in *Les Carabiniers;* the billboards, posters, record sleeves, and magazine ads in *My Life to Live, A Married Woman,* and *Masculine Feminine;* the pages from Ferdinand's journal, only part of which can be read, in *Pierrot le Fou;* the conversation with book covers in *A Woman Is a Woman;* the cover of the paperback series *"Idées"* used thematically in *Deux ou Trois Choses;* the Maoist slogans on the apartment walls in *La Chinoise.*) Not only does Godard not regard cinema as essentially moving photographs; for him, the fact that movies, which purport to be a pictorial medium, admit of language, precisely gives cinema its superior range and freedom compared with other art forms. Pictorial or photographic elements are in a sense only the raw materials of Godard's cinema; the transformative ingredient is language. Thus, to cavil at Godard for the talkiness of his films is to misunderstand his materials and his intentions. It is almost as if the pictorial image had a static quality, too close to "art," that Godard wants to infect with the blight of words. In *La Chinoise,* a sign on the wall of the student Maoist commune reads: "One must replace vague ideas with clear images." But that's only one side of the issue, as Godard knows. Sometimes images are too clear, too simple. (*La Chinoise* is Godard's sympathetic, witty treatment of the arch-romantic wish to make oneself entirely simple, altogether clear.) The highly permutated dialectic between image and language is far from stable. As he declares in his own voice at the beginning of *Alphaville:* "Some things in life are too complex for oral transmission. So we make fiction out of them, to make them universal." But again, it's clear that making things universal can bring oversimplification, which must be combated by the concreteness and ambiguity of words.

Godard has always been fascinated by the opaqueness and coerciveness of language, and a recurrent feature of the film narratives is some sort of deformation of speech. At perhaps its most innocent but still oppressive stage, speech can become hysterical monologue, as in *Charlotte et son Jules* and *Une Histoire d'Eau*. Speech can become halting and incomplete, as in Godard's early use of interview passages—in *Le Grand Escroc*, and in *Breathless*, where Patricia interviews a novelist (played by the director J.-P. Melville) at Orly Airport. Speech can become repetitive, as in the hallucinatory doubling of the dialogue by the quadrilingual translator in *Contempt* and, in *Band of Outsiders*, the English teacher's oddly intense repetitions of end phrases during her dictation. There are several instances of the outright dehumanization of speech—like the slow-motion croaking of the computer Alpha 60 and the mechanized impoverished speech of its catatonic human subjects in *Alphaville;* and the "broken" speech of the traveler in *Anticipation*. The dialogue may be out of step with the action, as in the antiphonal commentary in *Pierrot le Fou;* or simply fail to make sense, as in the account of "the death of logic" following a nuclear explosion over Paris in *Le Nouveau Monde*. Sometimes Godard prevents speech from being completely understood—as in the first scene in *My Life to Live,* and with the sonically harsh, partly unintelligible tape of the voice of "Richard Po—" in *Made in U.S.A.,* and in the long erotic confession at the opening of *Weekend*. Complementing these mutilations of speech and language are the many explicit discussions of language-as-a-problem in Godard's films. The puzzle about how it's possible to make moral or intellectual sense by speaking, owing to the betrayal of consciousness by language, is debated in *My Life to Live* and *A Married Woman;* the mystery of "translating" from one language to another is a theme in *Contempt* and *Band of Outsiders;* the language of the future is a subject of speculation by Guillaume and Veronique in *La Chinoise* (words will be spoken as if they were sounds and matter); the nonsensical underside of language is demonstrated in the exchange in the café between Marianne, the laborer, and the bartender in *Made in U.S.A.;* and the effort to purify language of philosophical and cultural dissociation is the explicit, main theme of *Alphaville* and *Anticipation,* the success of an individual's efforts to do this providing the dramatic resolution of both films.

At this moment in Godard's work, the problem of language appears to have become his leading motif. Behind their obtrusive verbosity, Godard's films are haunted by the duplicity and banality of language. Insofar as there is a "voice" speaking in all his films, it is one that questions all voices. Language is the widest context in which Godard's recurrent theme of prostitution must be located. Beyond its direct sociological interest for Godard, prostitution is his extended metaphor for the fate of language, that is, of consciousness itself. The coalescing of the two themes is clearest in the science-fiction nightmare of *Anticipation:* in an airport hotel some time in the future (that is, now), travelers have the choice of two kinds of temporary sexual companions, someone who makes bodily love without speaking or someone who can recite the words of love but can't take part in any physical embrace. This schizophrenia of the flesh and the soul is the menace that inspires Godard's preoccupation with language, and confers on him the painful, self-interrogatory terms of his restless art. As Natasha declares at the end of *Alphaville,* "There are words I don't know." But it's that painful knowledge, according to Godard's controlling narrative myth, that marks the beginning of her redemption; and—by an extension of the same goal—the redemption of art itself.

(February 1968)

III

What's Happening in America (1966)

[What follows is a response to a questionnaire sent out by the editors of *Partisan Review* in the summer of 1966 to a number of people. The questionnaire began: "There is a good deal of anxiety about the direction of American life. In fact, there is reason to fear that America may be entering a moral and political crisis." After more along these lines of understatement, contributors were invited to organize their replies around seven specific questions: 1. Does it matter who is in the White House? Or is there something in our system which would force any President to act as Johnson is acting? 2. How serious is the problem of inflation? The problem of poverty? 3. What is the meaning of the split between the Administration and the American intellectuals? 4. Is white America committed to granting equality to the American Negro? 5. Where do you think our foreign policies are likely to lead us? 6. What, in general, do you think is likely to happen in America? 7. Do you think any promise is to be found in the activities of young people today?

My own response, reprinted below, appeared in the Winter 1967 issue of the magazine, along with contributions from Martin Duberman, Michael Harrington, Tom Hayden, Nat Hentoff, H. Stuart Hughes, Paul Jacobs, Tom Kahn, Leon H. Keyserling, Robert Lowell, Jack Ludwig, Jack Newfield, Harold Rosenberg, Richard H. Rovere, Richard Schlatter, and Diana Trilling.]

Everything that one feels about this country is, or ought to be, conditioned by the awareness of American *power:* of America as the arch-imperium of the planet, holding man's biological as well as his historical future in its King Kong paws. Today's America, with Ronald Reagan the new daddy of California and John Wayne chawing spareribs in the White House, is pretty much the same Yahooland that Mencken was describing. The main difference is that what's happening in America matters so much more in the late 1960's than it did in the 1920's. Then, if one had tough innards, one might jeer, sometimes affectionately, at American barbarism and find American innocence somewhat endearing. Both the barbarism and the innocence are lethal, outsized today.

First of all, then, American power is indecent in its scale. But also the quality of American life is an insult to the possibilities of human growth; and the pollution of American space, with gadgetry and cars and TV and box architecture, brutalizes the senses, making gray neurotics of most of us, and perverse spiritual athletes and strident self-transcenders of the best of us.

Gertrude Stein said that America is the oldest country in the world. Certainly, it's the most conservative. It has the most to lose by change (sixty percent of the world's wealth owned by a country containing six percent of the world's population). Americans know their backs are against the wall: "they" want to take all that away from "us." And, I think, America deserves to have it taken away.

Three facts about this country.

America was founded on a genocide, on the unquestioned assumption of the right of white Europeans to exterminate a resident, technologically backward, colored population in order to take over the continent.

America had not only the most brutal system of slavery in modern times but a unique juridical system (compared with other slaveries, say in Latin America and the British colonies) which did not, in a single respect, recognize slaves as persons.

As a country—as distinct from a colony—America was created mainly by the surplus poor of Europe, reinforced by a small group who were just *Europamüde*, tired of Europe (a literary catchword of the 1840s). Yet even the poorest knew both a "culture," largely invented by his social betters and administered from above, and a "nature" that had been pacified for centuries. These people arrived in a country where the indigenous culture was simply the enemy and was in process of being ruthlessly annihilated, and where nature, too, was the enemy, a pristine force, unmodified by civilization, that is, by human wants, which had to be defeated. After America was "won," it was filled up by new generations of the poor and built up according to the tawdry fantasy of the good life that culturally deprived, uprooted people might have at the beginning of the industrial era. And the country looks it.

Foreigners extol the American "energy," attributing to it both our unparalleled economic prosperity and the splendid vivacity of our arts and entertainments. But surely this is energy bad at its source and for which we pay too high a price, a hypernatural and humanly disproportionate dynamism that flays everyone's nerves raw. Basically it is the energy of violence, of free-floating resentment and anxiety unleashed by chronic cultural dislocations which must be, for the most part, ferociously sublimated. This energy has mainly been sublimated into crude materialism and acquisitiveness. Into hectic philanthropy. Into benighted moral crusades, the most spectacular of which was Prohibition. Into an awesome talent for uglifying countryside and cities. Into the loquacity and torment of a minority of gadflies: artists, prophets, muckrakers, cranks, and nuts. And into self-punishing neuroses. But the naked violence keeps breaking through, throwing everything into question.

Needless to say, America is not the only violent, ugly, and unhappy country on this earth. Again, it is a matter of scale. Only three million Indians lived here when the white man arrived, rifle in hand, for his fresh start. Today American hegemony menaces the lives not of three million but of countless millions who, like the Indians, have never even *heard* of the "United States of America," much less of its mythical empire, the "free world." American policy is still powered by the fantasy of Manifest Destiny, though the limits were once set by the borders of the continent, whereas today America's destiny embraces the entire world. There are still more hordes of redskins to be mowed down before virtue triumphs; as the classic Western movies explain, the only good Red is a dead Red. This may sound like an exaggeration to those who live in the special and more finely modulated atmosphere of New York and its environs. Cross the Hudson. You find out that not just *some* Americans but virtually all Americans feel that way.

Of course, these people don't know what they're saying, literally. But that's no excuse. That, in fact, is what makes it all possible. The unquenchable American moralism and the American faith in violence are not just twin symptoms of some character neurosis taking the form of a protracted adolescence, which presages an eventual maturity. They constitute a full-grown, firmly installed national psychosis, founded, as are all psychoses, on the efficacious denial of reality. So far it's worked. Except for portions of the South a hundred years ago, America has never known war. A taxi driver said to me on the day that could have been Armageddon, when America and Russia were on collision course off the shores of Cuba: "Me, I'm not worried. I served in the last one, and now I'm over draft age. They can't get me again. But I'm all for letting 'em have it right now. What are we waiting for? Let's get it over with." Since wars always happen Over There, and we always win, why not drop the bomb? If all it takes is pushing a button, even better. For America is that curious hybrid—an apocalyptic country and a valetudinarian country. The average citizen may harbor the fantasies of John Wayne, but he as often has the temperament of Jane Austen's Mr. Woodhouse.

To answer, briefly, some of the questions:

1. I do *not* think that Johnson is forced by "our system" to act as he is acting: for instance, in Vietnam, where each evening he personally chooses the bombing targets for the next day's missions. But I think there is something awfully wrong with a *de facto* system which allows the President virtually unlimited discretion in pursuing an immoral and imprudent foreign policy, so that the strenuous opposition of, say, the Chairman of the Senate Foreign Relations Committee counts for exactly nothing. The *de jure* system vests the power to make war in the Congress—with the exception, apparently, of imperialist ventures and genocidal expeditions. These are best left undeclared.

However, I don't mean to suggest that Johnson's foreign policy is the whim of a clique which has seized control, escalated the power of the Chief Executive, castrated the Congress, and manipulated public opinion. Johnson is, alas, all too representative. As Kennedy was not. If there is a conspiracy, it is (or was) that of the more enlightened national leaders hitherto largely selected by the Eastern-seaboard plutocracy. They engineered the precarious acquiescence to liberal goals that has prevailed in this country for over a generation—a

superficial consensus made possible by the strongly apolitical
character of a decentralized electorate mainly preoccupied
with local issues. If the Bill of Rights were put to a national
referendum as a new piece of legislation, it would meet the
same fate as New York City's Civilian Review Board. Most of
the people in this country believe what Goldwater believes,
and always have. But most of them don't know it. Let's hope
they don't find out.

4. I do not think white America is committed to granting
equality to the American Negro. So committed are only a
minority of white Americans, mostly educated and affluent,
few of whom have had any prolonged social contact with
Negroes. This is a passionately racist country; it will continue
to be so in the foreseeable future.

5. I think that this administration's foreign policies are likely
to lead to more wars and to wider wars. Our main hope, and
the chief restraint on American bellicosity and paranoia, lies in
the fatigue and depoliticization of Western Europe, the lively
fear of America and of another world war in Russia and the
Eastern European countries, and the corruption and unrelia-
bility of our client states in the Third World. It's hard to lead a
holy war without allies. But America is just crazy enough to
try to do it.

6. The meaning of the split between the Administration and
the intellectuals? Simply that our leaders are genuine yahoos,
with all the exhibitionist traits of their kind, and that liberal
intellectuals (whose deepest loyalties are to an international
fraternity of the reasonable) are not *that* blind. At this point,
moreover, they have nothing to lose by proclaiming their discontent and frustration. But it's well to remember that liberal
intellectuals, like Jews, tend to have a classical theory of politics, in which the state has a monopoly of power; hoping that
those in positions of authority may prove to be enlightened
men, wielding power justly, they are natural, if cautious, allies
of the "establishment." As the Russian Jews knew they had at
least a chance with the Czar's officials but none at all with

marauding Cossacks and drunken peasants (Milton Himmel-
farb has pointed this out), liberal intellectuals more naturally
expect to influence the "decisions" of administrators than they
do the volatile "feelings" of masses. Only when it becomes
clear that, in fact, the government itself is being staffed by
Cossacks and peasants, can a rupture like the present one take
place. When (and if) the man in the White House who paws
people and scratches his balls in public is replaced by the man
who dislikes being touched and finds Yevtushenko "an interesting fellow," American intellectuals won't be so disheart-
ened. The vast majority of them are not revolutionaries,
wouldn't know how to be if they tried. Mostly a salaried pro-
fessoriat, they're as much at home in the system when it functions a little better than it does right now as anyone else.

7. A somewhat longer comment on this last question.

Yes, I do find much promise in the activities of young
people. About the only promise one can find anywhere in this
country today is in the way some young people are carrying
on, making a fuss. I include both their renewed interest in
politics (as protest and as community action, rather than as
theory) and the way they dance, dress, wear their hair, riot,
make love. I also include the homage they pay to Oriental
thought and rituals. And I include, not least of all, their interest in taking drugs—despite the unspeakable vulgarization of
this project by Leary and others.

A year ago Leslie Fiedler, in a remarkably wrongheaded
and interesting essay titled "The New Mutants," called attention to the fact that the new style of young people indicated a
deliberate blurring of sexual differences, signaling the creation
of a new breed of youthful androgens. The longhaired pop
groups with their mass teenage following and the tiny elite of
turned-on kids from Berkeley to the East Village were both
lumped together as representatives of the "post-humanist" era
now upon us, in which we witness a "radical metamorphosis of
the Western male," a "revolt against masculinity," even "a rejection of conventional male potency." For Fiedler, this new

turn in personal mores, diagnosed as illustrating a "programmatic espousal of an anti-puritanical mode of existence," is something to deplore. (Though sometimes, in his characteristic have-it-both-ways manner, Fiedler seemed to be vicariously relishing this development, *mainly* he appeared to be lamenting it.) But why, he never made explicit. I think it is because he is sure such a mode of existence undercuts radical politics, and its moral visions, altogether. Being radical in the older sense (some version of Marxism or socialism or anarchism) meant to be attached still to traditional "puritan" values of work, sobriety, achievement, and family-founding. Fiedler suggests, as have Philip Rahv and Irving Howe and Malcolm Muggeridge among others, that the new style of youth must be, at bottom, apolitical, and their revolutionary spirit a species of infantilism. The fact that the same kid joins SNCC or boards a Polaris submarine or agrees with Conor Cruise O'Brien *and* smokes pot and is bisexual and adores the Supremes is seen as a contradiction, a kind of ethical fraud or intellectual weak-mindedness.

I don't believe this to be so. The depolarizing of the sexes, to mention the element that Fiedler observes with such fascination, is the natural, and desirable, next stage of the sexual revolution (its dissolution, perhaps) which has moved beyond the idea of sex as a damaged but discrete zone of human activity, beyond the discovery that "society" represses the free expression of sexuality (by fomenting guilt), to the discovery that the way we live and the ordinarily available options of character repress almost entirely the deep experience of pleasure, and the possibility of self-knowledge. "Sexual freedom" is a shallow, outmoded slogan. What, who is being liberated? For older people, the sexual revolution is an idea that remains meaningful. One can be for it or against it; if one is for it, the idea remains confined within the norms of Freudianism and its derivatives. But Freud *was* a puritan, or "a fink," as one of Fiedler's students distressingly blurted out. So was Marx. It is right that young people see beyond Freud and Marx. Let the professors be the caretakers of this indeed precious legacy, and discharge all the obligations of piety. No need for dismay if the kids don't continue to pay the old dissenter-gods obeisance.

It seems to me obtuse, though understandable, to patronize the new kind of radicalism, which is post-Freudian and post-Marxist. For this radicalism is as much an experience as an idea. Without the personal experience, if one is looking in from the outside, it does look messy and almost pointless. It's easy to be put off by the youngsters throwing themselves around with their eyes closed to the near-deafening music of the discothèques (unless you're dancing, too), by the longhaired marchers carrying flowers and temple bells as often as "Get Out of Vietnam" placards, by the inarticulateness of a Mario Savio. One is also aware of the high casualty rate among this gifted, visionary minority among the young, the tremendous cost in personal suffering and in mental strain. The fakers, the slobs, and the merely flipped-out are plentiful among them. But the complex desires of the best of them: to engage and to "drop out"; to be beautiful to look at and touch as well as to be good; to be loving and quiet as well as militant and effective—these desires make sense in our present situation. To sympathize, of course, you have to be convinced that things in America really are as desperately bad as I have indicated. This is hard to see; the desperateness of things is obscured by the comforts and liberties that America does offer. Most people, understandably, don't really believe things are that bad. That's why, for them, the antics of this youth can be no more than a startling item in the passing parade of cultural fashions, to be appraised with a friendly but essentially weary and knowing look. The sorrowful look that says: I was a radical, too, when I was young. When are these kids going to grow up and realize what we had to realize, that things never are going to be really different, except maybe worse?

From my own experience and observation, I can testify that there is a profound concordance between the sexual revolution, redefined, and the political revolution, redefined. That being a socialist and taking certain drugs (in a fully serious spirit: as a technique for exploring one's consciousness, not as an anodyne or a crutch) are not incompatible, that there is no incompatibility between the exploration of inner space and the rectification of social space. What some of the kids understand is that it's the whole character structure of modern American man, and his imitators, that needs rehauling. (Old folks like Paul Goodman and Edgar Z. Friedenberg have, of course, been suggesting this for a long time.) That rehauling includes Western "masculinity," too. They believe that some socialist remodeling of institutions and the ascendance, through electoral means or otherwise, of better leaders won't really change anything. And they are right.

Neither do I dare deride the turn toward the East (or more generally, to the wisdoms of the non-white world) on the part of a tiny group of young people—however uninformed and jejune the adherence usually is. (But then, nothing could be more ignorant than Fiedler's insinuation that Oriental modes of thought are "feminine" and "passive," which is the reason the demasculinized kids are drawn to them.) Why shouldn't they look for wisdom elsewhere? If America *is* the culmination of Western white civilization, as everyone from the Left to the Right declares, then there must be something terribly wrong with Western white civilization. This is a painful truth; few of us want to go that far. It's easier, much easier, to accuse the kids, to reproach them for being "non-participants in the past" and "drop-outs from history." But it isn't real history Fiedler is referring to with such solicitude. It's just *our* history, which he claims is identical with "the tradition of the human," the tradition of "reason" itself. Of course, it's hard to assess life on this planet from a genuinely world-historical perspective; the effort induces vertigo and seems like an invitation to suicide. But from a world-historical perspective, that local history which some young people are repudiating (with their fondness for dirty words, their peyote, their macrobiotic rice, their

Dadaist art, etc.) looks a good deal less pleasing and less self-evidently worthy of perpetuation. The truth is that Mozart, Pascal, Boolean algebra, Shakespeare, parliamentary government, baroque churches, Newton, the emancipation of women, Kant, Marx, and Balanchine ballets don't redeem what this particular civilization has wrought upon the world. The white race *is* the cancer of human history; it is the white race and it alone—its ideologies and inventions—which eradicates autonomous civilizations wherever it spreads, which has upset the ecological balance of the planet, which now threatens the very existence of life itself. What the Mongol hordes threaten is far less frightening than the damage that Western "Faustian" man, with his idealism, his magnificent art, his sense of intellectual adventure, his world-devouring energies for conquest, has already done, and further threatens to do.

This is what some of the kids sense, though few of them could put it in words. Again, I believe them to be right. I'm not arguing that they're going to prevail, or even that they're likely to change much of anything in this country. But a few of them may save their own souls. America is a fine country for inflaming people, from Emerson and Thoreau to Mailer and Burroughs and Leo Szilard and John Cage and Judith and Julian Beck, with the project of trying to save their own souls. Salvation becomes almost a mundane, inevitable goal when things are so bad, really intolerable.

One last comparison, which I hope won't seem farfetched. The Jews left the ghetto in the early nineteenth century, thus becoming a people doomed to disappear. But one of the by-products of their fateful absorption into the modern world was an incredible burst of creativity in the arts, science, and secular scholarship—the relocation of a powerful but frustrated spiritual energy. These innovating artists and intellectuals were not alienated Jews, as is said so often, but people who were alienated *as* Jews.

I'm scarcely more hopeful for America than I am for the

Jews. This is a doomed country, it seems to me; I only pray that, when America founders, it doesn't drag the rest of the planet down, too. But one should notice that, during its long elephantine agony, America is also producing its subtlest minority generation of the decent and sensitive, young people who are alienated *as* Americans. They are not drawn to the stale truths of their sad elders (though these are truths). More of their elders should be listening to them.

(1966)

Trip to Hanoi

Though I have been and am passionately opposed to the American aggression in Vietnam, I accepted the unexpected invitation to go to Hanoi that came in mid-April with the pretty firm idea that I wouldn't write about the trip upon my return. Being neither a journalist nor a political activist (though a veteran signer of petitions and anti-war demonstrator) nor an Asian specialist, but rather a stubbornly unspecialized writer who has so far been largely unable to incorporate into either novels or essays my evolving radical political convictions and sense of moral dilemma at being a citizen of the American empire, I doubted that my account of such a trip could add anything new to the already eloquent opposition to the war. And contributing to the anti-war polemic seemed to me the only worthwhile reason for an American to be writing about Vietnam now.

Perhaps the difficulty started there, with the lack of a purpose that really justified in my own mind my being invited to North Vietnam. Had I brought some clear intentions about the usefulness (to me or to anyone else) of my visit, I probably would have found it easier to sort out and assimilate what I saw. If occasionally I could have reminded myself that I was a writer and Vietnam was "material," I might have fended off some of the confusions that beset me. As it was, the first days of my stay were profoundly discouraging, with most of my energies going toward trying to keep my gloom within tolerable limits. But now that I'm back, and since returning want after all to write about North Vietnam, I don't regret that early decision. By denying myself a role that could have shielded me from my ignorance and spared me a lot of personal discomfort, I unwittingly assisted what discoveries I eventually did make during the trip.

Of course, it wasn't only this original refusal to envisage the trip as a professional task that opened the way to my confusion. In part, my bewilderment was direct and unavoidable: the honest reflex of being culturally dislocated. Also, I should mention that few Americans who visit Hanoi at this time go alone, the usual practice being, for the convenience of the Vietnamese, to assemble groups of sometimes two, usually three, four, or five people who often don't know each other before the trip. I traveled to North Vietnam as one of three. And I had met neither of the two other Americans in whose company I made the trip—Andrew Kopkind, the journalist, and Robert Greenblatt, a mathematician from Cornell now working full time for the anti-war movement—before our rendezvous in Cambodia in late April. Yet this trip involves unremitting and not wholly voluntary proximity, the kind befitting a romance or a dangerous emergency, lasting without pause for at least a month. (We were invited for two weeks. It took us ten days, because of delays and missed connections, to go from New York via Paris and Phnom Penh to Hanoi, and just under a week to make the return trip.) Naturally, the situation with my companions claimed a sizable part of the attention that, had I traveled alone, would have gone to the Vietnamese: sometimes in the form of an obligation, most often as a pleasure. There was the practical necessity of learning to live amicably and intelligently with two strangers in circumstances of instant intimacy, strangers even if, or perhaps especially since, they were people already known to me by reputation and, in the case of Andy Kopkind, by his writing, which I admired. We were further drawn together by being in what was to all three of us an alien part of the world (neither Bob Greenblatt nor I had ever been to Asia before; Andy Kopkind had made one trip five years ago, visiting Saigon, Bangkok, the Philippines, and Japan), and meeting no one whose native language was English (except a U.S.I.S. official and an American journalist in Laos, where we were stuck for four days on our way "in," and four American college students sponsored by S.D.S. who arrived in Hanoi at the beginning of our second week). All this added together, it seems inevitable that we spent a great deal of time talking—gratefully, often feverishly—to each other.

Still, I don't mean to suggest that these elements of my situation account for the wistfully negative tone of my early impressions of Vietnam. The serious explanation for that I would locate not in the distractions and pressures of being one of an arbitrarily assembled yet inseparable trio in a new land, but in the demands and limitations of the approach to Vietnam I myself was capable of. Made miserable and angry for four years by knowledge of the excruciating suffering of the Vietnamese people at the hands of my government, now that I was actually there and being plied with gifts and flowers and rhetoric and tea and seemingly exaggerated kindness, I didn't *feel* any more than I already had ten thousand miles away. But being in Hanoi was far more mysterious, more puzzling intellectually, than I expected. I found that I couldn't avoid worrying and wondering how well I understood the Vietnamese, and they me and my country.

Yet this problem I posed for myself, frustrating as it proved, was perhaps the most important and fruitful one, at least to me. For it was not information (at least in the ordinary sense) that I'd come to find. Like anyone who cared about Vietnam in the last years, I already knew a great deal; and I could not hope to collect more or significantly better information in a mere two weeks than was already available. Ranging from the early reports in *The New York Times* by Harrison Salisbury of his visit in December and January of 1965–66 (later expanded into a book, *Behind the Lines—Hanoi*) and *The Other Side,* the book written jointly by Staughton Lynd and Tom Hayden, the first Americans from the anti-war movement to visit North Vietnam, to the analyses of Philippe Devillers and Jean Lacouture in the French press, to the recent articles by Mary McCarthy which I've been reading since my return to the United States, a multiple account has accumulated which conveys in vivid detail how Hanoi and large parts of North Vietnam appear to a sympathetic or at least reasonably objective outsider looking on. Anyone who wants to can get information on the achievements of the country since the French left in 1954: the expansion of medical services, the reorganization of education, the creation of a modest industrial base, and the beginnings of diversified agriculture. Even easier to obtain are the facts about the years of merciless bombing by the United States of all the population centers of North Vietnam—with the exception of downtown Hanoi (which has, however, been doused with "anti-personnel" or fragmentation bombs, those that don't harm buildings but only kill people)—and the destruction of virtually all the new schools and hospitals and factories built since 1954, as well as most bridges, theatres, pagodas, and Catholic churches and cathedrals. In my own case, several years of reading and of viewing newsreels had furnished a large portfolio of miscellaneous images of Vietnam: napalmed corpses, live citizens on bicycles, the hamlets of thatched huts, the razed cities like Nam Dinh and Phu Ly, the cylindrical, one-person bomb shelters spaced along the sidewalks of Hanoi, the thick yellow straw hats worn by schoolchildren as protection against fragmentation bombs. (Indelible horrors, pictorial and statistical, supplied by courtesy of television and *The New York Times* and *Life,* without one's even having to bestir oneself to consult the frankly partisan books of Wilfred Burchett or the documentation assembled by the Russell Foundation's International War Crimes Tribunal.) But the confrontation with the originals of these images didn't prove to be a simple experience; actually to see and touch them produced an effect both exhilarating and numbing. Matching concrete reality with mental image was at best a mechanical or merely additive process, while prying new facts from the Vietnamese officials and ordinary citizens I was meeting was a task for which I'm not particularly well equipped. Unless I could effect in myself some change of awareness, of consciousness, it would scarcely matter that I'd actually been to Vietnam. But that was exactly what was so hard, since I had only my own culture-bound, disoriented sensibility for an instrument.

Indeed, the problem was that Vietnam had become so much a fact of my consciousness as an American that I was having enormous difficulty getting it outside my head. The first experience of being there absurdly resembled meeting a favorite movie star, one who for years has played a role in one's fantasy life, and finding the actual person so much smaller, less vivid, less erotically charged, and mainly different. Most convincing were the experiences that were least real, like the evening of our arrival. I was nervous throughout the flight in the small International Control Commission plane that had belatedly taken off from Vientiane; and landing in Hanoi's Gia Lam airport at night several hours later, I was mainly relieved just to be alive and on the ground, and hardly bothered that I knew neither where I was nor whom I was with. Hugging my flowers, I crossed the dark landing area, trying to keep straight the names of the four smiling men from the Peace Committee who had come to meet us. And if our flight and landing had the quality of a hallucination, the rest of that night seemed like one vast back projection, with overvivid extensions and fore-shortenings of time, scale, and movement. First, there were either the few minutes or the hour spent waiting for our luggage in the bleak airport building, awkwardly chatting with the Vietnamese. Then, when we were distributed in three cars and started into the darkness, there was the rhythm of the ride into Hanoi. A little way from the airport, the cars lurched down a bumpy dirt road onto the narrow, shuddering pontoon bridge over the Red River that has replaced the bombed-out iron one, and inched across that; but once on the other side, the cars seemed to go too fast and, entering Hanoi, passing through dim streets, opened a rude swathe in the stream of indistinguishable figures on bicycles, until we halted in front of our hotel. Its name, Thong Nhat, means Reunification, someone said: a huge building, and indeterminate in style. A dozen people were sitting about the very plain lobby, mostly non-Orientals but at that point otherwise unidentifiable. After we were taken upstairs and shown to our large rooms, there was a late supper for us in a stark, deserted dining room with rows of propeller fans slowly turning overhead. "Our" Viet-namese waited for us in the lobby. When we joined them, we asked if, late as it was, they would mind going out with us for a walk. So out we went, weak with excitement. Along the streets, now almost empty of people, we passed clusters of trucks parked between tents which, they told us, sheltered all-night "mobile workshops" or "dispersed factories." We went as far as the Mot Cot pagoda in the Petit Lac, and lingering there, heard some—to me, barely intelligible—tales of ancient Vietnamese history. Once back in the hotel lobby, Oanh, evidently the leader of the group from the Peace Committee, gently urged us to go to bed. People in Hanoi, he explained, rise and eat breakfast very early (since the bombing started, most stores open at 5 A.M. and close a few hours later), and they would be coming by for us at 8 A.M. the next day, which happened to be Buddha's birthday, to take us to a pagoda. I remember reluctantly saying good night to the Vietnamese and to my two companions; in my room, spending a quarter of an hour trying to cope with the high vault of white mosquito netting covering the bed; and finally sinking into a difficult, agitated, but happy sleep.

Of course, North Vietnam was unreal that first night. But it continued to seem unreal, or at least incomprehensible, for days afterwards. To be sure, that initial haunting vision of wartime Hanoi at night was corrected by more mundane daytime experiences. The Thong Nhat Hotel shrank to ordinary size (one could even visualize it in its former incarnation, the Metropole of French colonial days); individuals of varying age and character emerged out of the silent collective traffic of bicyclists and pedestrians; and the Petit Lac and the nearby tree-shaded streets became places of daily resort, where we walked casually, without our guides, whenever it wasn't too hot and one or two or all three of us had a spare hour. Though so far from and so unlike the only cities I knew, those of America and Europe, Hanoi quickly gained an eerie familiarity. Yet when I was honest with myself I had to admit that the place was simply too foreign, that I really understood nothing at all, except at a "distance."

In his brilliant episode in the film *Far from Vietnam*, Godard reflects (as we hear his voice, we see him sitting behind an idle movie camera) that it would be good if we each made a Vietnam inside ourselves, especially if we cannot actually go there (Godard had wanted to shoot his episode in North Vietnam, but was denied a visa). Godard's point—a variant on Che's maxim that, in order to crack the American hegemony, revolutionaries have the duty to create "two, three, many Vietnams"—had seemed to me exactly right. What I'd been creating and enduring for the last four years was a Vietnam inside my head, under my skin, in the pit of my stomach. But the Vietnam I'd been thinking about for years was scarcely filled out at all. It was really only the mold into which the American seal was cutting. My problem was not to try to feel more inside myself. My problem was that I (luckier than Godard) was now actually in Vietnam for a brief time, yet somehow was unable to make the full intellectual and emotional connections that my political and moral solidarity with Vietnam implied.

The most economical way, I think, of conveying these early difficulties is to transcribe from journal entries I made during the first week after our arrival on the third of May.

MAY 5

The cultural difference is the hardest thing to estimate, to overcome. A difference of manners, style, therefore of substance. (And how much of what I'm struck by is Asian, how much specifically Vietnamese, I am unlikely to find out on my first trip to Asia.) Clearly, they have a different way here of treating the guest, the stranger, the foreigner, not to mention the enemy. Also, I'm convinced, the Vietnamese have a different relation to language. The difference can't just be due to the fact that my sentences, already slowed down and simplified, more often than not have to be mediated by a translator. For even when I'm in conversation with someone who speaks English or French, it seems to me we're both talking baby talk.

To all this add the constraint of being reduced to the status of a child: scheduled, led about, explained to, fussed over, pampered, kept under benign surveillance. Not only a child individually but, even more exasperating, one of a group of children. The four Vietnamese from the Peace Committee who are seeing us around act as our nurses, our teachers. I try to discover the differences between each of them, but can't; and I worry that they don't see what's different or special about me. All too often I catch myself trying to please them, to make a good impression—to get the best mark of the class. I present myself as an intelligent, well-mannered, cooperative, uncomplicated person. So not only do I feel like a rather corrupt child but, being neither a child nor in fact as simple and easy to know as the way I'm coming on would indicate, I feel somewhat of a fraud. (It's no extenuation that this open, legible person is perhaps who I would like to be.)

Maybe, if I'm cheating, with the best intentions, trying to make it easier for them, they're doing the same for us. Is that why, though I know they must be different from each other, I can't get beyond the surface markings? Oanh has the most personal authority, walks and sits with that charming "American" slouch, and sometimes seems moody or distracted. (We've learned that his wife has been ill ever since she was captured and tortured for a year by the French in the early 1950's; and he has several small children.) Hieu alternates between boyishness—he giggles—and the pointed composure of a junior bureaucrat. Phan has the most affable manners; he usually seems out of breath when he talks, which he loves doing; he's also one of the very few plump Vietnamese I've seen. Toan generally looks eager and slightly intimidated, and never speaks unless you ask him a question. But what else? Phan is the oldest, I think. Today we learned, to our great surprise, that Oanh is forty-six. It doesn't help that every Vietnamese (especially the men, who rarely go bald or even gray) looks at least ten years younger than he is.

What makes it especially hard to see people as individuals is that everybody here seems to talk in the same style and to have the same things to say. This impression is reinforced by the exact repetition of the ritual of hospitality at each place we visit. A bare room, a low table, wooden chairs, perhaps a couch. We all shake hands, then sit around the table, which holds several plates of overripe green bananas, Vietnamese cigarettes, damp cookies, a dish of paper-wrapped candies made in China, cups for tea. We are introduced. They tell us their names. We shake hands again. Pause. The spokesman of their group, wherever we are visiting (a factory, a school, a government ministry, a museum), gazes at us benignly, smiles, "*Cac ban* . . ." ("Friends . . .") He has started his speech of welcome. Someone comes through a curtain and begins serving tea.

MAY 6

Of course, I'm not sorry to have come. Being in Hanoi is at the very least a duty, for me an important act of personal and political affirmation. What I'm not yet reconciled to is that it's also a piece of political theatre. They are playing their roles, we (I) must play ours (mine). The heaviness of it all comes from the fact that the script is written entirely by them; and they're directing the play, too. Though this is how it has to be—it's their country, their life-and-death struggle, while we are volunteers, extras, figurants who retain the option of getting off the stage and sitting safely in the audience—it makes my acts here appear to me largely dutiful, and the whole performance a little sad.

We have a role: American friends of the Vietnamese struggle. (About forty Americans in some way connected with the anti-war movement in the States have made this trip before us.) The trip to Hanoi is a kind of reward or patronage. We are being given a treat, being thanked for our unsolicited efforts; and then we are to return home with a reinforced sense of solidarity, to continue our separate ways of opposing the current American policy.

There is, of course, an exquisite politeness in this corporate identity. We are not asked, separately or collectively, to say why we merit this trip. Our being recommended (by Americans who were invited earlier and retain the confidence of the Vietnamese) and our willingness to come (all this way, at our own expense, and facing the risk of prosecution when we return to the States) seem to put Bob's, Andy's, and my efforts on the same level. Nobody here poses questions about what we specifically do for the anti-war movement, or asks us to justify the quality of our activities; it seems to be assumed that

we each do what we can. Though our Vietnamese hosts evidently know we are not Communists, and indeed seem to have
no illusions about the American Communist Party—"We know
our Communist friends in the United States are not in great
number," a government official remarked dryly—nobody in-
quires into our political beliefs. We are *cac ban* all.

Everybody says, "We know the American people are our
friends. Only the present American government is our enemy."
A journalist we met commended our efforts to "safeguard the
freedom and prestige of the United States." Though I honor
the nobility of this attitude, I'm exasperated by their naïveté.
Do they really believe what they're saying? Don't they understand anything about America? Part of me can't help regarding them as children—beautiful, patient, heroic, martyred,
stubborn children. And I know that I'm not a child, though the
theatre of this visit requires that I play the role of one. The
same shy, tender smile appears on the face of the soldier we
pass in the park, the elderly Buddhist scholar, and the waitress
in the hotel dining room as on the faces of the children lined
up to greet us at the evacuated primary school we visited
today just outside Hanoi; and we're smiling at them like that,
too. We get little presents and souvenirs wherever we go, and
at the end of each visit Bob distributes a handful of anti-war
buttons (how lucky that he thought to bring a bagful of
them). The most impressive of his random collection are the
jumbo blue and white buttons from last October's March on
the Pentagon, which we save for special occasions. How could
we not be moved at the moment we are pinning on their tiny
red and gold badges while they are adorning themselves with
our big anti-war buttons? How could we not also be in bad
faith?

The root of my bad faith: that I long for the three-dimensional, textured, "adult" world in which I live in America—
even as I go about my (their) business in this two-dimensional
world of the ethical fairy tale where I am paying a visit, and in
which I do believe.

Part of the role (theirs and mine) is the stylizing of language: speaking mostly in simple declarative sentences, making all discourse either expository or interrogative. Everything is on one level here. All the words belong to the same vocabulary: struggle, bombings, friend, aggressor, imperialist, patriot, victory, brother, freedom, unity, peace. Though my strong impulse is to resist their flattening out of language, I've realized that I must talk this way—with moderation—if I'm to say anything that's useful to them. That even includes using the more loaded local epithets like "the puppet troops" (for the forces of the Saigon government) and "the American movement" (they mean *us!*). Luckily, I'm already comfortable with some of the key words. Within the last year, back in the States, I had started saying "the Front" (instead of Viet Cong) and "black people" (instead of Negroes) and "liberated zones" (for territory controlled by the National Liberation Front). But I'm far from getting it right, from their point of view. I notice that when I say "Marxism," it's usually rendered by our translator as "Marxism-Leninism." And while they may speak of "the socialist camp," it's hardly possible for me to say anything other than "Communist countries."

It's not that I judge their words to be false. For once, I think, the political and moral reality is as simple as the Communist rhetoric would have it. The French *were* "the French colonialists"; the Americans *are* "imperialist aggressors"; the Thieu-Ky regime *is* a "puppet government." Then what finicky private standard or bad vibrations make me balk? Is it just the old conviction of the inadequacy of that language, to which I was first introduced during my precociously political childhood when I read *PM* and Corliss Lamont and the Webbs on Russia, and later, by the time I was a junior at North Hollywood High School, worked in the Wallace campaign and attended screenings of Eisenstein films at the American-Soviet Friendship Society? But surely neither the philistine fraud of the American CP nor the special pathos of fellow-traveling in the 1940's is relevant here: North Vietnam, spring 1968. Yet how difficult it is, once words have been betrayed, to take them seriously again. Only within the last two years (and that very much because of the impact of the Vietnam war) have I been able to pronounce the words "capitalism" and "imperialism" again. For more than fifteen years, though capitalism and imperialism hardly ceased to be facts in the world, the words themselves had seemed to me simply unusable, dead, dishonest (because a tool in the hands of dishonest people). A great deal is involved in these recent linguistic decisions: a new connection with my historical memory, my aesthetic sensibility, my very idea of the future. That I've begun to use some elements of Marxist or neo-Marxist language again seems almost a miracle, an unexpected remission of historical muteness, a new chance to address problems that I'd renounced ever understanding.

Still, when I hear these tag words here, spoken by the Vietnamese, I can't help experiencing them as elements of an *official* language, and they become again an alien way of talking. I'm not referring now to the truth of this language (the realities that the words point to), which I do acknowledge, but to the context and range of sensibility it presupposes. What's painfully exposed for me, by the way the Vietnamese talk, is the gap between ethics and aesthetics. As far as I can tell, the Vietnamese possess—even within the terribly austere and materially deprived existence they are forced to lead now—a lively, even passionate aesthetic sense. More than once, for instance, people have quite unaffectedly expressed their indignation and sadness at the disfigurement of the *beauty* of the Vietnamese countryside by the American bombing. Someone even commented on the "many beautiful names," like Cedar Falls and Junction City, that the Americans have given their "savage operations in the south." But the leading way of thinking and speaking in Vietnam is unreservedly moralistic. (I suspect this is quite natural to the Vietnamese, a cultural trait that precedes any grafting on of the moralizing framework of Communist language.) And perhaps it's the general tendency of aesthetic consciousness, when developed, to make judgments more complex and more highly qualified, while it's in the very nature of moral consciousness to be simplifying, even simplistic, and to sound—in translation at least—stiff and old-fashioned. There's a committee here (someone had left a piece of stationery in the hotel lobby) for maintaining contact with South Vietnamese intellectuals, called "Committee of Struggle Against U.S. Imperialists and Henchmen's Persecution of Intellectuals in South Vietnam." Henchmen! But aren't they? In today's Vietnam News Agency bulletin the American soldiers are called "cruel thugs." Although again the quaintness of phrase makes me smile, that is just what they are—from the vantage point of helpless peasants being napalmed by swooping diving metal birds. Still, quite apart from the quaintness of particular words, such language does make me uncomfortable. Whether because I am laggard or maybe just dissociated, I both assent to the unreserved moral judgment and shy away from it, too. I believe they are right. At the same time, nothing here can make me forget that events are much more complicated than the Vietnamese represent them. But exactly what complexities would I have them acknowledge? Isn't it enough that their struggle is, objectively, just? Can they ever afford subtleties when they need to mobilize every bit of energy to continue standing up to the American Goliath? . . . Whatever I conclude, it seems to me I end up patronizing them.

Perhaps all I'm expressing is the difference between being an actor (them) and being a spectator (me). But that's a big difference, and I don't see how I can bridge it. My sense of solidarity with the Vietnamese, however genuine and felt, is a moral abstraction developed (and meant to be lived out) at a great distance from them. Since my arrival in Hanoi, I must maintain that sense of solidarity alongside new unexpected feelings which indicate that, unhappily, it will always remain a moral abstraction. For me—a spectator?—it's monochromatic here, and I feel oppressed by that.

MAY 7

Now, I think, I really understand—for the first time—the difference between history and psychology. It's the world of psychology that I miss. (What I meant yesterday by the "adult" world.) They live exclusively in the world of history.

And not only in history, but in a monothematic history that people allude to in more or less the same terms wherever we go. Today we got it in full, during a long, guided tour of the Historical Museum: four thousand years of continuous history, more than two thousand years of being overrun by foreign aggressors. The first successful Vietnamese uprising against foreign rule, in A.D. 40, was led by two women generals, the Trung sisters. That was over a thousand years before Joan of Arc, our woman guide at the museum added, as if to indicate we hadn't registered the proper surprise at the idea of a woman general. And you also have two of them, I joked back. She smiled slightly, then went on: "The tradition of the two sisters remains until now. In the present struggle many ladies have shown themselves worthwhile." No pleasantry, that. Oanh, who we've learned is one of the leading composers in North Vietnam, has written a song about the two sisters, and many temples in Hanoi and nearby are dedicated to them. . . . As the Vietnamese understand their history, it consists essentially of one scenario, which has been played out over and over again. Particular historical identities dissolve into instructive equivalences. The Americans = the French (who first entered Vietnam in 1787 with missionaries, and officially invaded the country in 1858) = the Japanese (in World War II) = the "Northern feudalists" (our guide's usual way of referring to the millennia of invading Chinese, I suppose out of politeness to the nominal ally of today). The general who repelled the Chinese invasion of 1075–76, Ly Thuong Kiet, was a poet as well and used his poems to rouse the Vietnamese people to take up arms—just like Ho Chi Minh, the guide pointed out. She told us the generals who defended the country against three invasions by "the Mongols" (another euphemism for the Chinese?) in the thirteenth century—in 1257, 1284–85, and 1287–88—originated the basic techniques of guerrilla warfare that General Giap successfully employed against the French between 1946 and 1954 and now uses against the Americans. In one room, examining a terrain map of the battle site, we learned that the turning point in a struggle against an invasion by two hundred thousand Manchu dynasty troops in 1789 was a surprise Tet offensive. As she relates, with the aid of maps and dioramas, the great sea battles on the Bach Dang River in 938 and 1288 which successfully terminated other wars of resistance, I detect unmistakable parallels to the strategies used at Dien Bien Phu. (The other night we saw an hour film on the Dien Bien Phu campaign, part original footage and part reconstruction. To-day, by the way, is the anniversary of that victory, though I've seen no signs in Hanoi of any festivities.)

My first reaction to the didactically positive way the Viet-namese have of recounting their history is to find it simple-minded ("childish" again). I have to remind myself that historical understanding can have other purposes than the ones I take for granted: objectivity and completeness. This is history for use—for survival, to be precise—and it is an entirely *felt* history, not the preserve of detached intellectual concern. The past continues in the form of the present, and the present extends backwards in time. I see that there's nothing arbitrary or merely quaint (as I'd thought) in the standard epithet for Americans which I've seen on billboards and wall posters: giac My xan luoc, "pirate American aggressors." The very first foreign invaders were pirates. So the Chinese, the French, the Japanese, now the Americans, and anybody else who invades Vietnam will always be pirates, too.

Even more than the Jews, the Vietnamese seem to suffer from an appalling lack of variety in their collective existence. History is one long martyrdom: in the case of Vietnam, the chain of episodes of victimization at the hands of great powers. And one of their proudest boasts is that people here have succeeded in retaining "Vietnamese characteristics, though we live close to the Chinese superpower and were under complete French domination for eighty years," in the words of our guide today. Perhaps only a martyr people, one which has managed to survive against crushing odds, develops so acute and personal a historical concern. And this extraordinarily vivid sense of history—of living simultaneously in the past, the present, and the future—must be one of the great sources of Vietnamese strength.

But the decision to survive at all costs in suffering obviously imposes its own aesthetic, its own peculiar and (to people not consciously driven by the imperative of survival) maddening sensibility. The Vietnamese historical sense, being, above all, a sense of the sameness of history, is reflected, naturally, in the sameness of what they say—what they feel we ought to listen to. I've become aware here of how greatly prized, and taken for granted, the value of *variety* is in Western culture. In Vietnam, apparently, something doesn't become less valuable or useful because it has been done (or said) before. On the contrary, repetition confers value on something. It is a positive moral style. Hence, the capsule summaries of Vietnamese history we get from most people we visit, almost as much a part of the ritual as the tea and green bananas and expressions of friendship for the American people whom we're supposed to represent.

But further, these speeches of historical recital that we hear almost daily are just one symptom of the general predilection of the Vietnamese for putting all information into a historical narrative. I've noticed that when we're discussing or asking questions about the country today, each account given to us is formulated around a pivotal date: usually either August 1945 (victory of the Vietnamese revolution, the founding of the state by Ho Chi Minh) or 1954 (expulsion of the French

colonialists) or 1965 (beginning of "the escalation," as they
call the American bombing). Everything is either before or
after something else.

Their framework is chronological. Mine is both chronological and geographical. I am continually reaching toward cross-
cultural comparisons, and these are the context of most of my
questions. But because they don't share this context, they seem
mildly puzzled by many things I ask. How hard it was yesterday, for instance, to get the affable, French-educated Minister
of Higher Education, Professor Ta Quang Buu, to explore the
differences between the French lycée curriculum used until
1954 and the program the Vietnamese have devised to replace
it. Though he heard my question, for a while he simply didn't
see the point of it. All he wanted was to outline the Vietnamese system (kindergarten plus ten grades), report how
few schools of any kind existed before 1954 and how many
have been opened since (except for a good medical school
inherited from the French, almost all university-level facilities
have had to be developed from scratch), cite figures on rising
literacy, tell how increasing numbers of teachers have been
trained and young people given access to higher education
and older people enrolled in adult-education courses since that
date. The same thing happened when we talked to the Minister
of Public Health, Dr. Pham Ngoc Thach, in his office in Hanoi,
and when we met the young doctor of the tiny hamlet of Vy
Ban in Hoa Binh province. After explaining that most of the
Vietnamese population had no medical services of any kind
under the French, they were eager to tell us how many
hospitals and infirmaries have been built and how many
doctors have been trained and to describe the programs
undertaken since 1954 that have brought malaria under control and virtually eliminated opium addiction, but were quite
taken aback when we wanted to know whether Vietnamese
medicine was entirely Western in orientation or whether, as
we suspected, Western techniques were mixed with Chinese
methods such as herbal medicines and acupuncture. They

must find us dilettantish, and may even regard such questions as a means of refusing full emotional solidarity with the unity and urgency of their struggle. Perhaps. It's still true that since Andy, Bob, and I don't share a history with the Vietnamese the historical view does narrow our understanding. To gain insight into what the Vietnamese are trying to build we must relate what they tell us to knowledge and perspectives we already have. But what we know, of course, is just what they don't know. And so most of our questions are a kind of rudeness, to which they respond with unfailing courtesy and patience, but sometimes obtusely.

MAY 8

Judging from these first days, I think it's hopeless. There is a barrier I can't cross. I'm overcome by how exotic the Vietnamese are—impossible for us to understand them, clearly impossible for them to understand us. No, I'm hedging here. The truth is: I feel I *can* in fact understand them (if not relate to them, except on their simplistic terms). But it seems to me that while my consciousness does include theirs, or could, theirs could never include mine. They may be nobler, more heroic, more generous than I am, but I have more on my mind than they do—probably just what precludes my ever being that virtuous. Despite my admiration for the Vietnamese and my shame over the deeds of my country, I still feel like someone from a "big" culture visiting a "little" culture. My consciousness, reared in that "big" culture, is a creature with many organs, accustomed to being fed by a stream of cultural goods, and infected by irony. While I don't think I'm lacking in moral seriousness, I shrink from having my seriousness ironed out; I know I'd feel reduced if there were no place for its contradictions and paradoxes, not to mention its diversions and distractions. Thus, the gluttonous habits of my consciousness prevent me from being at home with what I most admire, and—for all my raging against America—firmly unite me to what I condemn. "American friend" indeed!

Of course, I *could* live in Vietnam, or an ethical society like this one—but not without the loss of a big part of myself. Though I believe incorporation into such a society will greatly improve the lives of most people in the world (and therefore support the advent of such societies), I imagine it will in many ways impoverish mine. I live in an unethical society that coarsens the sensibilities and thwarts the capacities for goodness of most people but makes available for minority consumption an astonishing array of intellectual and aesthetic pleasures. Those who don't enjoy (in both senses) my pleasures have every right, from their side, to regard my consciousness as spoiled, corrupt, decadent. I, from my side, can't deny the immense richness of these pleasures, or my addiction to them. What came to mind this afternoon was the sentence of Talleyrand that Bertolucci used as the motto of his sad, beautiful film: "He who has not lived before the revolution has never known the sweetness of life." I told Andy, who knows the film, what I'd been thinking, and he confessed to similar feelings. We were walking alone in a quarter of Hanoi far from the hotel and, like truants, began talking—nostalgically?—about San Francisco rock groups and *The New York Review of Books.*

Does all this mental appetitiveness and lust for variety disqualify me from entering, at least partially, into the singular reality of North Vietnam? I suspect it does, that it already has, as indicated by my baffled, frustrated reactions to the Vietnamese so far. Maybe I'm only fit to share a people's revolutionary aspirations at a comfortable distance from them and their struggle—one more volunteer in the armchair army of bourgeois intellectuals with radical sympathies in the head. Before I give up, though, I must make sure I've read these feelings correctly. My impulse is to follow the old, severe rule: if you can't put your life where your head (heart) is, then what you think (feel) is a fraud. But it's premature to talk of fraud and hypocrisy. If the test is whether I can put my life (even imaginatively) in Vietnam, the time to take it isn't now but when I have a somewhat less meager grasp of the country.

Even if I fail the test of being able to identify myself with the Vietnamese, what have I actually proven? Perhaps I haven't experienced the constraints, real or imaginary, of ethical—or revolutionary—societies in general, only of this one. Maybe I'm only saying I find something uncongenial about North Vietnam. . . . And yet I do like the Vietnamese, respond to them, feel good with them, sometimes really happy here. Doesn't it all come down to the absurd complaint—the complaint of a real child, me—that people here aren't making it easier for me to perceive them, the wish that the Vietnamese "show" themselves to me clearly so that I can't find them opaque, simple-minded, naïve? Now I'm back where I started. The sense of the barrier between them and me. My not understanding them, their not understanding me. No judgments now (at least none I really believe).

MAY 9

How odd to feel estranged from Vietnam here, when Vietnam has been present in my thoughts every day in America. But if the Vietnam I've carried around like a wound in my heart and mind is not invalidated by what I see in Hanoi, it doesn't seem particularly related to this place at this time either. Having arrived after March 31, we are not under bombardment, though along with everyone else in Hanoi we take shelter at least once a day when the American reconnaissance planes come over. Where civilians are being slaughtered, villages burned, and crops poisoned, we aren't permitted to go. (Not for reasons of military security, since earlier American visitors were taken to areas under bombardment, but out of concern for our safety: where there's American bombing now, it goes on almost round the clock. The average daily tonnage of bombs being dropped on North Vietnam since March 31, though confined to the area below the 19th parallel, *exceeds* the daily average unloaded on the whole country before the "limited bombing pause.") We see only a handsome, evenly impoverished, clean Asian city; we see charming, dignified people living amid bleak material scarcity and the most rigorous demands on their energies and patience. The leveled towns and villages in the countryside to which we drive on short trips already constitute a tableau from the past, a thoroughly *accepted* environment in which people go on functioning, working toward their victory, making their revolution. I wasn't prepared for all this calm. Thinking about Vietnam in America, it seems natural to dwell on destruction and suffering. But not here. In Vietnam, there is also a peaceful, fiercely industrious present with which a visitor must be connected; and I'm not. I want their victory. But I don't understand their revolution.

It's all around me, of course, but I feel I'm in a glass box. We're supposed to be learning about it through the "activities" Oanh & Co. have set up in consultation with us since our arrival. In principle, we wanted to see anything and everything, and that's what's happening—though individual interests are swiftly catered to. (It was at my request that we spent an afternoon watching a movie being shot at the principal film studio in Hanoi; because Bob wanted to meet some mathematicians, a meeting with six math professors from the University of Hanoi was arranged, to which we all ended up going.) We are truly seeing and doing a great deal: at least one visit or meeting is planned for every morning and afternoon, and often in the evening as well, though we have an hour and a half each for lunch and dinner and are encouraged to rest after lunch until three o'clock, when the worst heat of the day is over. In other words, we're in the hands of skilled bureaucrats specializing in relations with foreigners. (Yes, even Oanh—whom I like more and more. Especially he.) All right, I see the inevitability of that. Who else could possibly take charge of us? But even within that framework, shouldn't we be able to go beyond it? I don't think I can. I'm obsessed

by the protocol of our situation, which leaves me unable to
believe I'm seeing a genuine sample of what this country is
like. That suggests the trip isn't going to teach me something
usable about revolutionary societies, as I'd assumed it would
—unless I count getting so shaken up, as I was yesterday, that
I question my right to profess a radical politics at all.

But perhaps there isn't much an American radical *can* learn
from the Vietnamese revolution, because the Vietnamese themselves are too alien, in contrast to the considerable amount I
think one can learn from the Cuban revolution, because—
especially from this perspective—the Cubans are pretty much
like us. Though it's probably an error, I can't help comparing
the Vietnamese with the Cuban revolution: that is, my experience of it during a three-month stay in Cuba in 1960, plus
accounts of how it has developed from friends who've visited
more recently. (I probably won't understand anything here
until I put Cuba out of my mind. But I can't ignore an experience that seems to me comparable to this one which I felt I
did understand and do have imaginative access to.) And
almost all my comparisons turn out favorable to the Cubans,
unfavorable to the Vietnamese—by the standard of what's
useful, instructive, imitable, relevant to American radicalism.

Take, for instance, the populist manners of the Cuban revolution. The Cubans, as I remember well, are informal, impulsive, easily intimate, and manic, even marathon talkers. These
may not always be virtues, but they seem so in the context of a
successful, entrenched revolutionary society. In Vietnam,
everything seems formal, measured, controlled, planned. I
long for someone to be indiscreet here. To talk about his personal life, his emotions. To be carried away by "feeling." Instead, everyone is exquisitely polite, yet somehow bland. It fits
with the impression Vietnam gives of being an almost sexless
culture, from all that I've observed, and from the evidence of
the three movies I've seen so far in Hanoi this week and the
novel I read last night in English translation. (Hieu confirmed,
when I asked him, that there is no kissing in Vietnamese plays

and films; obviously there's none in the streets or parks. I haven't seen people touching each other even in a casual way.) As Cuba has proved, a country doesn't have to adopt the puritan style when it goes Communist. And, probably, the Vietnamese attitudes toward sex and the expression of private feeling formed part of this culture long before the advent of revolutionary Marxist idealism. Nevertheless, they do discomfort a Western neo-radical like myself for whom revolution means not only creating political and economic justice but releasing and validating personal (as well as social) energies of all kinds, including erotic ones. And this *is* what revolution has meant in Cuba—despite waves of interference mainly by old-style orthodox Communist bureaucrats, who have been contested by Fidel precisely on this point.

I can't help contrasting the casual egalitarianism I observed among Cubans, whatever their rank or degree of responsibility, with the strongly hierarchical features of this society. No one is in the least servile here, but people know their place. While the deference I notice given to some by others is always graceful, there is clearly the feeling that certain people are more important or valuable than others and deserve a bigger share of the pitifully few comforts available. Hence, the store to which we were taken the third day to get tire sandals and have us each fitted for a pair of Vietnamese trousers. Hieu and Phan told us, with an almost proprietary pride, that this was a special store, reserved for foreigners (diplomatic personnel, guests) and important government people. I thought they should recognize that the existence of such facilities is "un-Communist." But maybe I'm showing here how "American" I am.

I'm troubled, too, by the meals at the Thong Nhat. While every lunch and dinner consists of several delicious meat and fish courses (we're eating only Vietnamese food) and whenever we eat everything in one of the large serving bowls a waitress instantly appears to put another one on our table, ninety-nine percent of the Vietnamese will have rice and bean curd for dinner tonight and are lucky to eat meat or fish once a month. Of course I haven't said anything. They'd probably be mystified, even insulted, if I suggested that we shouldn't be eating so much more than the average citizen's rations. It's well known that lavish and (what would be to us) self-sacrificing hospitality to guests is a staple of Oriental culture. Do I really expect them to violate their own sense of decorum? Still, it bothers me. . . . It also exasperates me that we're driven even very short distances; the Peace Committee has rented two cars, in fact—Volgas—that wait with their drivers in front of the hotel whenever we're due to go anywhere. The office of the NLF delegation in Hanoi, which we visited the other day, was all of two blocks from the hotel. And some of our destinations proved to be no more than fifteen or twenty blocks away. Why don't they let us walk, as Bob, Andy, and I have agreed among ourselves we'd feel more comfortable doing? Do they have a rule: only the best for the guests? But that kind of politeness, it seems to me, could well be abolished in a Communist society. Or must we go by car because they think we're weak, effete foreigners (Westerners? Americans?) who also need to be reminded to get out of the sun? It disquiets me to think that Vietnamese might regard walking as beneath our dignity (as official guests, celebrities, or something). Whatever their reason, there's no budging them on this. We roll through the crowded streets in our big ugly black cars—the chauffeurs blasting away on their horns to make people on foot and on bicycles watch out, give way. . . . Best, of course, would be if they would lend us, or let us rent, bicycles. But though we've dropped hints to Oanh more than once, it's clear they don't or won't take the request seriously. When we broach it, are they at least amused? Or do they just think we're being silly or impolite or dumb?

All I seem to have figured out about this place is that it's a very complex self that an American brings to Hanoi. At least this American! I sometimes have the miserable feeling that my being here (I won't speak for Andy and Bob) is a big waste of our Vietnamese hosts' time. Oanh should be spending these days writing music. Phan could reread Molière (he taught literature before he started working full-time for the Peace Committee) or visit his teenage daughters, who have been evacuated to the countryside. Hieu, whose profession turns out to be journalism, could be usefully composing articles in the dreadful prose of the North Vietnamese press. Only Toan, who apparently has some clerical job, might lose out; tagging along with the three others to entertain and keep busy the overgrown obtuse foreign guests is probably more amusing than that. What do the Vietnamese imagine is happening to us here? Do they grasp when we understand and when we don't? I'm thinking particularly of Oanh, who is obviously very shrewd and has traveled a lot in Europe, but also of all the smiling people who talk to us, flatter us ("We know your struggle is hard," someone said today), explain things to us. I fear they don't know the difference. They are simply too generous, too credulous.

But I'm also drawn to that kindly credulity. I like how people stare, often gape at us wherever we go in Hanoi. I feel they are enjoying us, that it's a pleasant experience for them to see us. I asked Oanh today if he thought people in the streets realized that we are Americans. He said that most wouldn't. Then who do they think we are, I asked. Probably Russians, was his answer; and indeed, several people have called out *tovarich* and some other Russian word at us. Most people, though, don't say anything in our direction. They stare calmly, point, then discuss us with their neighbors. Hieu says the comment most frequently made about us when we stroll or go to the movies is—delivered with good-natured amazement— how tall we are.

I go out for walks more often by myself now, whenever it's not too hot—trying to relate to the looks people give me, enjoying the ambiguities of my identity, protected by the fact that I don't speak Vietnamese and can only look back and smile. I'm no longer even surprised, as I first was, at how comfortable I am walking alone, even when I get lost in obscure neighborhoods far from the hotel. Though I'm aware of the possibility of an unpleasant incident occurring when I'm in another part of the city, unable to explain who I am or even read signs, I still feel entirely safe. There must be very few foreigners in Hanoi—except within a few blocks of the Thong Nhat, I've seen no one on the streets who isn't Vietnamese; yet here I walk unescorted among these people as if I had a perfect right to be prowling around Hanoi and to expect them all, down to the last old man squatting by the curb selling wooden flutes, to understand that and to ignore me in their amiable way. The impression of civility and lack of violence Hanoi gives is astounding, not just in comparison with any big American city but with Phnom Penh and Vientiane as well. People here are animated, plainly gregarious, but notably unquarrelsome among themselves. Even when the streets are most crowded, there's scarcely any strident noise. Though I see many small but not too well-nourished children and babies, I've yet to hear one cry.

Perhaps I feel so secure because I don't take the Vietnamese altogether seriously as "real people," according to the grim view popular where I come from that "real people" are dangerous, volatile; one is never altogether safe with them. I hope it's not that. I know I wouldn't prefer the Vietnamese to be mean or ill-tempered. But as much as I love the deep, sweet silence of Hanoi, I do miss among the Vietnamese a certain element of abrasiveness, a bigger—it doesn't have to be louder —range in their feelings.

For instance, it seems to me a defect that the North Vietnamese aren't good enough haters. How else to explain the odd fact that they actually appear to be quite fond of America? One of the recurrent themes of Dr. Thach's conversation with us was his fervent admiration for America's eminence in technology and science. (This from a cabinet minister of the country being ravaged by the cruelly perfect weapons produced by that very science and technology.) And I suspect that the extent to which the Vietnamese are so interested in and well informed about American politics—as I learned answering some questions put to me in the last days about the Nebraska primary, about Lindsay's influence in Harlem, and about American student radicalism—isn't mere expediency, part of the policy of knowing your enemy, but springs from just plain fascination with the United States. The government and professional people here who have radios listen regularly to the Voice of America and, to be sure, chuckle away at the American version of the war: this week, it's the VOA's denial that any serious military engagements are taking place in Saigon. But at the same time they seem quite respectful of American political processes and even a little sympathetic to the problems America faces as the leading world power. Poets read us verses about "your Walt Whitman" and "your Edgar Allan Poe." At the Writers Union tonight someone asked me if I knew Arthur Miller and flushed with shy pleasure when I said I did and could pass on to him the copy of the Vietnamese translation of *Death of a Salesman* I'd just been shown. "Tell us about your Norman Mailer," a young novelist asked me, and then apologized because Mailer hasn't yet been translated into Vietnamese. And they all wanted to know what kind of books I write, and made me promise to send them copies when I got back to the States. "We are very interested in American literature," someone repeated. Few translations of fiction are being published in Hanoi now, but one of the few this year was an anthology of American short stories: Mark Twain, Jack London, Hemingway, Dorothy Parker, plus some of the "progressive" writers from the 1930's favored in Eastern Europe. When I mentioned that Americans didn't consider Howard Fast and Albert Maltz in the same class as most others in the collection, one Vietnamese writer assured me they knew that. The trouble was that they actually had very few books—their main library, at the University of Hanoi, was bombed—and most of the volumes of American literature in Hanoi are the choices, and editions, of the Foreign Languages

Press in Moscow. "In socialist countries with whom we have normal relations, we can't find modern American writers," he added with a laugh. Another writer who was listening to our conversation grinned.

Of course, I'm delighted to learn that some Vietnamese are not unaware that belonging to the "socialist camp" has its disadvantages—among them, cultural isolation and intellectual provincialism. But it's also sad to think of them carrying the burden of that awareness as well, when they're so acutely conscious of Vietnam as an isolated, provincial country in its own right. Doctors, writers, academics we've talked to speak of feeling desperately cut off. As one professor said, after describing the growth of the science faculties since 1954: "But we still fail to grasp the main tendencies of work going on in the rest of the world. The material we receive is late and not adequate." For all their pride in the progress made since the French were expelled, people often mention to us, apologetically, what a "backward" country Vietnam still is. And then I realize how aware they are that we come from the world's most "advanced" country; their respect for the United States is there, whether voiced or not.

It's at these moments that I also feel like the visitor from America, though in another way. It must be because I'm so American after all, too profoundly a citizen of the nation that thinks itself the greatest in everything, that I feel actually embarrassed by the modest (if proud) self-affirmation of citizens of a small, weak nation. Their cordial interest in America is so evidently sincere that it would be boorish not to respond to it. Yet somehow it chills me, for it seems a little indecent. I'm aware now how their unexpectedly complex, yet ingenuous, relation to the United States overlays every situation between individual Vietnamese and Bob, Andy, and me. But I don't have the insight or the moral authority to strip us down to our "real" situation, beyond pathos. My political sympathies being what they are, perhaps there's no way for me or someone like me to be here except in some stereotyped capacity (as an "American friend"), no way to avoid being either self-effacing or passive or sentimental or patronizing— just as there's no way for Americans, myself included, not to measure a good six inches taller than the average Vietnamese.

There are pages more of the same in the first half of the journal I kept during my stay, interspersed with pages and pages of detailed notes on each of our visits and encounters. The strictly reportorial body of my journal, full of factual information and physical descriptions and summaries of conversations, conveys an attitude of intense, uncomplicatedly attentive concentration. But the subjective interludes, which I have partly transcribed, convey something else—the callowness and stinginess of my response.

It wasn't that I'd expected to feel at ease in North Vietnam, or to find the Vietnamese as a people exactly like Europeans and Americans. But neither had I expected to be so baffled, so mistrustful of my experiences there—and unable to subdue the backlash of my ignorance. My understanding of the country was limited to Vietnam's election as the target of what's most ugly in America: the principle of "will," the self-righteous taste for violence, the insensate prestige of technological solutions to human problems. I had some knowledge of the style of American will, from living at various times in the Southwest, in California, in the Midwest, in New England, and in recent years in New York, and from observing its impact on Western Europe during the last decade. What I didn't understand, hadn't even a clue to, was the nature of Vietnamese will—its styles, its range, its nuances. Breton has distinguished two forms of the will in authentic revolutionary struggle: "revolutionary patience" and "the cry." But these can't be confronted without grasping something of the specific quality of a people—just what I was finding so difficult in North Vietnam. Whether I concluded that my limitations, or theirs, were being exposed by my inability to have a satisfactory contact with the

Vietnamese, the impasse was the same. By around the fifth day, as the extracts from my journal indicate, I was ready to give up—on myself, which meant on the Vietnamese as well.

And then, suddenly, my experience started changing. The psychic cramp with which I was afflicted in the early part of my stay began to ease and the Vietnamese as real people, and North Vietnam as a real place, came into view.

The first sign was that I became more comfortable in talking to people: not only to Oanh, our chief guide—I talked to him more than to any other Vietnamese during my stay—but also to a militia girl or factory worker or schoolteacher or doctor or village leader whom we'd spend an hour with and never see again. I became less preoccupied with the constrictions of their language (a great deal of which I knew must be put down to that "abstractness" or "vagueness" of speech remarked on by Western visitors to every Oriental country) and with the reduction of my own resources of expression, and more sensitive to distinctions in the way the Vietnamese talked. For a start, I could distinguish between a propagandistic level of language (which still may convey the truth, but nevertheless sounds oppressive and wrong) and a merely simple kind of language. I learned, too, to pay more rather than less attention to whatever was constantly reiterated, and discovered the standard words and phrases to be richer than I'd thought.

Take, for instance, the notion of respect. "We respect your Norman Morrison" was a phrase often used in the ceremonial speeches of greeting made to us at each of our visits in Hanoi and in the countryside. We learned that Oanh had written a popular "Song to Emily"—Norman Morrison's youngest daughter, whom he took along with him when he went to immolate himself in front of the Pentagon. At the Writers Union, someone chanted for us a beautiful poem (which I'd read beforehand in English and French translation) called "The Flame of Morrison." Truck drivers taking supplies along the perilous route down to the 17th parallel are likely to have a

picture of Norman Morrison pasted on their sun visors, perhaps alongside a photograph of Nguyen Van Troi, the Saigonese youth who was executed several years ago for plotting
to assassinate McNamara during his visit to South Vietnam. At
first a visitor is likely to be both moved by this cult of Norman
Morrison and made uncomfortable by it. Although the emotion of individuals is plainly unfeigned, it seems excessive,
sentimental, and redolent of the hagiography of exemplary
cardboard heroes that has been a regular feature of Stalinist
and Maoist culture. But after the twentieth time that Norman
Morrison's name was invoked (often shyly, always affectionately, with an evident desire to be friendly and gracious to *us*,
who were Americans), I started understanding the very specific relation the Vietnamese have with Norman Morrison. The
Vietnamese believe that the life of a people, its very will, is
nourished and sustained by heroes. And Norman Morrison
really is a hero, in a precise sense. (The Vietnamese don't, as I
suspected at first, overestimate the actual impact of his sacrifice upon the conscience of America; far more than its practical
efficacy, what matters to them is the moral success of his deed,
its *completeness* as an act of self-transcendence.) Therefore,
they're speaking quite accurately when they declare their "respect" for him and when they call him, as they often do, their
"benefactor." Norman Morrison has become genuinely important for the Vietnamese, so much so that they can't comprehend that he mightn't be an equally important aliment of consciousness to us, three of their "American friends."

That very definition of us as friends, initially a source of
some embarrassment and malaise, now seemed—another sign
of the change in me—more comprehensible. Whereas at first
I'd felt both moved, sometimes to tears, and constrained by
the friendliness shown to us, eventually I could simply appreciate it, becoming more genuine and flexible in my own response. I surely had no grounds for suspecting the Vietnamese
of duplicity, or for dismissing their attitude as naïve. Since,
after all, I was a friend, why was it naïve or gullible of them to

know that? Instead of being so amazed at their ability to transcend their situation as America's victims and our identity as citizens of the enemy nation, I began to imagine concretely how it was indeed possible for the Vietnamese, at this moment in their history, to welcome American citizens as friends. It was important, I realized, not to be abashed by all the small gifts and flowers thrust on us wherever we went. I'd minded that we weren't allowed to pay for anything during our stay—not even the numerous books I asked for or the cables I sent my son in New York every few days to let him know I was all right (despite my insistence that at least I be allowed to pay for these). Gradually, I could see it was just stingy of me to resist, or feel oppressed by, the material generosity of our hosts.

But the change didn't consist only in my becoming a more graceful recipient of Vietnamese generosity, a better audience for their elaborate courtesy. Here, too, there was something further to be understood; and through more contact with people in Vietnam, I discovered their politeness to be quite unlike "ours," and not only because there was so much more of it. In America and Europe, being polite (whether in large or small doses) always carries a latent hint of insincerity, a mild imputation of coercion. For us, politeness means conventions of amiable behavior people have agreed to practice, whether or not they "really" feel like it, because their "real" feelings aren't consistently civil or generous enough to guarantee a working social order. By definition, politeness is never truly honest; it testifies to the disparity between social behavior and authentic feeling. Perhaps this disparity, accepted in this part of the world as an article of faith concerning the human condition, is what gives us our taste for irony. Irony becomes essential as a mode of indicating the truth, a whole life-truth: namely, that we both mean and don't mean what we're saying or doing. I had originally been disconcerted by the absence of irony among the Vietnamese. But if I could renounce, at least imaginatively, my conviction of the inevitability of irony, the

Vietnamese suddenly looked far less undecipherable. Their language didn't seem quite so imprisoning and simplistic, either. (For the development of ironic truths, one needs lots of words. Without irony, not so many words are required.)

The Vietnamese operate by another notion of civility than the one we're accustomed to, and that implies a shift in the meaning of honesty and sincerity. Honesty as it is understood in Vietnam bears little resemblance to the sense of honesty that has been elevated by secular Western culture virtually above all other values. In Vietnam, honesty and sincerity are functions of the dignity of the individual. A Vietnamese, by being sincere, reinforces and enhances his personal dignity. In this society, being sincere often means precisely forfeiting one's claim to dignity, to an attractive appearance; it means the willingness to be shameless. The difference is acute. This culture subscribes to an empirical or descriptive notion of sincerity, which measures whether a man is sincere by how fully and accurately his words mirror his hidden thoughts and feelings. The Vietnamese have a normative or prescriptive notion of sincerity. While our aim is to make the right alignment—correspondence—between one's words and behavior and one's inner life (on the assumption that the truth voiced by the speaker is ethically neutral, or rather is rendered ethically neutral or even praiseworthy by the speaker's willingness to avow it), theirs is to construct an appropriate relation between the speaker's words and behavior and his social identity. Sincerity, in Vietnam, means behaving in a manner *worthy* of one's role; sincerity is a mode of ethical aspiration.

Thus, it's off the point to speculate whether the warmth of Pham Van Dong during the hour conversation Bob, Andy, and I had with him in the late afternoon of May 16 was sincere in our sense, or whether the Prime Minister "really" wanted to embrace us as we left his office, before walking us out the front door and across the gravel driveway to our waiting cars. He was sincere in the Vietnamese sense: his behavior was attractive, it was becoming, it intended good. Nor is it quite right to ask whether the Vietnamese "really" hate the Americans, even though they say they don't; or to wonder why they don't hate Americans, if indeed they do not. One basic unit of Vietnamese culture is the extraordinary, beautiful gesture. But gesture mustn't be interpreted in our sense—something put on, theatrical. The gestures a Vietnamese makes aren't a performance external to his real personality. By means of gestures, those acts brought off according to whatever standards he affirms, his self is constituted. And in certain cases, personality can be wholly redefined by a single, unique gesture: for a person to do something finer than he ever has done may promote him, without residue, to a new level on which such acts are regularly possible. (In Vietnam, moral ambition is a truth—an already confirmed reality—in a way it isn't among us, because of our psychological criteria of "the typical" and "the consistent." This contrast sheds light on the quite different role political and moral exhortation plays in a society like Vietnam. Much of the discourse we would dismiss as propagandistic or manipulative possesses a depth for the Vietnamese to which we are insensitive.)

Vietnam—at least in its official view of itself—may strike the secular Western eye as a society tremendously overextended ethically, that is, psychologically. But such a judgment depends entirely on our current, modest standards of how much virtue human beings are capable of. And Vietnam is, in many ways, an affront to these standards. I remember feeling just so affronted when, during the first afternoon of a two-day drive into mountainous Hoa Binh province north of Hanoi, we stopped briefly somewhere in the countryside to visit the grave of an American pilot. As we got out of our cars and walked off the road about fifty yards through the high grass, Oanh told us that it was the pilot of an F-105 brought down by a farmer with a rifle about a year ago. The pilot had failed to eject and crashed with his plane on this very spot; some villagers recovered his body from the wreckage. Coming into a clearing, we saw not a simple grave but an elevated mound decorated with chunks of the plane's engine and a crumpled piece of wing, like a Chamberlain sculpture, and with flowers, and topped by a wooden marker on which was written the pilot's name and the date of his death. I stood there some minutes feeling haunted, barely able to comprehend that initial act of burial, astonished by the look of the site and the evidence that it was still being looked after. And afterwards, when the vice-chairman of the province's administrative council, who was traveling in my car, explained that the pilot had been buried, and in "a coffin of good wood," so that his family in America could come after the war and take his body home, I felt almost undone. What is one to make of this amazing act? How could these people, who have had spouses and parents and children murdered by this pilot and his comrades (the load of one F-105, four canisters of CBU's, kills every unsheltered living creature within an area of one square kilometer), quietly take up their shovels and tastefully arrange his grave? What did they feel? Did they realize that whatever his objective guilt, he, just as much as their dead, was a precious, irreplaceable human being who should not have died? Could they pity him? Did they forgive him? But maybe these questions are misleading. What's likely is that the villagers thought burying the pilot was a beautiful (they would probably say "humane") thing to do—a standard that both overrides and transforms their personal feelings, so far as these might enter the matter.

Such transpersonal gestures are hard for a visitor to credit on their own terms. Certainly, I wasn't entirely able to put aside my own habitual understanding of how people function. Throughout the two weeks, I was continually tempted to frame psychological questions about the Vietnamese—all the while knowing how loaded such questions are with arbitrary, Western ethical assumptions. If it even makes sense to inquire, for instance, what "ego" is for the Vietnamese, I could observe that it doesn't take many of the expressive forms familiar to us. People in North Vietnam seem astonishingly calm, and though they talk of little else but the war, their discourse is singularly unmarked by hate. Even when they use the melodramatic Communist language of denunciation, it comes out sounding dutiful and a little flat. They talk of atrocities, the marrow of their history, with an almost gentle sorrow, and still with amazement. Can these things really have happened, their manner says. Did the French really disembowel that row of handcuffed plantation workers who had gone on strike, as the photograph we saw in the Revolutionary Museum shows? How can the Americans not be *ashamed* of what they're doing here? was the unspoken question that echoed throughout our tour of another, smaller "museum" in Hanoi devoted to a display of the various genocidal weapons used by the Americans on North Vietnam in the last three years. Indeed, I think, they don't quite understand—which, after all, is just the failure of understanding one might expect to find in a culture built on shame that's currently under attack by a culture whose energies come from deploying huge increments of guilt.

That Vietnam is a culture founded on shame probably accounts for much of what one sees (and does not see) there in the range of people's expressiveness. And my formation in a culture founded on guilt is surely one reason I found it hard to understand them. I would guess that guilt-cultures are typically prone to intellectual doubt and moral convolutedness, so that, from the point of view of guilt, all cultures founded on shame are indeed "naïve." The relation to moral demands tends to be much less ambivalently felt in shame-cultures, and collective action and the existence of public standards have an inherent validity they do not possess for us.

Prominent among these public standards in Vietnam is decorum—more generally, the concern for maintaining in all exchanges between people an exacting moral tone. I might have imagined this concern to be simply Asian if I hadn't already seen something of Cambodians and Laotians, in contrast with whom the Vietnamese are much more dignified and reserved, even prudish in their manner, and also more discreet in their dress. No matter how fiercely hot it gets, nowhere does one see in Vietnam (as one does throughout Cambodia and Laos) a man in shorts or without a shirt. Everyone is neatly, if shabbily, dressed from neck to ankles—women as well as men wear long trousers—and great value is placed on being clean. The pride of people in Na Phon when they showed us their two-stall brick and cement public latrine, the first such facility in the hamlet and completed just a day earlier, had to do with more than hygiene or convenience. The new latrine was a kind of moral victory. "All the water of the Eastern Sea could not wash away the dirt left by the enemy" is a saying that dates from one of the innumerable Vietnamese struggles against the Chinese, a war which began in 1418 and ended victoriously in 1427. No doubt the North Vietnamese regard with a similar anguish the three years of American assault: once again, and most horrendously, their country has been defiled. The moral metaphor of cleanliness and dirt is, of course, found almost universally, in all cultures; still, I felt it to be especially strong in Vietnam. Its strength is strikingly expressed in the eighteenth-century epic *Kieu*, the most famous work of Vietnamese literature. (The poem is studied in detail in the schools and recited often on the radio; practically every Vietnamese knows long passages from it by heart.) When the story begins, the heroine, Kieu, is a young girl. A young man sees her, falls in love with her, secretly, and patiently courts her, but family duties suddenly call him away before he can explain. Believing herself abandoned and faced by a family crisis of her own, Kieu sells herself as a concubine to a rich man, to save her father from debtors' prison. Only after twenty years of mistreatment and degradation, in which she ends up in a brothel and from there escapes to become a bonze, is Kieu able to return home, where she meets again the man she loved. He asks her to marry him. In the long final scene, which takes place on their wedding night, Kieu tells her husband that, although she loves him deeply and has never enjoyed sexual relations with any other man, their marriage can't be consummated. He protests that her unfortunate life during their long separation means nothing to him; but she insists that she is not clean. Precisely as they love each other, she argues, they must make this sacrifice. Eventually, out of respect and love for her, he agrees. The poem ends with a description of the harmony and joy of their married life. To a Western sensibility, such a happy ending is hardly happy at all. We would rather have Kieu die of tuberculosis in the arms of her true love, just after they are reunited, than award them a lifetime together of renunciation. But to the Vietnamese, even today, the resolution of the story is both satisfying and just. What may appear to us as their being "closed," secretive, or unexpressive, I think, is partly that they are a remarkably fastidious people.

Needless to say, the standards of today are not the same as those proposed in *Kieu*. Sexual self-control, however, is still much admired. In present-day Vietnam, women and men work, eat, fight, and sleep together without raising any issue of sexual temptation. By now the Vietnamese understand that Westerners don't have the same standards of sexual propriety. Oanh, when he told me that it's very unusual for Vietnamese husbands and wives to be unfaithful to each other, even in circumstances of lengthy separation caused by war, said he knew marital fidelity was "not common" in the West. With an edge of self-mockery, he mentioned how shocked he was on one of his first trips to Europe—it was to Russia—to hear people at parties telling "indecent" jokes to each other. Now, he assured me, it bothers him less. With their incorrigible politeness, the Vietnamese have concluded that we arrange such matters differently. Thus, whenever Andy Kopkind, Bob Greenblatt, and I traveled in the countryside, no matter how primitive and small the sleeping accommodations, we were always given separate rooms (or something that passed for rooms); but on one of these trips, when we were accompanied by a nurse because Bob had become slightly ill in Hanoi the day before our departure, I noticed that the young, pretty nurse slept in the same room as our guides and drivers, who were all men. . . . Sexual self-discipline, I imagine, must be taken for granted in Vietnam. It's only a single aspect of the general demand made on the individual to maintain his dignity and to put himself at the disposal of others for the common good. In contrast to Laos and Cambodia, with their "Indian" or "southern" atmosphere that derives from an eclectic blend of Hindu and Buddhist influences, Vietnam presents the paradox of a country sharing the same severely tropical climate but living by the classical values—hard work, discipline, seriousness—of a country with a temperate or cold climate. This "northern" atmosphere is undoubtedly the legacy of those hordes of "Northern feudalists." (I also gathered that it is more attenuated in the southern region of the country. People in Hanoi describe the Saigonese as more easygoing, more emotional, more charming, but also less honest and sexually looser—in short, the conventional northern clichés about southerners.)

Thus, while the exacting demands the Vietnamese make upon themselves, in their present form, are undoubtedly reinforced by the paramilitary ethos of a left-revolutionary society under invasion, their basic form has deep historical roots, particularly in the Confucian as distinct from the Buddhist strands in Vietnamese culture. In some societies, notably Chinese, these two traditions have been experienced as sharply antagonistic. But in Vietnam, I suspect, they have not. Most Vietnamese, of course, apart from a large Catholic minority, are Buddhists. Even though we saw mostly old people praying in the pagodas, a good deal of domestic ritual still takes place (we saw altars in many homes); beyond that, there appears to be a considerable secular continuity with Buddhist values. Nevertheless, whatever in Vietnam persists of the Buddhist ethos—with its fatalism, its intellectual playfulness, its stress on charity—seems quite compatible with the ethos of discipline characteristic of Confucianism. The behavior of the Vietnamese reflects the Confucian idea that both the body politic and an individual's well-being depend on cultivating the rules of appropriate and just behavior. Also intact is the Confucian view expressed by Hsün Tzu: "All rules of decorum and righteousness are the product of the acquired virtue of the sage and not the products of the nature of man." This Confucian idea of a people's dependence on its sages partly explains the veneration felt by the Vietnamese for Ho Chi Minh, their sage-poet-leader. But only partly. As indeed the Vietnamese often insist, their regard for Ho has nothing in common with the mindless adulation surrounding Mao today. Ho's birthday is mainly an annual occasion for the North Vietnamese to show their good taste, the delicacy of their feeling toward him. "We love and respect our leader," commented the monthly journal *Hoc Tap* on Ho's birthday last year, "but we do not deify him." Far from treating him like the usual bigger-than-life, heroic, all-wise leader, people I met spoke of Ho as if they knew him personally, and what fascinates and stirs them is their sense of him as a real man. Humorous anecdotes illustrating his modesty and shyness are legion. People find him charming, even a little eccentric. And they are moved when they speak of him, reminiscing about his years of privation in exile and his sufferings in Chinese jails throughout the 1930's, and worrying over his physical frailty. *Bac Ho*, Uncle Ho, is no special title, with Orwellian Big Brother overtones, but ordinary courtesy; a Vietnamese of any age addresses someone of an older generation to whom he's not related as "Uncle" or "Aunt." (Swedish has the same usage, except that *tant* and *farbror* are used only by children or young people to address adults who are strangers, and wouldn't be said by a middle-aged person to a seventy-year-old.) The feeling for Ho Chi Minh, an intimate affection and gratitude, is only the apex of the feeling that exists between people in a small, beleaguered nation who are able to regard each other as members of one big family. Indeed, almost all the virtues admired by the Vietnamese—such as frugality, loyalty, self-sacrifice, and sexual fidelity—have, as their basic supporting metaphor, the authority of family life. Here is still another feature pointing back to

Confucianism—as distinct from Buddhism, which attaches the highest prestige to monastic separation from society and the renunciation of family ties—and away from the austerity and "puritanism" of Vietnamese culture considered as something relatively new, the graft of revolutionary ideology. (Considered as "Marxist-Leninist *thought,*" Vietnamese Communism seems conveniently vague and outstandingly platitudinous.) Though a visitor is tempted to attribute the extraordinary discipline of the country in large measure to the influence of Communist ideology, it's probably the other way around: that the influence of Communist moral demands derived its authority from the indigenous Vietnamese respect for a highly moralized social and personal order.

But I am making the Vietnamese sound more solemn than they are, when actually what is particularly noticeable is the grace with which these ends are pursued. In conversation, the Vietnamese are low-keyed; even in public meetings, they are laconic and not particularly hortatory. It is hard to recognize the passionate consciousness when it lacks the signs of passion as we know them—such as agitation and pathos. One realizes that these are people living through the most exalted moment of their consciousness, the climax of more than a quarter of a century of continuous struggle. They have already beaten the French against incredible odds. (The French first brought napalm to Vietnam. Between 1950 and 1954, eighty percent of the French budget for the war was paid for by the United States.) Now, even more incredibly, they've demonstrated they can endure whatever punishment the Americans can inflict on them, and still cohere and prosper as a people, while in the South the National Liberation Front is steadily extending its support and control of territory. Yet most of the time this mood of exaltation has to be inferred by the sympathetic observer—not because the Vietnamese are unemotional, but because of their habitual emotional tact, a cultural principle of the conservation of emotional energy. We were told that in heavily bombed places in the countryside it's common for the farmers to take their coffins with them each day when they go to the rice fields, so that if someone dies, he can be buried right then while the others continue working. In the evacuated schools, children pack up their personal belongings and bedding before they leave the dormitory hut each morning for classes and pile the tiny bundles neatly in the nearest dirt shelter, in case there is a bombing raid during the day and the hut burns down; each evening they take their bundles out of the shelter, unpack them, and set up the dormitory again. . . . More than once, observing the incredible matter-of-factness of the Vietnamese, I thought of the Jews' more wasteful and more brilliant style of meeting their historical destiny of chronic suffering and struggle. One advantage of the Vietnamese over the Jews as a martyr people, perhaps, is simply that of any culture dominated by the peasant type over a culture that has crystallized into an urban bourgeoisie. Unlike the Jews, the Vietnamese belong to a culture whose various psychic types have not yet reached a high degree of articulation (forcing them to reflect upon *each other*). It is also the advantage of having a history, albeit mainly of cruel persecution, that is anchored to a land with which people identify themselves, rather than simply (and, therefore, complicatedly) to an "identity."

The Jews' manner of experiencing their suffering was direct, emotional, persuasive. It ran the gamut from stark declamation to ironic self-mockery. It attempted to engage the sympathy of others. At the same time, it projected a despair over the difficulties of engaging others. The source of the Jewish stubbornness, of their miraculous talent for survival, is their surrender to a complex kind of pessimism. Perhaps something like the Jewish (and also "Western") style of overt expressive suffering was what I unconsciously expected to find when I came to Vietnam. That would explain why at first I took for opaqueness and naïveté the quite different way the Vietnamese have of experiencing a comparably tragic history.

It took me a while, for instance, to realize that the Vietnamese were genuinely constrained by a kind of modesty about showing us the unspeakable sufferings they have endured. Even when describing the American atrocities, they hastened to emphasize—almost as if it would be bad taste not to—that the full horror of America's war on Vietnam couldn't be seen anywhere in the North. For that, they said, one must see "what is happening to our brothers in the South." We heard the statistics of civilian casualties since February 7, 1965: sixty percent of all people killed are women and children; twenty percent of those killed and seriously wounded are elderly people. We were taken to see towns where formerly no fewer than twenty thousand and as many as eighty thousand people lived, in which not a single building was standing. We saw photographs of bodies riddled with pellets from fragmentation bombs or charred by incendiary weapons (besides napalm, the Americans also drop white phosphorus, Thermit, and magnesium on the Vietnamese). We met briefly with some forlorn victims of "the escalation," among them a girl of twenty-four whose husband and mother-in-law and children had been killed in a single raid, and an elderly Mother Superior and two young nuns who were the only survivors of the bombing of a Catholic convent located just south of Hanoi. Nevertheless, our North Vietnamese hosts seemed anything but eager to ply us with atrocities. They seemed more pleased to tell us, as we visited ruin after ruin, when there had been no casualties—as was the case when the new 170-bed hospital outside of Hoa Binh City was destroyed. (The hospital had been evacuated just before the first raid in September 1967; it was bombed several times afterwards and of course has never been reoccupied.) The impression the Vietnamese prefer to give, and do, is of a peaceful, viable, optimistic society. Ho Chi Minh has even given, in a speech after August 1945, a five-point recipe "for making life optimistic": each person must (1) be good in politics, (2) be able to draw or paint, (3) know music, (4) practice some sport, and (5) know at least one foreign language. Thus, by optimism among the Vietnamese, I mean not only their implacable conviction that they are going to win, but their espousal of optimism as a form of understanding, the emphasis placed throughout the whole society on continuous improvement.

Indeed, one of the most striking aspects of Vietnam is the positiveness of their approach to almost any problem. As Professor Buu, the Minister of Higher Education, remarked without a trace of irony: "The Americans have taught us a lot. For instance, we see that what's necessary for education is not beautiful buildings, like the brand-new Polytechnic School in Hanoi which we had to abandon in 1965 with the start of the escalation. When we went into the jungle and built the decentralized schools, education improved. We'd like better food and more colorful clothes, of course, but in these three years we've learned one can do many things without them. We don't regard them as fundamental, though very important all the same." Among the advantages, he said, in having been forced to evacuate the colleges of Hanoi into the countryside were that the college students had to put up their new school buildings themselves and learn how to grow their own food (every evacuated school or factory forms a new community and is asked not to be parasitic on the nearest village but to become self-sufficient on the level of a subsistence economy). Through these ordeals, "a new man" is being formed. Somehow, incredibly, the Vietnamese appreciate the assets of their situation, particularly its effect on character. When Ho Chi Minh said that bombing heightens the "spirit" of people, he meant more than a stiffening of morale. There is the belief that the war has effected a permanent improvement in the moral level of people. For instance, for a family to be uprooted and have all its possessions destroyed (many families have relics going back ten centuries) has always been considered in Vietnam the worst possible fate, but now that just this has happened to so many tens of thousands of families, people have discovered the positive advantages of being stripped of everything: that one becomes more generous, less attached to "things." (This is the theme of a movie I saw, *The Forest of Miss Tham*, in which at the end, to facilitate the repair of a truck route after bombing, an old peasant volunteers to cut down the two trees he has spent his whole life growing.) The bombing has also been, for instance, an occasion for developing people's poise and articulateness and administrative talents. Each village or hamlet, through an elected team, does its own reporting on the bombing; in Hanoi and Haiphong, several residents from each street are delegated to make out detailed reports. I remember, on our inspection of the bombed areas of Hanoi, receiving such a report from the leader of the "investigation team" of Quan Than Street (two kilometers from our hotel), an elderly uneducated worker who, since he was elected to this job by his neighbors, had learned a whole new set of skills. The war has made people cleverer and also democratized the use of intelligence, since everybody has essentially the same task: protecting the country, repelling the aggressors. Throughout North Vietnam, self-help plus cooperation has become the regular form of social and economic life. This may sound like the conventional code of a socialist economy applied in an underdeveloped country. But North Vietnam is not just one more small, economically backward member of the Third World, afflicted with the standard handicaps of an over-specialized economy (imposed by colonial rule), illiteracy, disease, and hard-to-assimilate tribal peoples culturally anterior to the majority population. (Vietnam has sixty "ethnic minorities.") It is a country that has literally been gashed and poisoned and leveled by steel, toxic chemicals, and fire. Under these circumstances, self-sufficiency would hardly be enough —were it not for the remarkable ability of the Vietnamese somehow to nourish themselves on disaster.

People there put it much more simply: it's just a question of being sufficiently ingenious. The overwhelming superiority of the United States in manpower, weapons, and resources and the extent of the devastation already wrought on their country pose a definite "problem," as the Vietnamese often said, but one they fully expect to solve by their unlimited and "creative" devotion to work. Everywhere we went, we saw evidence of the tremendous output of toil needed to keep North Vietnam going. Work is, as it were, evenly distributed over the whole surface of the country—like the huge wooden crates lying, unguarded, on the edges of sidewalks on many streets in Hanoi ("our evacuated warehouses," Oanh said) and on country roads, or the piles of tools and other material left in the open alongside the railroad tracks so that repair of the track can start within minutes after a bombing. Nevertheless, willing as the Vietnamese are to rebuild the country inch by inch with shovel and hammer, they have a rather elegant sense of priorities. For instance, it was usual for the craters blasted in rice fields by the B-52's to be filled in by the farmers within days after the raid. But we saw several craters, made by 2,000- and 3,000-pound bombs, so big it had been judged that the time and labor needed to fill them would be prohibitive; these had been converted into fish-breeding ponds. Though the on-going and endless work of repairing bomb-damaged sites and facilities or constructing new, better-protected ones consumes most of their energies now, the Vietnamese think a great deal about the future. Mindful of their postwar need for people with sophisticated skills, the Vietnamese have not mobilized teachers and professors or any of the 200,000 students in colleges and vocational schools; indeed, the number of students enrolled in programs of higher education has steadily risen since 1965. Architects have already drawn up plans for the completely new cities (including Hanoi, which the North Vietnamese fully expect to be razed before the Americans finally withdraw) that must be built after the war.

A visitor may conclude that this work, for all its ingenuity, is mainly conservative in purpose—the means whereby the society can survive—and only secondarily expresses a revolutionary vision—the instrument of a society bent on radical change. But the two purposes, I think, cannot be separated. The war seems to have democratized North Vietnam more profoundly, and radically, than any of the socialist economic reforms undertaken between 1954 and 1965. For instance, the war has broken down one of the few strong articulations in Vietnamese society: between the city and the country. (Peasants still make up eighty percent of the North Vietnamese population.) When the American bombing started, over a million and a half people left Hanoi, Haiphong, and other smaller cities and scattered throughout the countryside, where they have been living now for several years; the population of Hanoi alone dropped from around one million before 1965 to less than 200,000. And this migration, several Vietnamese told me, has already effected a marked change in manners and sensibility, both among peasants who have had to absorb a colony of motley refugees with urban habits and tastes, and among people from Hanoi or Haiphong, many of whom knew nothing about the starkly primitive conditions of daily existence that still prevail in the villages and hamlets but find themselves thriving psychically on physical austerity and the community-mindedness of rural life.

The war has also democratized the society by destroying most of the modest physical means as well as restricting the social space Vietnam had at its disposal for differentiated kinds of production (I include everything from industry to the arts). Thus, more and more people are working at all kinds of activities at the same level—with their bare hands. Each small, low building in the complexes of evacuated schools that have been set up throughout the countryside had to be made in the simplest way: mud walls and a straw roof. All those kilometers of neat trenches connecting and leading away from every building, to get the children out in case of attack, had to be painstakingly dug out of the red clay. The omnipresent bomb shelters—throughout Hanoi, in each village and hamlet, at intervals on the side of every road, in every tilled field—had to be put up, one by one, by people living nearby, in their spare time. (Since 1965, the Vietnamese have dug more than 50,000 kilometers of trenches and constructed, for a population of

17,000,000, more than 21,000,000 bomb shelters.) Late one night, on our way back to Hanoi from a trip to the north, we visited a decentralized factory housed in crude sheds at the foot of a mountain. While several hundred women and young boys were operating the machines by the light of kerosene lamps, a dozen men using only hammers were widening the walls of a small adjacent cave to make a shelter safe from bombing for the biggest machinery. Almost everything in North Vietnam has to be done manually, with a minimum of tools. Time enough to wonder what the vaunted aid from Russia and China amounts to: however much there is of it, it's scarcely enough. The country is pitifully lacking in such elementary hospital equipment as sterilizers and X-ray machines, in typewriters, in basic tools like lathes and pneumatic drills and welding machines; there seem to be plenty of bicycles and quite a few transistor radios, but books of all kinds, paper, pens, phonographs, clocks, and cameras are very scarce; the most modest consumer goods are virtually nonexistent. Clothing, too, exists only in a limited supply. A Vietnamese is lucky if he owns two sets of clothes and one pair of shoes; rationing allows each person six meters of cotton fabric a year. (The cotton comes in only a few colors and most garments are almost identically cut: black trousers and white blouses for the women; tan, gray, or beige trousers and tan or white shirts for the men. Ties are never worn, and jackets only rarely.) Even the clothes of very high officials are frayed, dully stained, shiny from repeated washings. Dr. Thach, cousin of the former puppet emperor Bao Dai and, before throwing in his lot with the revolution, one of the richest landowners in Vietnam, mentioned that he hasn't had any new clothes in two years. Food is very short, too, though no one starves. Industrial workers get a monthly ration of 24 kilos of rice; everyone else, including the highest government officials, gets 13.5 kilos a month.

Lacking almost everything, the Vietnamese are forced to put everything they do have to use, sometimes multiple use. Part of this ingenuity is traditional; for example, the Vietnamese make an astonishing number of things out of bamboo—houses, bridges, irrigation devices, scaffolding, carrying poles, cups, tobacco pipes, furniture. But there are many new inventions. Thus, American planes have become virtual mines in the sky. (The supply is still far from cut off. During our stay in Hanoi, the Vietnamese bagged a dozen of the unmanned reconnaissance planes that have been flying over several times a day since March 31; and they get more planes below the 19th parallel, where the air attack is more intense now than at any time before the "limited bombing pause.") Each plane that's shot down is methodically taken apart. The tires are cut up to make the rubber sandals that most people wear. Any component of the engine that's still intact is modified to be reused as part of a truck motor. The body of the plane is dismantled, and the metal is melted down to be made into tools, small machine parts, surgical instruments, wire, spokes for bicycle wheels, combs, ashtrays, and of course the famous numbered rings given as presents to visitors. Every last nut, bolt, and screw from the plane is used. The same holds for anything else the Americans drop. In several hamlets we visited, the bell hanging from a tree which summoned people to meetings or sounded the air-raid alert was the casing of an unexploded bomb. Being shown through the infirmary of a Thai hamlet, we saw that the protective canopy of the operating room, relocated, since the bombing, in a rock grotto, was a flare parachute.

In these circumstances, the notion of a "people's war" is no mere propagandistic slogan but takes on a real concreteness, as does that favorite hope of modern social planners, decentralization. A people's war means the total, voluntary, generous mobilization of every able-bodied person in the country, so that everyone is available for any task. It also means the division of the country into an indefinite number of small, self-sufficient communities which can survive isolation, make decisions, and continue contributing to production. People on a *local* level are expected, for instance, to solve any kind of problem put to them as the aftermath of enemy bombing.

To observe in some of its day-to-day functioning a society based on the principle of total use is particularly impressive to someone who comes from a society based on maximal waste. An unholy dialectic is at work here, in which the big wasteful society dumps its garbage, its partly unemployable proletarian conscripts, its poisons, and its bombs upon a small, virtually defenseless, frugal society whose citizens, those fortunate enough to survive, then go about picking up the debris, out of which they fashion materials for daily use and self-defense.

The principle of total use applies not only to things but to thoughts as well, and grasping this helped me to stop mechanically chafing at the intellectual flatness of Vietnamese discourse. As each material object must be made to go a long way, so must each idea. Vietnamese leaders specialize in an economical, laconic wisdom. Take the saying of Ho, repeated to us often: "Nothing is more precious than independence and liberty." Not until I'd heard the quote many many times did I actually consider it. But when I did, I thought, yes, it really does say a great deal. One could indeed, as the Vietnamese have, live spiritually from that simple sentence for a long time. The Vietnamese regard Ho not as a thinker but as a man of action; his words are for use. The same standard applies to the iconography of the Vietnamese struggle, which is hardly outstanding for either visual or ideological subtlety. (Of course, the utilitarian principle doesn't work equally well in all contexts, as evidenced by the rather low level of Vietnamese visual art, with the exception of posters. In contrast to the poor development not only of painting but of film, prose fiction, and dance as well, poetry and theatre seemed to me the only arts in a sophisticated condition, as arts, in Vietnam now.) The principle of getting maximal use from everything may partly explain why there are still quite a few pictures of Stalin in North Vietnam, hanging on the wall in some but hardly all government offices, factories, and schools. Stalin is the traditional figure on the right in the tintype pantheon Marx-Engels-Lenin-Stalin, and the Vietnamese lack both time and incentive for symbolic controversy. The composition of that quartet represents a form of politeness to the leading country and titular head of the "socialist camp" which was installed when the present government came to power in 1954. People in North Vietnam are perfectly well aware that the picture is out of date in 1968, and many North Vietnamese appeared to me to have grave reservations about the Soviet Union's domestic and foreign policies, even the character of its people. (Ho Chi Minh, whose picture is rarely to be seen in public buildings, pointedly refused the Lenin Prize a few years ago.) But whatever the Vietnamese, especially in Hanoi, might think, or even express privately, about the Russians—that they are collaborating with the Americans, that they don't genuinely back Vietnam's struggle, that they've abandoned the ideals of genuine Communism and of world revolution, that they're prone to be drunks and boors—does not yet invalidate the old icon. It remains, at least for the present, as a polite tribute to the *idea* of unity and solidarity among the Communist countries.

It's all part of the Vietnamese style, which seems guided by an almost principled avoidance of "heaviness," of making more complications than are necessary. No one can fail to credit the Vietnamese with subtlety in planning large-scale actions, as evidenced in the fabulous strategic sense of General Giap. But directness and plainness remain the rule when it comes to expressing something or making a gesture, and not out of any deeper artfulness. It was my impression that the Vietnamese, as a culture, genuinely believe that life is simple. They also believe, incredible as it may seem considering their present situation, that life is full of joy. Joy is to be discerned behind what is already so remarkable: the ease and total lack of self-pity with which people worked a backbreaking number of hours, or daily faced the possibility of their own death and the death of those they love. The phenomena of existential agony, of alienation, just don't appear among the Vietnamese—probably in part because they lack our kind of "ego" and our endowment of free-floating guilt. Of course, it's hard for a visitor to take all this at face value. I spent much of my early time in Vietnam wondering what lay "behind" the Vietnamese's apparent psychic equilibrium. The kind of seriousness—identified, Confucian-style, with unselfishness—that is deeply ingrained in Vietnamese culture is something which visitors from the Western capitalist world, equipped with their tools of psychological debunking, can hardly recognize, much less fully credit. Right away, the delicate build of the Vietnamese and their sheer physical gracefulness can set a gawky, big-boned American on edge. The Vietnamese behave with an unfaltering personal dignity that we tend to find suspect, either naïve or sham. And they appear so singularly and straightforwardly involved with the virtue of courage, and with the ideal of a noble, brave life. We live in an age marked by the discrediting of the heroic effort; hence, the awareness most people in this society have of their lives, whether they are appalled by it or not, as stale and flat. But in Vietnam one is confronted by a whole people possessed by a belief in what Lawrence called "the subtle, lifelong validity of the heroic impulse." Educated urban Americans, imbued with a sense of the decline of the heroic spirit, must find it especially difficult to perceive what animates the Vietnamese, to correlate the "known" historical dossier of their long, patient struggle to liberate their country with what can really be "believed" about people.

Ultimately, the difficulty encountered visiting North Vietnam reflects the crisis of credulity that is endemic in Western post-industrial society. Not only do the Vietnamese have virtues that thoughtful people in this part of the world simply don't believe in any more. They also mix virtues that we consider incompatible. For instance, we think war to be by its very nature "dehumanizing." But North Vietnam is simultaneously a martial society, completely mobilized for armed struggle, and a deeply civil society which places great value on gentleness and the demands of the heart. One of the more astonishing instances of Vietnamese concern for the heart, related to me by Phan, is the treatment accorded the thousands of prostitutes rounded up after the liberation of Hanoi from the French in 1954. They were put in charge of the Women's Union, which set up rehabilitation centers for them in the countryside, where they first passed months being elaborately pampered. Fairy tales were read to them; they were taught children's games and sent out to play. "That," Phan explained, "was to restore their innocence and give them faith again in man. You see, they had seen such a terrible side of human nature. The only way for them to forget that was to become little children again." Only after this period of mothering were they taught to read and write, instructed in a trade by which they could support themselves, and given dowries to improve their chances of eventually marrying. There seems no doubt that people who can think up such therapy really have a different moral imagination than we have. And as the quality of Vietnamese love differs from ours, so does the nature of their hate. Of course, the Vietnamese hate the Americans in some sense—but not as Americans would, if we had been subjected to equivalent punishment at the hands of a superior power. The North Vietnamese genuinely care about the welfare of the hundreds of captured American pilots and give them bigger rations than the Vietnamese population gets, "because they're bigger than we are," as a Vietnamese army officer told me, "and they're used to more meat than we are." People in North Vietnam really do believe in the goodness of man ("People in every country are good," Ho said in 1945, "only the governments are bad"), and in the perennial possibility of rehabilitating the morally fallen, among whom they include implacable enemies, even the Americans. In spite of all the stiff words disseminated by the Vietnamese, it's impossible not to be convinced by the genuineness of these concerns.

Still, apart from the general problem of credulity a Western visitor brings to a society like Vietnam, one may be doubly wary of any deeply positive reaction to the Vietnamese. The moment one begins to be affected by the moral beauty of the Vietnamese, not to mention their physical grace, a derisive inner voice starts calling it phony sentimentality. Understandably, one fears succumbing to that cut-rate sympathy for places like Vietnam which, lacking any real historical or psychological understanding, becomes another instance of the ideology of primitivism. The revolutionary politics of many people in capitalist countries is only a new guise for the old conservative culture-criticism: posing against overcomplex, hypocritical, devitalized, urban society choking on affluence the idea of a simple people living the simple life in a decentralized, uncoercive, passionate society with modest material means. As eighteenth-century *philosophes* pictured such a pastoral ideal in the Pacific islands or among the American Indians, and German romantic poets supposed it to have existed in ancient Greece, late twentieth-century intellectuals in New York and Paris are likely to locate it in the exotic revolutionary societies of the Third World. If some of what I've written evokes the very cliché of the Western left-wing intellectual idealizing an agrarian revolution that I was so set on not being, I must reply that a cliché is a cliché, truth is truth, and direct experience is—well—something one repudiates at one's peril. In the end I can only avow that, armed with these very self-suspicions, I found, through direct experience, North Vietnam to be a place which, in many respects, *deserves* to be idealized.

But, having stated my admiration for the Vietnamese (people, society) as bluntly and vulnerably as I can, I should emphasize that none of this amounts to a claim that North Vietnam is a model of a just state. One has only to recall the more notorious crimes committed by the present government: for example, the persecution of the Trotskyist faction and the execution of its leaders in 1946, and the forcible collectivization of agriculture in 1956, the brutalities and injustices of which high officials have recently admitted. Still, a foreigner should try to avoid padding out the lamentable facts with a reflex reaction to words. Upon learning that in North Vietnam today everyone belongs to at least one "organization" (usually several), a non-Communist visitor is likely to assume that the Vietnamese must be regimented and deprived of personal liberty. With the rise to dominance of the ideology of the bourgeoisie in the last two centuries, people in Europe and America have learned to associate membership in public organizations with becoming "depersonalized," and to identify achievement of the most valuable human goals with the autonomy of private life. But this apparently isn't how the threat of depersonalization arises in Vietnam; there, people rather experience themselves as dehumanized or depersonalized when they are not bound to each other in regular forms of collectivity. Again, a visitor of the independent Left will probably wince each time the Vietnamese mention "the Party." (The 1946 constitution does allow for a plurality of political groupings, and there is a Socialist Party and a Democratic Party, both of which publish weekly newspapers and have some representation in the government. But *Lao Dong*, the Workers Party, with nearly a hundred members on its Central Committee, is "the Party"; it runs the country, and the candidates it proposes are overwhelmingly favored by the electoral system.) But the preference for government by a single party of newly independent countries which have never known multi-party democracy is a fact that merits a more discriminating response than automatic disapproval. Several Vietnamese I met themselves brought up the dangers of single-party rule and claimed that in spite of these dangers the Workers Party had proved it deserves to hold power by being responsive to the concrete local demands of people. For the Vietnamese, "the Party" simply means the effective leadership of the country— from Ho Chi Minh, founder of the independent nation and of the Party (in 1930), to the young cadre just out of the Party School who comes to a village under bombardment to show its inhabitants how to build shelters or volunteers to live in the high mountains, among the Meo or Muong minorities, and teach them how to read and write. Of course, this conception of the Party as a vast corps of skilled, ethically impeccable, mostly unpaid public servants, tutoring and working alongside people in all their activities, sharing their hardships, doesn't exempt the Vietnamese system from terrible abuses. But neither does it preclude the possibility that the present system functions humanely, with genuine substantive democracy, much of the time.

In any case, I noticed that the word "democracy" was frequently invoked in Vietnam, far more often than in any other Communist country I've visited, including Cuba. The Vietnamese claim that democracy has deep roots in their culture, specifically in the customs of a fiercely independent peasantry. ("The law of the king must be subordinate to the law of the village," runs an old proverb.) Even in the past, Dr. Thach said, the form of the regime—kings and mandarins— was authoritarian, but its content—the traditions of village life—was democratic. Whether or not this account stands up to objective scrutiny, it's interesting that the Vietnamese *think* it true that their country is, and always has been, democratic. North Vietnam is the only Communist country I know in which people regularly praise the United States for being, after all and despite everything, "a great democracy." (As I've suggested, the Vietnamese don't show a very advanced command of Marxist thinking and critical analysis.) All this, myth as well as reality, must be taken into consideration when evaluating the nature of public institutions in North Vietnam and their role in promoting or discouraging individuality. The life of an institution cannot be appraised by examining a blueprint of its structure; run under the auspices of different feelings, similar structures can have a quite different quality. For instance, when love enters into the substance of social relations, the connection of people to a single party need not be dehumanizing. Though it's second nature for me to suspect the government of a Communist country of being oppressive and rigid, if not worse, most of my preconceptions about the misuses of state power in North Vietnam were really an abstraction. Against that abstract suspiciousness I must set (and be overruled by) what I actually saw when I was there —that the North Vietnamese genuinely love and admire their leaders; and, even more inconceivable to us, that the government loves the people. I remember the poignant, intimate tones in Pham Van Dong's voice as he described the sufferings the Vietnamese have endured in the last quarter of a century and their heroism, decency, and essential innocence. Seeing for the first time in my life a prime minister praising the moral character of his country's people with tears in his eyes has modified my ideas about the conceivable relations between rulers and ruled, and given me a more complex reaction to what I would ordinarily dismiss as mere propaganda.

For while no dearth of propaganda is put out by the North Vietnamese, what makes one despair is that this propaganda conveys so poorly, insensitively, and unconvincingly the most admirable qualities of the society built since 1954. Anyone who consults the publications about North Vietnam (on education, public health, the new role of women, literature, war crimes, etc.) issued in English and French by the Foreign Languages Press in Hanoi will not only get virtually nothing of the delicate texture of North Vietnamese society but be positively misled by the bombastic, shrill, and overly general character of these texts. Toward the close of my stay I mentioned to several government people that foreigners, reading these books and press releases, couldn't possibly form an idea of what North Vietnam is like, and explained my general impression that their revolution is being betrayed by its language. Though the Vietnamese I talked to seemed aware of the problem—they indicated I wasn't the first foreign visitor to tell them this—I felt they're far from knowing how to solve it. (I learned that Pham Van Dong had made a speech three years ago criticizing "the disease of rhetoric" that he charged was rife among the political cadres and appealing for an "improvement" of the Vietnamese language. But the only concrete advice he gave was that people spend less time talking about politics and more time reading classical Vietnamese literature.)

Can North Vietnam really be such an exceptional place? That's a question I have no way of answering. But I do know that North Vietnam, while definitely no Shangri-La, is a truly remarkable country; that the North Vietnamese is an extraordinary human being, and in ways not accounted for by the well-known fact that any keen struggle, a really desperate crisis, usually brings out the best (if not the worst) in people and promotes a euphoria of comradeship. What is admirable in the Vietnamese goes deeper than that. The Vietnamese are "whole" human beings, not "split" as we are. Inevitably, such people are likely to give outsiders the impression of great "simplicity." But while the Vietnamese are stripped down, they are hardly simple in any sense that grants us the right to patronize them.

It is *not* simple to be able to love calmly, to trust without ambivalence, to hope without self-mockery, to act courageously, to perform arduous tasks with unlimited resources of energy. In this society, a few people are able just faintly to imagine all these as achievable goals—though only in their private life. But in Vietnam the very distinction taken for granted here between the public and the private has not been strongly developed. This indistinct separation between public and private among the Vietnamese also informs their pragmatic, verbally and conceptually meager style of making their revolution. By way of contrast, the acute sense of the discontinuity of private and public in the West may partly explain the amount of talk, often very interesting talk, that accompanies every revolutionary gesture.* In our society, talk

---

* What brings about genuine revolutionary change is the shared experience of revolutionary *feelings*—not rhetoric, not the discovery of social injustice, not even intelligent analysis, and not any action

is perhaps the most intricately developed expression of private individuality. Conducted at this high pitch of development, talking becomes a double-edged activity: both an aggressive act and an attempted embrace. Thus talk often testifies to the poverty or inhibition of our feelings; it flourishes as a substitute for more organic connections between people. (When people really love, or are genuinely in touch with themselves, they tend to shut up.) But Vietnam is a culture in which people have not got the final devastating point about talking, have not gauged the subtle, ambivalent resources of language —because they don't experience as we do the isolation of a "private self." Talk is still a rather plain instrumentality for them, a less important means of being connected with their environment than direct feeling, love.

The absence of the sharp distinction between public and private spheres also allows the Vietnamese a relation to their country that must seem exotic to us. It is open to the Vietnamese to love their country passionately, every inch of it. One can't exaggerate the fervor of their patriotic passion and their intense attachment to particular places. Most people, I noticed, volunteer quickly where they are from, with a special

---

considered in itself. And one can indeed "talk" revolutions away, by a disproportion between consciousness and verbalization, on the one hand, and the amount of practical *will*, on the other. (Hence the failure of the recent revolution in France. The French students talked —and very beautifully, too—instead of reorganizing the administration of the captured universities. Their staging of street demonstrations and confrontations with the police was conceived as a rhetorical or symbolic, rather than a practical, act; it too was a kind of talking.)

In our society, "idealistic" tends to mean "disorganized"; "militant" tends to mean merely "emotional." Most of the people in Europe and the Americas who are quite vociferous in their denunciations of the society in which they live are profoundly confused and thoughtless not only about what they would prefer instead but about any plan for actually taking power, so radical change might be effected. Indeed, revolution in the Western capitalist countries seems, more often than not, to be an activity expressly designed never to succeed. For many people, it is an *a*social activity, a form of action designed for the assertion of individuality against the body politic. It is the ritual activity of outsiders, rather than of people united by a passionate bond to their country.

melancholy if they were born in the South and have therefore been prevented from returning there for many years. And I remember Oanh describing his childhood on his uncle's fishing boat in Ha Long Bay, a famous resort area during the French colonial period. (Oanh recalled the excitement he felt as a small boy in the late 1920's when Paulette Goddard spent a holiday there.) But when Oanh had gone on for a while about the splendors of the rock formations in the bay, now heavily bombed, he stopped, almost apologetically, to say something like: Of course your Rocky Mountains must be very beautiful, too.

But is it possible to feel like that about America now? That was something I often debated with the Vietnamese. They assured me that I must love America just as much as they love Vietnam. It's my patriotism that makes me oppose my country's foreign policy; I want to preserve the honor of the country I cherish above all others. There was some truth in what they said: all Americans—alas—believe that America is special, or ought to be. But I knew I didn't feel the positive emotion that Vietnamese attributed to me. Outrage and disappointment, yes. Love, no. Putting it in the baby language they and I shared (which I'd become rather skillful at), I explained: it's hard to love America right now, because of the violence which America is exporting all over the world; and given that the interests of humanity come before those of any particular people, a decent American today must be an internationalist first and a patriot second. Once at the Writers Union, when I had made this point (and not for the first time, so my voice may have been a little plaintive), a young poet answered me soothingly in English: "We are patriots, but in a happy way. You have more suffering in your patriotism." Sometimes they seemed to understand, but more often they didn't. Perhaps the difficulty is that, as I've already mentioned, they're quite fond of America themselves. People in Vietnam appear to take for granted that the United States *is* in many ways the greatest country in the world: the richest, the most advanced technologically, the most alive culturally, the most powerful, even the most free. They are not only endlessly curious about America—Oanh said several times how much he longs to visit the States as soon as the war is over—but genuinely admiring. I have described earlier the avidity of the poets and novelists for American literature. Pham Van Dong mentioned respectfully "your Declaration of Independence," from which Ho Chi Minh quoted when he declared the independence of Vietnam from the French on September 2, 1945. Hoang Tung, the editor of the principal daily paper, *Nhan Dan,* spoke of his "love" for the United States and praised to us "your tradition of freedom" which makes possible such creative political acts as the sit-in and the teach-in. The United States, he said, disposes of possibilities of good unmatched by any other country in the world.

If their view of the United States seemed at first improbable, then innocent and touching, the emotion the Vietnamese have for their own country seemed utterly alien, and even dangerous. But by the end of my visit I began to feel less estranged. Discovering the essential purity of their own patriotism showed me that such an emotion need not be identical with chauvinism. (How sensitive the Vietnamese are to the difference was clear in the only slightly concealed distaste of people I met in Hanoi for recent developments in China, like the cult of Mao and the cultural revolution.) If the Vietnamese could make such distinctions, so could I. Of course, I knew perfectly well why the attitude the Vietnamese expected of me was in fact so difficult. Ever since World War II, the rhetoric of patriotism in the United States has been in the hands of reactionaries and yahoos; by monopolizing it, they have succeeded in rendering the idea of loving America synonymous with bigotry, provincialism, and selfishness. But perhaps one shouldn't give up so easily. When the chairman of the Writers Union, Dang Thai Mai, said in his speech of welcome to Bob, Andy, and myself, "You are the very picture of the genuine American," why should I have slightly flinched?

If what I feel is that flag-waving Legionnaires and Irish cops and small-town car salesmen who will vote for George Wallace are the genuine Americans, not I—which I fear part of me does feel—isn't that cowardly, shallow, and simply untrue? Why should I (we) not think of myself (ourselves) as a genuine American? With a little more purity of vision—but one would have to close the seepage of private despair into public grievances—maybe an intelligent American who cares for the other ninety-six percent of the human population and for the bio-ecological future of the planet could love America, too. Probably no serious radical movement has any future in America unless it can revalidate the tarnished idea of patriotism. One of my thoughts in the closing days of my stay in North Vietnam was that I would like to try.

Unfortunately, the first test of my vow came much sooner than I expected, almost immediately, in the first hours after leaving Hanoi the evening of May 17, and I failed right off. I wish something could be arranged to insure a proper "coming down" for visitors to North Vietnam in the first days after their departure. Unprepared, the ex-guest of the Democratic Republic of North Vietnam is in for a series of brutal assaults. Thirty minutes out of Hanoi, it was the spectacle of the drunken Polish members of the International Control Commission sitting around a table in the forward part of the plane dealing out a deck of pornographic playing cards. As we made our first touchdown, in the small airfield of Vientiane, it was seeing the landing area crowded with planes marked Air America (the C.I.A.'s private airline) which leave daily from here to drop napalm on villages in Northern Laos held by the Pathet Lao. Then came the taxi ride into Vientiane itself, River City U.S.A. (as Andy dubbed it), sordid outpost of the American empire. Servile, aggressive Laotian pedi-cab drivers trying to hustle a fare, an elderly lady tourist or a freaked-out hippie or an American soldier, weaved in and out of Cadillacs driven by American businessmen and Laotian government personnel. We passed the movie theatres showing skin flicks for the GI's, the "American" bars, the strip joints, stores selling paperbacks and picture magazines that could have been transplanted directly from Times Square, the American Embassy, Air France, signs for the weekly meeting of the Rotary Club. In the lobby of the Lane Xang, the one "modern" hotel in Vientiane, we bought copies of *Newsweek* and *Time* to catch up on what had been going on, during our absence of two weeks, in our world. Minutes later, Bob, Andy, and I were sitting on benches covered with thick red plastic in the hotel's air-conditioned cocktail lounge, getting drunk, soaking up Muzak, and poring helplessly, incredulously, and eagerly through the magazines. We began cracking hysterical jokes, with Andy further amplifying on his running gag about the Lone Ranger and Tonto that had been Bob's and my delight since the beginning of the trip—only it wasn't funny now. We debated going out and buying some grass (what else could one do here?) but decided against it, mainly because we were reluctant to go into the street and get even more depressed. By midnight we were all feeling positively sick. When dawn came four insomniac hours later, I could see out the window of my room across the flat, almost dry Mekong River. The river bed is an unguarded frontier, for what lies on the far side is Thailand, another, much more important American colony, home of the bases from which most planes take off daily to bomb the country we had just left. . . . And so on, out and out, further away from North Vietnam.

Due to one of the misadventures typical of the ICC flights, we had already spent four days in Vientiane before we went to Hanoi, staying at this very hotel, walking all over the town we'd just driven through. And though we had been jolted by its sordidness then, it seemed now that we couldn't have taken its full measure. And yet, of course, it had all been there before, and we'd seen it. In contrast to her subtler dealings with Western Europe, America exports to Southeast Asia only the most degraded aspects of her culture. And in that part of the world there is no dressing up or concealing the visible signs of American might. Though it could be helpful anyway to abstain from *Time* and *Newsweek* for at least ten days after a visit to North Vietnam, an American must brace himself for a big cultural shock—reverse cultural dislocation, I suppose—when the first environment he sees after leaving Hanoi is a place like Vientiane.

Remembering the intimations I'd had in North Vietnam of the possibility of loving my own country, I wanted very much not to react crudely, moralistically, not to slip back into the old posture of alienation. And after a while the keenest part of my outrage did subside. For the anger an American is likely to direct toward the emblems of his country's imperial dominance isn't founded simply upon their inherent repulsiveness, which permits no reaction other than aversion, but rather upon the despairing conviction that American power in its present form and guided by its present purposes is *invincible*. But this may not be, probably isn't, the case. The Vietnamese, for one, don't think so. And their wilder judgments do, by this time, have a claim to be taken seriously. After all, who—except the Vietnamese themselves—would have predicted on February 7, 1965, that this small, poor nation could hold out against the awesome cruelty and thoroughness of American military force? But they have. Three years ago, enlightened world opinion pitied the Vietnamese, knowing that they couldn't possibly stand up to the United States; and the slogan of people protesting against the war was "Peace in Vietnam." Three years later, "Victory for Vietnam" is the only credible slogan. The Vietnamese don't want anybody's pity, as people in Hanoi told me; they want solidarity. The "tragedy" is Johnson's and the American government's, for continuing the war, Hoang Tung said. "There are many difficulties until the war ends," he added, "but we remain optimistic." For the Vietnamese, their victory is a "necessary fact."

The consequences for Vietnam of the eventual defeat of the American invasion are not hard to envisage. They will consist, for the most part, in unqualified improvements over the present situation: cessation of all bombing, withdrawal of American troops from the South, the collapse of the Thieu-Ky government, and the accession to power of a government dominated by the National Liberation Front, which some day, but not in the near future (according to the present leadership of the NLF), will unite with the Hanoi government so that at long last the divided country will be reunified. But one can only speculate about the consequences of this defeat for the United States. It could be a turning point in our national history, for good or bad. Or it could mean virtually nothing—just the liquidation of a bad investment that leaves the military-industrial establishment free for other adventures with more favorable odds. To believe that things in America could move either way doesn't seem to me overly optimistic. But then, if there's at least some hope for America, 1968 would be the wrong time for people in this country who look toward radical change to lose heart.

As Hegel said, the problem of history is the problem of consciousness. The interior journey I made during my recent stay in Hanoi made the truth of this grandiose maxim sharp and concrete for me. There, in North Vietnam, what was ostensibly a somewhat passive experience of historical education became, as I think now it had to, an active confrontation with the limits of my own thinking.

The Vietnam that, before my trip to Hanoi, I supposed myself imaginatively connected with, proved when I was there to have lacked reality. During these last years, Vietnam has been stationed inside my consciousness as a quintessential image of the suffering and heroism of "the weak." But it was really America "the strong" that obsessed me—the contours of American power, of American cruelty, of American self-righteousness. In order eventually to encounter what was there in Vietnam, I had to forget about America; even more ambitiously, to push against the boundaries of the overall Western sensibility from which my American one derives. But

I always knew I hadn't made more than a brief, amateurish foray into the Vietnamese reality. And anything really serious I'd gotten from my trip would return me to my starting point: the dilemmas of being an American, an unaffiliated radical American, an American writer.

For in the end, of course, an American has no way of incorporating Vietnam into his consciousness. It can glow in the remote distance like a navigator's star, it can be the seat of geological tremors that make the political ground shake under our own feet. But the virtues of the Vietnamese are certainly not directly emulatable by Americans; they're even hard to describe plausibly. And the revolution that remains to be made in this country must be made in American terms, not those of an Asian peasant society. Radical Americans have profited from the war in Vietnam, profited from having a clear-cut moral issue on which to mobilize discontent and expose the camouflaged contradictions in the system. Beyond isolated private disenchantment or despair over America's betrayal of its ideals, Vietnam offered the key to a systematic criticism of America. In this scheme of use, Vietnam becomes an ideal Other. But such a status only makes Vietnam, already so alien culturally, even further removed from this country. Hence the task awaiting any sympathetic person who goes there: to understand what one is nevertheless barred from understanding. When American radicals visit North Vietnam, all things are thrown into question—their necessarily American attitudes to Communism, to revolution, to patriotism, to violence, to language, to courtesy, to eros, not to mention the more general Western features of their identity. I can testify that, at the very least, the world seems much bigger since I went to North Vietnam than it did before.

I came back from Hanoi considerably chastened. Life here looks both uglier and more promising. To describe what is promising, it's perhaps imprudent to invoke the promiscuous ideal of revolution. Still, it would be a mistake to underestimate the amount of diffuse yearning for radical change pulsing through this society. Increasing numbers of people do realize that we must have a more generous, more humane way of being with each other; and great, probably convulsive, social changes are needed to create these psychic changes. To prepare intelligently for radical change requires not only lucid and truthful social analysis: for instance, understanding better the realities of the distribution of political and economic power in the world which have secured for America its present hegemony. An equally relevant weapon is the analysis of psychic geography and history: for instance, getting more perspective on the human type that gradually became ascendant in the West from the time of the Reformation to the industrial revolution to modern post-industrial society. Almost everyone would agree that this isn't the only way human beings could have evolved, but very few people in Europe and America really, organically *believe* that there is any other way for a person to be or can *imagine* what they might be like. How can they when, after all, that's what they are, more or less? It's hard to step over one's own feet.

And yet, I think, the path isn't altogether blocked. Of course, most people are unlikely to come to a direct awareness of how local is the human type they embody, and even less likely to appreciate how arbitrary, drastically impoverished, and in urgent need of replacement it is. But they do know something else: that they are unhappy and that their lives are cramped and savorless and embittered. If that discontent isn't channeled off to be repaired by the kind of psycho-therapeutic awareness which robs it of social and political, of historical, dimension, the wide prevalence of unfocused unhappiness in modern Western culture could be the beginning of *real* knowledge—by which I mean the knowing that leads simultaneously to action and to self-transcendence, the knowing that would lead to a new version of human nature in this part of the world.

Ordinarily, changes in the human type (which is to say, in the quality of human relations) evolve very slowly, almost imperceptibly. Unfortunately, the exigencies of modern history being what they are, we can't be content to wait for the course of natural deliverance. There may not be enough time, given this society's strong taste for self-destructiveness. And even if Western man refrains from blowing himself up, his continuing as he is makes it so awfully hard, perhaps soon intolerably so, on the rest of the world—that is, most of the world, the more than two billion people who are neither white nor rich nor as expansionist as we are. Just possibly, the process of recasting the particular historical form of our human nature prevalent in Europe and America can be hurried a little, by more people becoming aware of capacities for sentiments and behavior that this culture's values have obscured and slandered.

An event that makes new feelings conscious is always the most important experience a person can have. These days, it's a pressing moral imperative as well. I was very lucky, I think: my ignorance, my empathic talents, and the habit of being dissatisfied with myself worked together to allow just such an experience by the end of my trip to North Vietnam in May. (Though the new feelings that were revealed to me are undoubtedly quite old in a historical sense, I personally had never experienced them before, or been able to name them, or been hitherto capable of believing in them.) Now, once again, I am far from Vietnam, trying to make these feelings live here in an appropriate and authentic form. That sounds difficult. Still, I doubt that what's required is a great effort of "holding on." In and by itself, such an experience is transformative. It is indelible.

I recognized a limited analogy to my present state in Paris in early July when, talking to acquaintances who had been on the barricades in May, I discovered they don't really accept the failure of their revolution. The reason for their lack of "realism," I think, is that they're still possessed by the new feelings revealed to them during those weeks—those precious weeks in which vast numbers of ordinarily suspicious, cynical urban people, workers and students, behaved with an unprecedented generosity and warmth and spontaneity toward each other. In a way, then, the young veterans of the barricades are right in not altogether acknowledging their defeat, in being unable fully to believe that things have returned to pre-May normality, if not worse. Actually it is they who are being realistic. Someone who has enjoyed new feelings of that kind—a reprieve, however brief, from the inhibitions on love and trust this society enforces—is never the same again. In him, the "revolution" has just started, and it continues. So I discover that what happened to me in North Vietnam did not end with my return to America, but is still going on.

(June–July 1968)